Universal Lord Shiva
&
the Married life of the Trinity

Prafulla Chandra Sharma

BLUEROSE PUBLISHERS
India | U.K.

Copyright © Prafulla Chandra Sharma 2025

All rights reserved by author. No part of this publication may be reproduced, stored in a retrieval system or transmitted in any form or by any means, electronic, mechanical, photocopying, recording or otherwise, without the prior permission of the author. Although every precaution has been taken to verify the accuracy of the information contained herein, the publisher assume no responsibility for any errors or omissions. No liability is assumed for damages that may result from the use of information contained within.

BlueRose Publishers takes no responsibility for any damages, losses, or liabilities that may arise from the use or misuse of the information, products, or services provided in this publication.

For permissions requests or inquiries regarding this publication, please contact:

BLUEROSE PUBLISHERS
www.BlueRoseONE.com
info@bluerosepublishers.com
+91 8882 898 898
+4407342408967

ISBN: 978-93-6261-941-9

Cover design: Daksh
Typesetting: Tanya Raj Upadhyay

First Edition: January 2025

Preface

I have great pleasure and satisfaction to write this book which is my first book describing the greatness and vastness of Lord Shiva who is a supreme god of the Trinity. He is the god of destruction, who destroys the universe in order to recreate a new universe when Adharma and evil dominate over Dharma and good. He also destroys evil, misconception and darkness. He is regarded as Mahadeva means a supreme god or a deity of all deities.

It is believed that unlike other deities he leads an ascetic life on the Mount of Kailash and as a severe hermit who is totally detached from the physical attachments. In Rig Veda, he is mentioned as Rudra and praised Lord Shiva as Mightiest of the mighty.

Lord Shiva has many contradictory natures and behaviors, sometimes he is Bholenath and sometimes he is Rudra. He is an ascetic hermit as Shiva and also sitting with his family as Shankar. It is believed that Shiva is Absolute and Nothingness as everything begins with Shiva and ends with him. He is like a cipher which is infinite having no start point and no end point. Shiva is a universe which contains innumerous stars, planets, galaxies, constellations of celestial bodies and meteoroids, appears infinite or zero, but seems real. So Shiva is everything and tangible, but actually infinite and zero. Shiva is husband, father and house holder, but he is also hermit, apathetic to the earthly world and involved in meditation. He is a householder but mendicant and yogi too. He is father and sitting with family, but no physical attachments and easement. He is the start point (aadi) and end point (anta). So, my book has the title "Universal Lord Shiva and the Married Life of the Trinity. ". First part of the book describes that lord Shiva is everything and every breath and every drop of blood circulating in the body. Second part narrates the characteristics of the married life of Brahma, Vishnu and Shiva.

After retirement as an Income Tax officer I thought of writing something then to sit idle. As I had some idea of the specifications of the married life of the gods of the Trinity, I started writing /typing on my laptop slowly.

I am grateful to my Shakti, my wife Mrs. Mala Sharma, for her constant encouragement.

I would like to express my appreciation for my son, Major Avichal Sharma, for his constant reminders and encouragement. Also, I wish to convey my heartfelt appreciation to my daughter, Pallavi, for her support. Gratitude is also due to the publisher for motivating me to expedite the completion of the book and ensuring its publication.

In today's hostile environment, where people face numerous challenges—mentally, financially, socially, and more—without finding solutions, I hope my book will guide you toward the ultimate refuge in Lord Shiva, bringing eternal peace through His blessings.

As this is my first book, there may be some errors in word choice, sentence structure, or other aspects. I kindly request readers to offer constructive suggestions, if any.

Table of Contents

Lord Shiva's Glory..1
Shiva cuts Brahma's 5th head: -..............................9
Shiva (Virabhadra) cuts Daksha's head:-................12
Shiva incinerates Kama:-.......................................17
Shiva impales Andhaka:-..21
Shiva beheads Vinayaka:-......................................26
Shiva killed Yama:-..31
Shiva kills Shankhachuda:-....................................35
Shiva kills Jalandhar:...39
Shiva gives boons:-..45
Shiva's boon to Bhasmasura:-................................47
Shiva's boon to Shukracharya:-..............................53
Shiva's boon to Banasura:-.....................................57
Shiva's boon to Draupadi:-.....................................61
Shiva's boon to Arjuna:-...67
Shiva's boon to Jayadratha:- -................................72
Shiva's boon to Lord Krishna:-...............................80
Shiva's boon to Ravana:-..92
Shiva 's boon to river Narmada :...........................117
Shiva's boon to Nandi:-...127
Shiva's boon to Markandeya:-..............................136
Incarnation of Shiva:-:..146

Piplaad Avatar:. 156
Nandi Avatar: 158
Virabhadra Avatar:...............................159
Bhairava Avatar: 166
Ashwathama Avatar:...........................173
Sharabh Avatar:....................................185
Grihapati Avatar:................................. 190
Durvasa Avatar: 194
Rishabha Avatar:-.................................213
YathinathAvatar:- 218
Bhikshuvarya Avatar:-......................... 225
Sureshwar Avatar:-.............................. 230
Keerat Avatar:- 232
Sunatnartak Avatar:-........................... 236
Brahmachari Avatar:- 242
Yaksheshewar Avavatr:-.......................244
Avdhut Avatar:- 249
Hanuman Avatar:-............................... 254
Shiva as a tapasvi - 279
Shiva as Adiguru:-.................................282
Shiva as Rudra - 284
As First Story Teller 288
Shiva's Unique Trishul: 294
As Arms Inventor:-................................296
Shiva as first Surgeon -..........................307

- Different Offerings to Shiva:. 313
- Third Eye as Fire Missile:-. 324
- Shiva as Engineer:.. 327
- As a Householder:-... 329
- As an Environmentalist:-... 330
- Other Episodes:-.. 336
- Jyotirlinga- 349
- Shiva Temples Outside India: 387
- Shiva's Simplicity:-... 388
- The married life of the Trinity :-. 395
- The married life of Brahma:- 396
- The married life of Vishnu:-....................................404
- Married life of Shiva:-,.. 419
- About Book 437
- About Author.. 438

Om Shri Ganeshay Namah

Lord Shiva's Glory

As per Hindu mythology the entire universe is created, sustained and destroyed. This cycle of creation, preservation and destruction of the universe is continued infinitely. The present age of the universe wherein we are living is estimated to be at least 13. 8 billion years old. Researchers and scientists are still trying to find the exact age of the universe. According to the researchers, 22 billion years in the future is the possible end of the Universe. In Hinduism, the universe is believed to regenerate in a cyclical pattern. (every 2, 160, 000, 000 years). Shiva destroys the universe at the end of each cycle, allowing for a new creation to begin.

The Trimurty consists of three prime gods who are responsible for the creation, maintenance and destruction of the universe. These supreme gods are Brahma, Vishnu and Shiva. Brahma is the creator of the universe; Vishnu is the preserver of the universe, while Shiva destroys it to enable its recreation.

It is believed that Shiva's powers of destruction and recreation are continuously used for destroying the delusions and deficiencies of the world, paving the way for positive changes. This destruction is not arbitrary but constructive. Actually, the destruction is deconstruction and for new construction the destruction is essential, otherwise, the status quo would be an obstruction in the path of novelty. Shiva is therefore regarded as the source of both demolition and construction and the bliss and the fear.

Shiva is generally depicted in paintings and sculptures as having a white body (smeared with the ashes of corpses) and a blue neck (from holding the halahala poison, which turned his neck blue). His hair is shown in matted locks from which the Ganga flows, and he is adorned with a crescent moon. He has three eyes, the third eye being the transcendental eye that neither desires nor shuns. Moreover, it bestows inward vision but is capable of causing destruction by burning when the third eye focuses outward. Shiva has a garland of skulls and a serpent around his neck. He holds a trident tied with a Damroo or sometimes a club with a skull at the top. He wears animal hides and no other clothing. He resides at the abode of Mount Kailash, usually in meditation. He leads the hermit's way of life; indifferent to worldly things. His ash smeared ascetic appearance represents the realized soul who withdraws from the world.

Since Tapa, which is performed by all Rishis and sages, cleanses the mind, eliminates all memories and prejudices, it experiences sat-chit ananda. Tapasya is the process of lighting the fire of consciousness. The Tapas are fire churning ascetics. Shiva is the greatest Tapasvi and expends no energy engaging with the external world.

All the heat he generates is contained within his body. Naturally, the world around Shiva gradually loses all warmth and becomes cold. As a result, water becomes still and transforms into snow, turning his mountain into the Himalayas, the abode of snow. Shiva being a tapasvi practices celibacy, refuses to part with women and does not believe in fathering children. He is indifferent to all physical engagements and wanders as a hermit.

But Shakti, (nature) always tries to urge Shiva who is Purusha to be a householder for the generation of humanity. The Goddess in different forms as radiant Gauri and Kali stands in opposition to Shiva for generation and sustenance of life. While Shiva remains in the north, she comes from the south as dakshina Kali. During that time, Shiva's eyes are shut showing he is indifferent to the outer world. But Shakti does not want that. Ultimately Shiva must generate and sustain life in the world first. That is why, Shiva is regarded as "Adideva".

Shiva has two forms: physical and formless. His true nature is always intended to be formless, without beginning or end. Physically he is finite, but he is in fact infinite, representing the entire universe. His color represents that of the sky, and the Ganga flows from his matted hair, symbolizing its flow from the Himalayas.

The moon that rises in the sky is depicted as an ornament of Shiva. The snakes around his neck are symbols of creatures moving on the earth. Shiva is limitless and dimensionless like the universe as it is impossible to fathom the dimension of the universe. All the galaxy, sun, planets, stars, milky ways, dust clouds, light and living things are contained in the universe. It is believed that Shiva is the entire universe. Symbolically, he is depicted with the Ganga River, crescent moon and snakes indicating that only the universe can contain these things, not a normal deity. Like the universe, Shiva is infinite and beyond the boundaries of time and space. Shiva is regarded as Mahakal and Jagdish means timeless and God of the world.

According to the Hindu scriptures, Shiva has created the entire universe. He also created 5 elements of nature i. e Earth, Water, Air, Fire and Sky and all matters are composed of these basic elements, even human body structure is made up of these five elements. Hence, Shiva is also called "Bhootnath" (god of elements, Bhoot means element). He has created the Sun (the source of energy to the Universe), moon and all species in the universe.

Shiva is actually the entire universe and resides in everything –living and nonliving. In every soul, Shiva exists. Hence Shiva is the supreme soul. He imparts truth about the soul, God and creation and inspires humans to purify themselves by linking their hearts and minds with him. Swami Dayanand Saraswati once said that "Shiva is the one who is bliss and the giver of happiness to all". Supreme soul Shiv brings liberation (mukti) and salvation (jeevan mukti) to all. Shiva, an essential deity within the Trimurti, is known as "the Destroyer, " who clears the way for the reconstruction of a new universe and creation.

So, Shiva, the supreme god, creates, protects and transforms the universe. He is respected to be the most divine among all Hindu gods ``Maha Dev "god of gods. He is also considered as the father of the whole universe and all living and nonliving creatures. He is Adi-guru, the first guru (teacher) who teaches all aspects of humanity and life. He leads an ascetic life and has no physical attachments and amenities. Lord Shiva's body is adorned with ash, draped in a tiger skin. He bears a crescent moon on his forehead and a snake around his neck. His third eye symbolizes divine wisdom, complementing his matted hair from which flows the sacred River Ganga. He wields a trident and carries a damroo, the rattle drum, tied to it.

He sometimes is involved in a cosmic dance and sometimes sits still like a rock. Sometimes he sits with his family and sometimes alone like a hermit. The whole concept of Shiva is sublime. As per Hindu mythology, Shiva's sublimity is described as Arupa (without any form and Shiva is formless, shapeless and colorless) implying that he is cipher or zero. He is also described as a Sarupa (with a defined form where Shiva manifests into diverse forms). So, Sarupa-Arupa (Formless manifesting into form or form emerging from formless) is a transitional state from subtle (minute) to gross (coarse). The personality of Shiva cannot be put in one form, because he is formless like zero and at the same time, he is infinite.

Defacto, Shiva is the whole universe and he contains all celestial bodies i. e. stars, nebulas, planets and galaxies, the earth, rivers and mountains. This is why Shiva is visualized as blue like the sky. The crescent moon and flowing river (Ganga) represent the sky and the earth and sitting on Mount Kailash signifies the whole nature and environmental sceneries. He is omnipresent, omnipotent and omniscient. He is Adi-Aanta (Beginning and ending).

Shiva is a god having contrasting and divergent natures. He can be Bholenath (innocent) and he can also be Rudra (dreadful, horrific) depending on the deeds of the others. As Bholenath, he is very easily pleased with the devotees, without discriminating the antecedents and manners of their prayers, but considering their emotions. Once Shiva told Parvati `It is not what I am offered. It is the emotion that accompanies it that matters to me. " So, most of the demons, who want boons, make their tapasya's (penances) to him and Shiva is easily pleased to offer boons to them without worrying for the outcomes of his offered boons to Demons. But seeing the misdeed and arrogance of any deity and others, he turns into Rudra (fearsome) and either chops their heads or slays them.

"Shiva, the Divine Destroyer, who severs heads with a graceful yet powerful sweep. "

<u>Shiva cuts Brahma's 5th head:</u> - As per Hindu mythology, Brahma is creator of all living and nonliving creatures in the universe and is still creating. Naturally, he is the father of all creatures. Brahma is visualized as an aged god who has 4 heads with white beard and is absorbed in reading 4 Vedas. It is a belief that 4 heads of Brahma symbolize 4 directions of nature and the universe and knowledge of 4 Vedas.

While Brahma was creating the universe, he created a female deity, known as Shatpura (a hundred beautiful forms). "Initially, she was created to assist Brahma in the act of creation. However, upon catching a glimpse of Shatpura's unparalleled beauty and charm, Brahma became instantly infatuated, relentlessly pursuing her wherever she ventured. ". She comes to realize the hidden and nefarious intentions behind Brahma's pursuit and desire to control her, despite his role as the creator, akin to a father figure to her. There is a description in the Brihadaranyaka Upanishad that Shatarupa has the supernatural power to take the forms of different animals and birds, so she runs, taking the forms of various animals. But Brahma also possesses the same power to reform himself into any male animal/bird, so he pursues her, taking the form of a similar male counterpart. When she runs as a goose, he chases as a gander. When she runs as a cow, he pursues as a bull. Similarly, she becomes the mare, when he runs as a stallion. Shatarupa moves in various directions to avoid his stare and chasing, but fails, as Brahma has 4 heads, one for each direction of compass. Desperate and helpless, she leads him over, keeping away from his gaze even for a moment, Brahma has developed a fifth head atop the first four, solely to keep her within his sight. "She is distressed about how to escape from the gaze of Brahma. "The fifth head also strengthens Brahma's ego (Ahm), driving him to believe he can conquer both Shatarupa and nature itself.

Observing the distress of Shatarupa and Brahma's unrighteous and immoral obsession with her, despite being his own creation, Shiva manifests and severs the fifth head atop Brahma.

Additionally, Shiva decreed that there shall be no worship of the unholy Brahma anywhere. Since the incident, Brahma has been reciting the four Vedas, one from each of his mouths, in an attempt at repentance.

As per Linga Purana, Shiva (Rudra) howls when he observes how Brahma chases Shatarupa /Prakriti (nature) and his own creation. Shiva laments the corrupted mind of Brahma. Shiva watches how Brahma develops four heads, facing the four directions as he seeks to gaze upon Shatarupa at all times in his attempt to control her. He then sprouts a fifth head on the top of the first four. This 5th head symbolizes the gradual increase of corruption of the mind, its binding and crumpling with fear and insecurity as the desire to dominate and control to take over.

The first four faces represent the reality of nature in every direction, while the fifth simply disregards it. It is the head of delusion and ego (ahm) that Brahma develops as a symbol of his ego or self-appreciation. The 5th head implies that Brahma is not only creator, but also lord and master of Nature (Prakriti). This type of claim over nature is humanity's great illusion.

Shiva, i. e. the Rudra, always destroys such a type of ahm or delusion. He chops off the fifth head of Brahma to shatter his illusion and ego. Shiva therefore becomes Kapalika, the skull bearer. By cutting the 5th head delusion of Brahma is destroyed which led him to believe that he created objective reality (Prakriti). Brahmananda reveals that Brahma, in fact, creates only his own subjective reality.

<u>Shiva (Virabhadra) cuts Daksha's head:-</u> As per Hindu literature, Daksha is the son of Brahma (manas putra) and he is Prajapati, emperor of the world. He belongs to the deity reign and believes in purity, control over all people and supremacy. The culture, customs and tradition are the following paths of Daksha, whereas God Shiva is free from all boundaries of social customs and cultural values, followed by Aryas and deities. Shiva wanders as a hermit, smears his body with ash, wears tiger skin and lives in caves and mountains and his companions are dogs, ghosts, snakes, goblins and ganas. Moreover, he belongs to the Rudra clan. There is a cultural conflict between both the clans of Shiva and Daksha. Daksha is Prajapati who has ambition and desire to rule over the world, whereas Shiva is Pashupati, meaning he has triumphed over all basic and animal instincts i. e. sex, greed, violence, anger, disillusion and fear.

Daksha's hatred and enmity increased when Shiva saved Chandra from the curse made by Daksha that Chandra would be ugly, and his brightness will decrease day by day. Chandra gets married to Rohini and the other 26 daughters of Daksha, but at the same time Chandra loves Rohini and ignores the other 26 wives. Being ignored and dejected, they approach their father, Daksha. He invites Chandra and warns him to treat them at par and to not show partiality between Rohini and other 26 wives. But Chandra does not amend himself, consequently leading the 26 daughters to visit Daksha again to complain about Chandra's behavior. An enraged Daksha curses Chandra to be ugly and waning. But on the advice of Narada, Chandra goes to Shiva's refuge and Shiva promises him to save from Daksha's curse. This is a big setback for Daksha and in result, he keeps enmity with Shiva.

Secondly, the youngest daughter, Sati falls in love with Shiva and expresses her desire to be his wife. She tells her father Daksha about her love and desire, but he refuses to give his consent, as he dislikes and envies Shiva. Sati is adamant about marrying him. So, she revolts against her father and leaves her father's house to become Shiva's wife. Sati's revolt for love marriage is the first incident in the world that a daughter is independent and determined to choose her husband as per her love and Sati's defiance of her father, Daksha, her marriage to Shiva, and Daksha's denial of their union, all enhance Daksha's feelings of inferiority and humiliation towards Shiva. This is because Shiva's power is affirmed when Daksha's own daughter defies him for Shiva

To recover his loss and gain more power, Daksha organizes a big yagna and all deities are invited to participate in the yagna, but Shiva and Sati are not invited by Daksha. However, after getting information from sage Narada and even after not being invited by her father, Devi Sati wishes to go to father's residence. But at the same time, Shiva is unmoved but Sati goes there. She is not welcomed by Daksha there. On the contrary, she is insulted. Being misbehaved and insulted, she leaps into the sacrificial fire and sets herself ablaze. On being informed of the death of Sati by self- immolation, Shiva feels the sudden anguish and pain and does not tolerate the unexpected death of Sati who lives with him without any expectation from him. She had been a devoted wife to him (therefore devoted wife is known as Sati), although Shiva was always indifferent to her as he was not willing to be the householder.Sati's absolute and undemanding companionship eroded Shiva's indifference. As a result, Shiva became impatient and restless with agony. He comes and takes the charred corpse of Sati on his shoulder and wanders in the hills. howling in pain. In his sorrow and anguish, he forgets that he restored Chandra and gave the Asuras the Sanjivani Vidya to resurrect themselves. This is an unique example of the highest level of love and affection of a husband for his wife. He cries with agony and moves everywhere to resurrect the burnt and dead body of his wife, Sati. His howling is so intense that the universe is unable to bear it. So, on the request of all deities, Vishnu hurls his Sudarshan Chakra and cuts Sati's body into 51 pieces. Each piece falls on the earth and transforms into Shaktipith, the seat of the Goddess.

Meanwhile, Shiva 's outrage takes the form of Virabhadra, a terrifying warrior and leads an army of ghosts, goblins, ganas, all inauspicious and wild creatures into Daksha's sacrificial hall and destroys everything there. Urine, sputum, blood and vomit are poured into the pots and pans, and everything is made filthy. Finally, Virabhadra finds Daksha and cuts him into pieces. After Shiva's composure, the Devas beg him to forgive Daksha as the yagna is left unfinished. As Shiva is Bholenath, he agrees to the Devas 's begs to resurrect Daksha. He replaces Daksha's head with the male goat's head and the male goats are generally considered as the sacrificial offerings. Shiva thus teaches a lesson to Daksha, Prajapati and son of Brahma, the creator of the universe, by revealing his weakness, likening him to a goat.

He always desires to dominate over the Prajas (people) and become more powerful. For various reasons, he harbors enmity and loathing towards the ascetic Shiva, who is Pashupati, free from all animal instincts and physical attachments. By replacing the beheaded Daksha with the head of a male goat, Shiva demonstrates that greed and the lust for power lead to devastation. Daksha is reminded of the true meaning of sacrifice: the sacrifice of one's animal nature and the understanding of one's human nature. The ultimate aim of life is to relinquish the senses in pursuit of tranquility.

Shiva incinerates Kama:- After Sati's self-immolation, her body is cut into pieces by Vishnu's Sudarshan Chakra, and Daksha's head is replaced with that of a male goat. Following these events, Shiva's senses cease to engage with Prakriti, and he isolates himself from all worldly affairs.

Meanwhile, there is a powerful Asura, Tarakasura, son of demon Vajranaka, king of demons. Tarakasura is very clever and a devotee of Shiva. He performs severe penance for a thousand years. After a long time, Shiva is moved with his severe penance and appears in front of him. Shiva asks Tarakasura about the boon he desires, and Tarakasura requests that he can only be killed by Shiva's son. Knowing that Sati had just died childless and that Shiva had withdrawn from worldly affairs, Tarakasura believed that Shiva would likely never become a householder again. Shiva as Bholenath grants him the boon and thus Tarakasura becomes invincible. With help of his brothers and huge army, Tarakasura repeatedly attacks the Devas and defeats all deities including Indra. Due to the blessing that Tarakasura can only be killed by the son of Shiva, any deity or king is unable to either defeat or kill him. Knowing the boon granted to Tarakasura, all devas along with Indra approach and pray to Rishi (sage) Narada to advise a plan regarding the birth of a son of Shiva. As per plan, they approach Himavanta (Himavan), king of mountains and his wife Maina as well as

Parvati to prepare them to wed Mahadeva. Parvati is also requested to go to Shiva who is in deep meditation. Parvati on listening decides that Shiva shall be her husband and begins to worship Shiva continuously to please him, but in vain. So, the Devas decided to help Parvati to awaken Shiva and sought the help of Kamadeva, God of carnal desire and enjoyment. Kamadeva is visualized as a passionate god who rides a parrot, carries a bow made of sugar cane and string made of bees. His arrows are made of flowers which stirs the five senses and sensual desires. His consort is Rati, goddess of love making and techniques of making love. It is a fact that arousing sensual desires can deviate many tapasvi from their tapasyas (penances). So, Indra uses Kamadeva to excite Shiva, but he is no ordinary Tapasyin or hermit. He is the Purusha and Pashupati who has control over all his senses. When Kamadeva shoots his arrows, Shiva remains unaffected and unmoved, but feels something was wrong. He simply opens his third eye and unleashes a missile of flames.

It sets Kamadeva ablaze, and he is reduced to ashes. Parvati and Rati watch in shock, Kamadeva blazing and reducing to ashes. Shiva remains as calm as ever and indifferent to Prakriti. Shiva by this act becomes Kamantaka, the destroyer of desire. Rati, the wife of Kamadeva, laments in anguish, feeling utterly lost and purposeless without her beloved Kama by her side. She requests Shiva to resurrect her husband to complete the pair of Kama (the deity of desire) and Rati (the goddess of love and passion), without which future generations will not be conceived, leaving the universe devoid of creatures. Shiva is moved by Rati's lament and compelling arguments and resurrects Kamadeva, but without any physical form, only invisible Kama. Setting Kamadeva ablaze and restoring him in invisible form represents that Kamadeva is no longer required to stimulate the sensual feeling and desire to anyone by appearing there personally, but now Kamadeva is reshaped into unseen carnal desire and feeling. This incidence is very beneficial for the creatures, especially deities, demons and men in order to maintain the personal and social sanctity. The act of sexuality confines to the person/persons involved and no Kamadeva is required. Thus, Shiva does a yeoman's service to mankind by reshaping bodily Kamadeva into invisible Kama or sensual desire and mood. On the other hand, this episode may be interpreted as Shiva experiencing sensual desire and passion during his meditation.

With help of inner will power, he sets Kama (sensual desire and feeling) ablaze into ashes. Because Shiva is not an ordinary tapasvin, he controls and triumphs over the carnal desire. Shiva is Pashupati, conqueror of all brutal instincts.

Shiva impales Andhaka:- In Hindu literature, Andhaka is a malevolent asura whose pride is ultimately defeated by Shiva and Parvati. As per Shiva Purana, Matsya purana, Kurma purana and Linga purana, Andhaka believed that he is a warrior, having one thousand heads, two thousand arms, two thousand eyes and feet. In some versions, Andhaka is sometimes described as a son of Shiva and Parvati. According to Shiva purana, once Shiva was meditating on Mount Mandara. Ma Parvati was in a playful mood and covered Shiva's eyes. As his both eyes are shut, the whole universe is plunged into darkness. Because Shiva is envisaged as the whole universe and his eyes are light of the universe. To get the Sun to shine again. Shiva opens his third eye. The sweat that oozed from Parvati's hands upon touching Shiva fell to the ground and created a horribly looking blind boy. Parvati became terrified on seeing him. Shiva informs that the boy, Andhaka took birth due to their physical contact, is their child.

When the demon king Hiranyaksa performed penance (tapasya) to please Shiva for having a child, Shiva gifted the boy to him and named him Andhaka due to his blindness. After the death of Hiranyaksha, Andhaka became the new king, but the demon clan does not regard him as demon (asura), since he is born of the Devas. Disowned by the majority, he begins to perform a severe penance to please Brahma. Seeing the hard tapasya of Andhaka, Brahma appears and asks him about his wish. Andhaka begs for his blindness to be healed and the grant of vision and immortality. Brahma replies that he cannot be immortal since all that take birth, must die, although he may choose the condition of his death. Andhaka says that if he lusts for a woman who is like a mother, then only he can only be killed. Brahma accepts his request and grants all his boons. Andhaka goes to his kingdom and takes control over all his opponents and the Deities.

One day Andhaka asks his minister if there is anyone who can be equal to him in strength, majesty and assets. The minister points out that he has no company of a beautiful woman, as the wife of ascetic Shiva ie. Parvati, who is the most beautiful woman in the world.

Shiva lives on Mount Kailash. Andhaka is advised that if he wants a beautiful woman who is matchless, he should possess her. Andhaka attacks Shiva with his great warriors, but they are defeated by Shiva's army. He again returns to the battle which has lasted for hundred years, no result.

On one side, Vishnu, Brahma, and the Devas join the battle against Andhaka and his soldiers. Andhaka has a demon general, Vighasa, who swallows all the gods, prompting Shiva to retaliate by charging with his bull and plowing into the demons.

Sukradev, the Guru of Demons brings all the dead demons back to life by using Vidya Sanjivini. Shiva orders the Ganas to capture Sukradev. When Sukradev was brought to Shiva, he swallowed him. One day Andhaka reaches Mount Kailash and challenges for a duel. Shiva, that time was lost in meditation therefore does not pay attention to Andhaka's challenge. Andhaka sees Parvati sitting beside Shiva. He is filled with lust for Parvati, without knowing that he has desire for his own mother. Parvati realizes the unthinkable lust Andhaka has for her, she immediately begs Shiva to open his eyes and prevent their son from doing an immoral act. Shiva comes out of meditation and opens his eyes and with his trident, he impales Andhaka and keeps him alive for a thousand years, draining him of blood until he is reduced to a skeleton. Once Andhaka realizes his mistake that the woman he has lusted for is actually his mother and Shiva is his father, he apologizes to the divine couples and chants Shiva in repentance This pleases Shiva who forgives him, makes him a Gana and allows him to live in Kailasha.

It is noteworthy to mention that Andhaka is born when the third eye of Shiva is opened while other eyes are closed by Parvati. This episode demonstrates the limitation of the gaze of the third eye which is the transcendental eye. The right and left eyes stand for a gaze which differentiates proper and improper conduct. But the third eye is indifferent to such distinctions. This eye of wisdom may find any merit in the existing culture and ethics which depend on various factors i. e distinctions, social traditions, customs and hierarchies. Cultures of two countries or continents or different societies may be different completely or partially. As per the prevailing culture and tradition when a woman is solemnized as wife and a man as husband, others are not allowed to disturb this relationship. But the transcendental gaze of the third eye looks at all traditions and cultures as invalid and hence causes delusion. The gaze of the third eye is not able to differentiate between woman and wife. So, the child born of the third eye is not capable of recognizing his mother and in resultant, he tries to treat his mother as a lover. This act or intention does not draw appreciation, but most immoral and condemnable acts as per culture and morality. So, Shiva impales Andhaka for a thousand years and makes him repent for his immoral act and apologies. The divine couple Shiva and Parvati forgive him and allow him to live as Gana.

Shiva beheads Vinayaka:- After the marriage, Parvati comes to mount Kailash, and it is known that Shiva is Purush and Parvati is Shakti or Nature. Parvati tries to persuade Shiva to have a child, but Shiva refuses to do so and says that he does not want a child. In Hinduism, there is a strong belief that if a couple is blessed with a male child, they will go to heaven after death. According to the Manu Smriti, those whose sons light their pyres and perform Shraddha go to heaven and are not required to take rebirth. Children are required to repay the debts they owe to their ancestors who gave them birth. This is called Pitra-rin (parental debt). During funeral rituals the pitrs are offered balls of meshed rice. This ritual implies that they will produce children, enabling the dead to regain a body and repay their debts. So having children is very essential to the couple for repaying the ancestors 'debts. On the other hand, Parvati (nature /shakti) intends to make Shiva Purusha), a hermit to be a householder and force him to be a father. The production of the next generation is the main aim of nature (Shakti), but for this purpose, the collaboration of Purusha (Shiva) is essential.

When Parvati expresses her desire to be a mother. Shiva (i. e Shankara) refuses and tells Parvati that "I don't owe any debt to any accentors as I have no ancestors. I am self-born and will never die. Therefore, I don't need to have children to enable my rebirth. " But Parvati as Shakti does not heed and persists. One day Shiva moves away from her to meditate in isolation in the dark and dense forest.

Children are a powerful means of true involvement with the material world and the complete fulfillment of marital life. Children are valuable assets to the family and serve as the adhesive for a good and stable married life. Parvati 's prime aim is to involve Shiva into domestic affairs. She has succeeded in opening the eyes of Shiva and he becomes Shankara to watch Nature (Shakti), but refuses to be responsive to nature's request. To infuse empathy for the world, having a child is necessary. So, Parvati decides to create a child on her own. She anoints her body with a paste of turmeric and oil, then scrapes it off and collects the residue, which is a mixture of turmeric paste, her sweat, and dirt. She makes a boy doll out of the rubbings and breathes it into life. Parvati calls this good-looking boy "Vinayaka (born without(vina) a man (Nayaka). The boy was very active and absolutely loyal to Parvati.

One day Parvati wants to take a bath and she instructs Vinayaka to guard the door and not let anyone come in until she finishes her bath. Meanwhile, Shiva comes out of his meditation and wants to see Parvati, but he is stopped by a strange boy. Shiva tries to convince the boy that he is the husband of Parvati and has come out of meditation after a long period, but the boy does not listen to him and does not let Shiva enter until his mother Parvati finishes her bath. Shiva gets angry because the boy is adamant, arrogant and strong enough to block his path. He decides to get rid of this boy who blocked his path to Parvati. So, Shiva raises his trident and beheads the boy and the head of Vinayaka is severed. He moves triumphantly covered with the boy's blood. When Parvati sees it, she cries in agony and runs outside and finds the body of her son without a head. She is so enraged and pained that she decides to destroy the entire creation. She transforms from gentle Gauri into fearsome Kali. She shouts in fury " You have killed my son and I will destroy everything. Shiva trembles with fear and tries to cool down furious and pained Parvati that he will resurrect the boy. He orders his Ganas to fetch the head of the first creature they encounter in the northern direction. The Ganas find an elephant. It should be added that as per the Brahma Vaivarta Purana that elephant was Airavata, the mount of Indra. Others say that it was one of the elephants that flank Lakshmi. Shiva places the head of the elephant on the severed neck of Vinayaka and brings back to life the boy.

Shiva declares him to be his son and names him Ganesha, lord of Ganas and Ganapati, master of the Ganas. All other deities are assembled to bless

Ganesha and shower him with flowers. It is also declared that Ganesha will be memorized and worshiped first, before starting any ceremony, rite, auspicious occasion or worshiping of another god/goddess. So Shri Ganeshaya Namah means initiation of any work or launching any mission.

Beheading Vinayaka and replacing his chopped head with that of an elephant represents that arrogance and obstinacy need to be removed. The elephant's head symbolizes strength, peace, wisdom, and a sharp mind, which is to be substituted. The boy becomes a unique deity possessing the essence of human nature, knowledge, consciousness, awareness, and the strength, wisdom, and long memory of an elephant. He is the God of evil destroyer with a sharp mind, consciousness and someone who removes obstacles & ignorance. On Deepawali, he is worshiped along with Goddess Lakshmi because there is a belief that while Lakshmi offers wealth, she does not necessarily impart the understanding of how to use it properly. Only Lord Ganesha teaches the sense of consciousness and proper thought. He helps and supports the human-beings in the fulfillment of the four aims of human life, namely duty (Dharma) wealth (Arth), enjoyment (Kama) and liberation (Moksha). Ganesha is a very important god in Hinduism. If the boy Vinayaka had not been reshaped as Ganesh by Shiva, who cut off Vinayaka's head and replaced it with that of an elephant, he might have remained an ordinary deity. Hence Shiva's beheading Vinayaka in anger transforms Vinayaka into one powerful and super god Ganesha who is worshiped not only in India, but in other parts of the world. He is widely worshiped by the Hindus, Buddhists and Jains.

Shiva killed Yama:- As per Hindu literature, there is a sage, Mrikanda (or Mrikandu) by name who has no child and to have child/ children, he undertakes severe penance (tapasya) to please Shiva. Shiva appears and asks him what he desires. The sage Mrikanda prays to Shiva for a son and Shiva offers him a choice: a wise son who would live for only 16 years or a foolish son who would live for 100 years. Mrikanda chooses for a wise son and is blessed with Markandeya, an ideal son fated to die at the age of 16 years. Since childhood, Markandeya was very brilliant and had a great learning attitude to learn and master the Vedas and the religious shastras and grew up to be a great devotee of Shiva. He used to utter a mantra "Mahamrityunjaya "mantra (the great death-conquering –mantra). When Markendeya comes to know of his death before 16 years he starts praying to Shiva, worshiping Shiva-linga and hymning Mahamrityunjaya mantra. Seeing his devotion to Shiva, the gods plead to Shiva to extend Markendaya's life. Shiva consents to the wishes of the sage.

As per destiny, the Yama-doota (the messenger of Yama)comes to take away Markendeya's life, but fails to reach him as Markendeya is continuously repeating Shiva's name. After Yama-Doota's failure, Yama (god of death) comes himself to carry away Markendeya' s soul and tells him to stop his worshiping and humming the Mahamrityunjaya mantra. He also asks him to come with him to yamloka as per his fate. Markendeya requests Yama to allow him to finish his prayers, after which he is ready to die. But death never waits for man or prayer. It is ultimate truth who takes birth, must die and death never distinguishes any creature and treats alike. Yama assumes a fearsome form and throws his noose to capture Markendeya hugs Shiva-linga very tightly. When the noose touches the linga; Shiva suddenly emerges from the Shiva-linga and kicks Yama away. Shiva strikes Yama with his trident, kicks his chest and thus kills Yama, god of Yama. Since then, Shiva is regarded as Yamantaka who destroyed Yama. Markandeya after that becomes the immortal sage.

Sages, gods, and other beings appear to praise Shiva. However, Yama is killed by Shiva, and as a result, no one therefore dies in the world, and all will become immortal. The earth will be burdened by evil beings and the population would manifold on the earth. The sages, deities and others pray and request Shiva to resurrect Yama, so that the natural circle of birth- death can continue for balancing the generation. Shiva touches dead Yama with his feet and revives Yama. After being alive, Yama prays to Shiva and promises to never touch any devotees of Shiva. He also gives up coming personally to take the life of anybody. instead of creating the causes for the death of the living creatures. So, the reason for the death may be diseases, old age, accidents, natural calamities, wars or pandemics.

The legend implies the superiority of Shiva who is omnipotent and omniscient. Due to his victory over Yama(death), Shiva is regarded as Mrityunjaya who won over death. Shiva also wins over all instincts which lead to the worldly temptations and attachments. As a hermit, he smears himself with ash, symbolizing its indestructibility. Ash burns away any living or non-living entity, converting it into ash which cannot be further destroyed. It is believed that the true devotees of Shiva can achieve freedom from the fear of death and hence the death and samsara(the cycle of the death and rebirth to which life in the material world is bound). The killing and resurrection of Yama, and the liberation of Markandeya from Yama, demonstrate that Shiva is the most supreme god who conquers death, an inevitable and cruel reality. Hence, Shiva is the vanquisher of time and death.

Shiva kills Shankhachuda:- As per Hindu mythology and Shiva Purana, Shankhachuda was born to the demon king Dambha. It is said that Shankhachuda is the incarnation of Sudama, friend of Lord Krishna. He was born in the demon family due to the curse of Radha. When he grows up, he goes to Pushkar and starts a tremendous tapasya to please Brahma. God Brahma is pleased to find his severe tapasya. God Brahma blesses him and says that he would be invincible and gives him the divine talisman that would yield victory everywhere and in absence of talisman he may be defeated. He also instructs Shankhachuda to go to Badarikashrama where he will find his would-be wife, Tulsi, daughter of Dharmdhwaja. He also says that he will continue to get power till his wife is chaste. As per instruction of God Brahma, Shankhachuda goes to Badarikashrama and gets married to Tulsi, daughter of Dharmadhwaja.

When Shankhachuda returns to his capital, alongwith his newly wedded wife, he is crowned as king of the demons by the demon guru Shukracharya. After coronation, he attacks

Indrapuri with his massive army and occupies Indrapuri by defeating the Deities. Shankhachuda goes to Badarikashrama, He is invincible by the dent of Brahma's boon and cannot be defeated by any warrior / king. Consequently, he has conquered all over the three lokas in the short span of time. The defeated, unpowered and harassed deities approach Brahma and seek his help in getting rid of Shankhachuda. Brahma takes them to God Vishnu for solution. But Vishnu also fails to solve their problems and he takes all deities and Brahma to lord Shiva. They all request Shiva to save them from the cruelty of Shankhachuda and help them to get back their kingdoms from him. Accepting their request and seeing their plight, Shiva agrees to kill Shankhachuda.

Shiva then sent his messenger Pushpadat to Shankhachuda asking him to return the kingdoms of the deities to them and to live peacefully. Instead of considering the advice of Shiva, he expresses his willingness to fight against god Shiva. Pushpadat, the messenger returns in despair and narrates the whole story to god Shiva. Shiva is fully convinced that Shankhachuda will never give up the enmity with deities and as a consequence he is ready for war. Hence Shiva sends all his ganas under the leadership of Kartikeya and Ganesha. Later on, Bhadrakali with a huge army proceeds towards the battlefield. Ultimately, Shiva along-with other deities reaches to the battlefield. On arrival of Shiva with the deities and huge army, Shankhachuda gives away all kingdoms conquered from the deities to his son and goes to his wife for consent. His wife does not agree with him to fight with Shiva, but after sometime she allows him to fight. He proceeds to the battlefield. A fierce battle started between the Deities and the Demons. Both of them attacked each other and used fatal and destructive weapons freely against each other. But the deities could not face Shankhachuda and ran away from the battlefield helplessly. They take the refuge of Shiva and tell their helplessness before Shankhachuda. Then, Kartikeya and Ganesha went to fight Shankhachuda and a bloody and brutal battle was fought between them. Meanwhile, Bhadrakali enters the battlefield. She can devour Shankhachuda very easily, but due to Brahma's boon, she neither devours nor kills him.

Shiva himself came forward to fight with him and they fought fiercely for hundreds of years.

As Shiva takes hold of his trident in order to slay Shankhachuda, a celestial voice is heard " O God, as long as Shankhchuda wears the talisman of Krishna and as long as his wife maintains her chastity, he can't be killed. " Therefore Shiva stops and on other hand god Vishnu goes to Shankhachuda in disguise of Brahman and requests for the amulet of Krishna as alms and he gives it to god Vishnu. He puts on that talisman and disguises himself as Shankhachuda. He approaches Tulsi and her chastity is sullied. Shiva in the battlefield chops off the head of Shankhachuda.

By chopping off the head of Shankhachuda, Shiva makes Sudama free from the curse of Radha that he would be born as demon Shankhachuda. Furious by the misdeed of Vishnu, Tulsi curses him to become rock. Shiva reaches there and consoles Tulsi and reveals to her that she had performed severe penance in the previous birth to get god Vishnu as her husband. After giving up her present body, she would become the secret river Gandaki and the Tulsi plant. He also tells that due to her curse, Vishnu will assume the form of rock on the banks of river Gandaki and it will be worshiped as Shaligrama. Shiva also declares that her husband Shankhchuda would be present as conch shells in the oceans. In future, anyone who worships the Tulsi plant, the conch shell and Shaligrama together will enlighten the devotee of the god. Therefore this is how, Shiva blesses Tulsi and makes her husband and rock form of Vishnu as holy and venerable.

Shiva kills Jalandhar:- The Shiva Purana states the birth and death of Jalandhar. Once Indra and Vrihaspati were going to Mount Kailash to meet Shiva. Their way was blocked by a hermit with matted hair and radiant face. The hermit was Shiva himself and he was there to test their knowledge, but they did not recognize him. They asked the hermit to move away to let them go, but he did not listen. Indra becomes furious and threatens him with his thunderbolt. Shiva becomes angry upon the action of Indra due to which his eyes turn red. The anger causes Shiva's third eye to open, but meanwhile, Vrihaspati recognizes god Shiva and prays him to pardon Indra. in the meantime a ball of fire emerges from his third eye and to prevent from turning Indra into ashes, Shiva diverts the ball of fire to the ocean. When the ball of fire falls into the ocean, a boy is born who begins to cry so terribly and continuously. It impels Brahma to descend from Brahmaloka. The ocean tells Brahma that it does not know where the child came from. Brahma foretells that this child will become the emperor of the demons and cannot be killed by anyone except Shiva. After his death, he will return to Shiva's eye.

By time, that boy grows as Jalandhara and becomes a mighty emperor and rules with justice and dignity. He marries Vrinda, daughter of demon Kalanemi. Once sage Bhrigu visits the kingdom of Jalandhara and narrates how demon Rahu 's head is chopped by Vishnu, because he tastes Amrit (nectar), comes out in Samundra –Manthan in which both Deities and Demons participate on the basic of equal sharing, but the deities deceive the demons by capturing the most of produces. Sage Bhrigu also told him how Indra took away his father's treasure. Jalandhar gets angry and declares war against Indra and other deities. After a severe war, he waged a war against gods. The defeated deities pleaded with God Vishnu who therefore fights with Jalandhara but fails to defeat him. Watching Jalandhar's fighting with skill and strategy Vishnu is very impressed and asks for boon. Jalandhara requests for Ksheer Sagar (ocean of milk). Jalandhara after that becomes king of three lokas (worlds).

Sage Narada once visits Jalandhar and narrates to him the beauty and splendor of Mount Kailash, uniqueness and greatness of God Shiva and his charmful and dutiful wife Parvati. On listening to sage Narada's description of the beauty of Parvati, he decides to get Parvati. He sends his messenger Rahu to Shiva with instructions to say that Shiva is a hypocrite for keeping a wife, Parvati, despite being an ascetic.

Rahu requests that Shiva should hand over Parvati to Demon king Jalandhara, failing which Jalandhara will capture Parvati by attacking on Shiva. On hearing these insulting words and proposals, Shiva is enraged and turns into a furious creature (Kirtimukha). He springs from his bow and hurts Rahu badly. Rahu ran away to save himself. He narrates the whole thing to Jalandhara. Jalandhara marches to Kailash, but he does not find Shiva and Parvati there. Shiva has forsaken Kailash and made his dwelling on a mountain near Lake Manasa.

He puts the position of his Ganas and troops surrounding the mountain. Nandi along with ganas and troops attacks forces of Jalandhar and destructs enemy forces but suffers a lot. Then Parvati requests Shiva to lead the war. Shiva warns Parvati to be more careful, as the demons in some disguise may visit her to harm her.

Shiva, accompanied by Virabhadra and Manibhadra, two forms of his anger, goes to the battlefield. Meanwhile, Kartikeya and Ganesha fight with Jalandhara and dominate initially, but later, both are defeated. On finding that Shiva and his avatars Virabhadra and Manibhadra are dominating the battlefield and there has been stampede on Jalandhara's troops, Jalandhara creates the illusion of beautiful apsaras singing and dancing in the battlefield to distract the troops.

Meanwhile, Jalandhara disguises himself as Shiva and goes to Parvati to attract her, but Parvati recognizes him and gets enraged. She turns into Kali, the fierce goddess and attacks Jalandhara. He runs away in fear of seeing the fierce goddess. Parvati then goes to Vishnu and urges him to play the same trick as Jalandhara played with her. Vishnu goes to Vrinda and creates the illusion that Jalandhara is killed by Shiva, but at the same time his life is restored. Seeing Jalandhara, who is actually Vishnu in disguise, she embraces Vishnu and thus infringes her morality and chastity. She recognizes and curses him that in future his wife would be abducted by someone. She enters in fire and blazes herself. Hearing of his wife's death, Jalandhara comes to the battlefield and a formidable war takes place between him and Shiva. Ultimately, Shiva kills Jalandhara by thrusting his Trident into chest and cutting his head with a chakra, created by his toe. Upon his death, his soil merges with Shiva. When the deities came to know about the killing of Jalandhara, they became overjoyed. They come to Shiva and eulogize him. After expressing their gratitude to him, they return to their respective abodes.

By killing Jalandhara, Shiva punishes him for his immorality that even being son of Shiva, he lures towards Parvati and tries to detain her. Even though he does not know about his father, it is an act of immorality and social sin to try to capture another's wife. In civil society and as per religious custom, lust for a woman who is the wife of another person and effort to make his wife is sin and offense also. Shiva shows that morality and social & religious ethics must stand for all and it must be followed. This episode also illustrates that a son born from Shiva's third eye would not be ordinary, as Shiva's third eye is transcendent, neither desiring nor rejecting. It does not distinguish between light and darkness, or morality and immorality.

So, the son has no conscience about what is correct and what is wrong. Besides, he also fails to differentiate between social ethics and offense. So, such a bewildering and unnatural son is killed by Shiva to destroy the impurities in the creations. Shiva is a destroyer who destroys impurities taking place in the human mind.

Shiva gives boons:- According to the Hindu mythology and scriptures, initially there are two dominated races Suras (also called Devas) and Asura (Danavs). Both are born out of the same father sage Kashyapa, but two different mothers. Suras are sons of Aditi and Asuras are sons of Diti. The deities are civilized and followers of cultures, social ethics and customs and they usually perform Yajnas and other rituals. They are known for Satvik traits. On the other hand, the Demons follow a path different from that of the Deities. They have tamasic traits and they undertake penance or tapasayas to achieve their desires. There are continuous conflicts between the deities and the demons It is alleged that the demons are power seeking individuals who are against the deities to gain and rule. To achieve powers and to conquer over the deities, they need to do tapas to please gods, because the gods of the Trinity have power to give boons to their devotees or tapasvins and boons have magnificent power to fulfill the desires of the devotees /tapasvins. It is observed that Shiva and Brahma gave so many blessings to the Asuras and others. Brahma gives boons with conditions of death, whereas Shiva's boon has no condition. Like Brahma gives boon to Hiranyaksha that no god, demon or human might ever kill him, so he is killed by the Varaha(boar) avatar of God Vishnu. Similarly, Brahma also gives boon to Hiranyakashyap that he would not be killed in day or night, inside or outside of a building, nor by a human or beast but he is killed by Narsingh(an avatar of Vishnu) on the pillar of the building in the evening. Whereas Shiva gives more boons without any condition, because he knows the outcome of the boon which will accelerate the process of destruction of Adharma.

Shiva, known as Ashutosha, is easily pleased and very kind to his devotees. More importantly, he never distinguishes between good and bad devotees and always considers their devotion and penance, whether they are demon, deity, or human. He is also called as Bholenath who is easily moved by the penances and sufferings of his devotees. Consequently, the demons prefer to do penance to Shiva to please him and receive boons from him.

He gives everything he has, without thinking about future consequences. Consequently, some demons also do tapasya (penances) to Shiva with malafide intention, Shiva, in return, gives boons to these demons, but later, the same demons create significant problems by dint of Shiva's boons. So, Shiva's boons should not be taken for granted. He also has fierce and destructive form as basically he is the Destroyer God ie. if evil dominates the good. Shiva or even Vishnu incarnates to destroy evil. Specially Shiva gives the boons to even evil demons acknowledging their tapasya's(penance) to destroy them easily and quickly. The outcome of his boons ultimately leads to the downfall of the evil and wicked devotees, thereby establishing the reign of Dharma over Adharma.

Shiva's boon to Bhasmasura:- As per mythology, Lord Siva took the decision of giving away a boon to Vrikasura (Bhasmasura), the son of Sakuni-one of the Epic Villains of Mahabharata He was not an intelligent boy and his foolishness annoyed his family in general especially his father. His father told him that due to his foolishness he would not be successful in his life but he decided to prove his father wrong. At the same time, he was a devotee of Lord Shiva.

Once, Bhasmasura meets Sage Narada, who has the ability to visit any place and meet any god without restriction. He requests Narada for proving his mettle, and Narada advises him to perform penance to Lord Shiva. Following Narada's advice, Bhasmasura searches for a peaceful area and begins performing penance (tapasya) to Lord Shiva to obtain a boon from him.

After a long and severe penance, Shiva is pleased and appears before Bhasmasura. He asks Bhasmapura for a boon. Since Bhasmasura is not clever, but an idiot so he requests Shiva for a boon that ' Let any creature on whom I place my hand turns into ash. ' (bhasma). At first Shiva is astonished to find this type of boon requested, but still Shiva blesses him with the boon. Bhasmasura then wants to test his new power or demonstrate his cunningness by placing his hand on Shiva first. Shiva immediately runs, not knowing how to tackle the foolish /cunning Asura. Bhasmasura does not think if Shiva is destroyed, the universe would be destroyed. Bhasmasura is thinking to prove how powerful he is, by testing his power on Shiva. So, the running of Shiva and chasing of Bhasmasura are ongoing. Ultimately Shiva seeks the help of Vishnu. He appears in the form of Mohini in front of Bhasmasura.

Mohini is so ravishing and beautiful that it enchants the foolish demon with her mesmerizing smile. Bhasmasura immediately falls in love with Mohini and forgets Shiva. Bhasmasura asks her to marry him. Mohini announces that she is very fond of dancing and anyone who matches her dance movements identically would be her husband. Without any hesitation he agrees to dance with Mohini and they start dancing. He tries to match her. The dance is in full swing and during the dance, at one moment, Mohini strikes a pose where she puts her hand on top of her own head. He in the intensity of movements of dance, also imitates her pose and puts his hand on his own head. Hence, he immediately gets burned down and turns into ashes due to the boon he got from Shiva.

The episode of Bhasmasura illustrates that the outcome of any work with malafide intention harms the person before hurting others. Any work with pure purpose results in happiness and satisfaction. The demon Bhasmasura wanted to misuse the boon; therefore, he had to be burned and turned into ashes. On the other hand, this episode brings unforgettable and great incarnations of Shiva. Shiva is running ahead and after some spell of time, he looks back, but does not see Bhasmasura chasing him. He stops and retreats and after some distance, he finds that there are ashes and a very attractive and charmful woman, Mohini standing there. Shiva asks about her purpose of standing midway. She tells Shiva that she is Vishnu. He has changed into Mohini so as to end Bhasmasura. Shiva at once is enchanted and embraces Mohini

Manikanta, also known as 'Hariharan Puthran' and 'Hariharaputra,' is said to have been born from the union of Lord Shiva and Lord Vishnu who was in his only female form ie. Mohini. When Vishnu took the form of Mohini, Shiva became enchanted with her beauty and embraced her. As a result of carnal desire, there was a generation of seed of Shiva which was kept in the tube of bamboo. It was later utilized by Vishnu to give birth to Manikanta who later became Ayyappa, a popular deity in Kerala. Ayyappa is often depicted squatting with cloth tied just below his knees. It is believed that his father, the Chera king, bound him in this manner to prevent him from escaping worldly life. As an ascetic warrior detached from worldly affairs, he resides atop the hill known as Sabarimala, where he protects and blesses all those who come to him.

According to the Shiva Purana, upon seeing Mohini, Shiva released his seed, which was then collected and placed into the ear of Añjanā. This act led to the birth of Hanuman, who is considered an incarnation of Shiva.

He is the force of yoga and celibacy that will be able to do anything. He is a great devotee of Rama, a very helpful and powerful god. Hanuman is the mighty monkey-god of the Hindus who is revered for his humanity, celibacy and strength.

Skanda, the Hindu god of war, is known as the firstborn son of Shiva, with various legends describing his birth. In Kalidasa's epic poem *Kumarasambhava* ("The Birth of the War God," 5th century CE), as in most versions of the story, the gods desired Skanda's birth to vanquish the demon Taraka, who could only be killed by a son of Shiva. To achieve this, they sent Parvati to convince Shiva to marry her. Yet Shiva, engrossed in meditation, was not attracted to Parvati until Kama, the god of love, struck him with an arrow. Shiva, infuriated, reduced Kama to ashes. After many years of abstinence, Shiva's seed became so powerful that the gods, concerned about its potential, sent Agni, the god of fire, to intervene. Agni received the seed and placed it into the Ganges, where Skanda was born.

Since Shiva's seed blazes with the power of tapa therefore Skanda is very hyper masculine, being capable of going to war. When he is only six days old, he defeats Taraka. Skanda thus helps the Devas from the torturous clutch of demon Tarakasura. Kartikeya is god of strength and handsome. In South India, he is popularly worshiped as god Murugan, boy-god and as Kumara, the eternal child. Most importantly, unlike Ayyappa and Hanuman, Kartikeya participates in worldly affairs and has two consorts, but In North India, Kartikeya is believed to be bachelor. The Bhasmasura, Vishnu's form as Mohini and Shiva's semen spill out result in the incarnation of three mighty gods. Shiva's any activity ushers some new big happening in the future and this is the charisma of Lord Shiva.

Shiva's boon to Shukracharya:- As Vedic mythology, Shukracharya was a son of sage Bhrigu and Kavya Mata. He is a great sage who is guru or counselor of Asuras (demons). According to Devi-Bhagawat purana, Sukracharya was a very bright child, he went to study Vedas under Rishi Angirasa. Due to Rishi Angirasa's favoritism towards his own son Brihaspati., Sukracharya left Angirasa and went to study under Rishi Gautama. When Brihaspati became the Guru of the deities, he had to become the Guru of the demons due to envy and rivalry with Brihaspati. As Guru, he guided his disciples and helped them wage war against the deities, thereby avenging his alienation. He always sought revenge for the insult of being considered less knowledgeable thanBrihaspati, who had become the Guru of the deities. The planet Venus in our solar system is named after him as Guru Sukracharya and holds great significance in individual horoscopes. Additionally, the fifth day of the week, Shukravar, is dedicated to him in the Hindu calendar.

Before waging war against the Devas, Sukrachaya wanted to get blessings from Shiva, so that he could be able to save his disciples from death. If the demons die on the battlefield, he can resurrect them. Therefore he starts to undertake severe penance to please Shiva.

He hangs upside down from a tree and gives up food and water. He only inhales smoke coming from burning leaves. On learning about Shukracharya's severe tapasya, the Devas became afraid. Consequently, Indra, the king of the Devas, made several attempts to disrupt his tapasya but failed.

Indra then sends his daughter Jayanti to try to disrupt the penance of Shukracharya. She puts chillies into burning leaves, hoping that smoke and burning smell of chillies will force him to stop the penance. But she is surprised to find that the sage is still hanging upside down even as blood comes out of his eyes, nose and mouth. After seeing Shukracharya in pain, Shiva appears and acknowledges his severe penance. Shiva is also pleased with Sukrachaya's commitment as well as devotion. Even knowing that Shukracharya is Guru of the Demons, he asks Shukracharya for boon. Shukracharya requests for Sanjivini Mantra and Shiva blesses him with the Sanjivnini Vidya with caution that the Vidya should not be misused. Jayanti, daughter apologizes to him for her misdeed and proposes to him for the marriage. Thus Indra's daughter becomes Guru Patni.

On the receipt of Sanjivani Mantra (Vidya), Shukracharya becomes very powerful and guides the demons to fight with the deities, In the battle, the demon who dies fighting, is resurrected by Sukracharya with help of the Sanjivini vidya. Consequently the demons are triumphant and the deities are defeated and humiliated. Because of this boon, the demons almost become invincible and acquire the supremacy and domination over the deities. So the deities, frightened and dejected, go for Shiva's refuge and request him to save them from the demons. They also tell Shiva how Sukracharya is misusing the Sanjivini Vidya to resurrect the evil demons who died in the battlefield. Shiva, enraged, searches for Sukracharya and swallows him. After millions of years of penance inside of Shiva's body, Shiva is pleased and redeems Sukracharya through penile passage. So, Sukra is a word that means semen. In another version, seeing Sukra, Shiva is ready to kill him, but is restrained by Parvati who says that since Sukra emerges from Shiva's stomach, so he is his son, does not deserve to be killed by him. Agreed, Shiva lets Sukra to go wherever he wishes. Being pardoned, Sukra returns to his place.

It is through Shukracharya that the Sanjivini (Mahamrityunjaya) mantra, which came to Earth from God Shiva, has become very beneficial to humankind. He is a great devotee of god Shiva and upon that he is righteous. According to Hindu scriptures, he has warned the demons many times to follow the right and correct path. At the same time, he has had the courage to oppose the deities. According to the Bhagavad Gita, Shukracharya is a form of Vishnu, and he works to balance good and evil, thereby maintaining the universe in harmony.

Shiva's boon to Banasura:- As per Hindu mythology, Banasura is son of Demon king Mahabali. There are different versions of the kingdoms of Banasura. One version says that he was king of Sonitpur (Tezpur, Assam) at present) and as per others, he was king of Kerala. This version also reflects the mythology and culture of Kerala. At present, there is a hill named "Banasura Hill" and a dam called "Banasura Sagar Dam" dedicated to the memory of King Banasura in Kerala. Banasura was a mighty demon who ruled over a large kingdom. He was so influential and powerful that even some deities and all other kings had to tremble before him.

He used to worship a Rasalingam which is believed to be given to him by Vishvakarma. Since his childhood, he had been a keen devotee of God Shiva. He used to worship Shiva with deep devotion and respect. According to the Hindu scripture, Bana had a thousand arms and he used his thousand arms to play the Mridangam when Shiva was performing the Tandav dance. Seeing his devotion and service, Shiva was pleased and gave a boon to Banasura to be invincible and long life. Bana also requested Shiva to be his protector. Then Banasura became unbeatable. As time passed, Bana became more cruel and arrogant. One day Banasura proudly told Shiva that he wanted to fight someone who might be as strong and mighty as him. Shiva felt his arrogance and ego and told that he would get a chance when his flag-staff would be broken and fall on the ground. Shiva also warned that there would be a great warrior who would crush his reputation and pride.

Banasura had a beautiful daughter named Usha. One night, she dreamed of a handsome prince and fell in love with him instantly. Upon waking, she could not find the prince from her dream and lamented that she would die without him. Usha had a clever and talented companion, Chitralekha, who wanted to help her. Chitralekha drew portraits of all the gods, but Usha said that none of them resembled the prince from her dream. Based on Usha's description, Chitralekha sketched a portrait of a young man, and Usha immediately recognized him.

Upon inquiry, it was revealed that the dream prince was Aniruddha, the grandson of Krishna.

Using her supernatural powers, Chitralekha abducted Aniruddha from Krishna's palace and brought him to Sonitpur. Upon meeting Usha, Aniruddha also fell deeply in love with her and decided to marry her. When Banasura learned about the love affair, he confined Usha in the fortress and attempted to capture Aniruddha. Aniruddha fought bravely and defeated the guards sent by Banasura, but ultimately, he was imprisoned.

In the meantime, Narada, a wandering sage, narrated the entire episode of Usha and Aniruddha's love affair and captivity to Krishna. Krishna, along with Balrama, Pradyumna, and others, led an army of 12 akshauhinis and surrounded Sonitpur on all sides. Banasura retaliated with equal force but felt powerless against Lord Krishna. He then invoked Lord Shiva to support him. Shiva, accompanied by Kartikeya, came to Banasura's aid. A fierce battle ensued between the two gods and continued for several days without any resolution, with other gods, heavenly beings, and sages merely observing.

At Krishna's request, it was decided that Krishna would use his divine weapons to put Shiva to sleep. Krishna then used his Sudarshan Chakra to sever Banasura's thousand arms, like branches from a huge tree. Just as Krishna was about to kill Banasura, Shiva awoke and requested Krishna to spare his devotee. Krishna agreed and spared Banasura.

The marriage between Aniruddha and Usha was then conducted, and the war concluded peacefully. Banasura later began penance to Brahma and received a boon that he could only be killed by an adolescent unmarried girl. According to Hindu mythology, Bhagwati Parvati manifested herself at the southern tip of Bharat to fulfill this prophecy. As an adolescent girl with immense devotion to Shiva, she attracted Banasura, who approached her without recognizing her true identity. Enraged, Bhagwati Parvati immediately slew Banasura, thus bringing about his end.

The story of Banasura illustrates the kindness and generosity of Lord Shiva, who is easily pleased with his devotees and grants boons readily. Shiva also defends his devotees, as seen when Banasura made Shiva his protector and called upon him to battle Krishna. This is why Shiva is revered as Bholenath.

Shiva's boon to Draupadi:- According to the epic *Mahabharata*, Panchala (present-day Bareilly region) is believed to be the birthplace of Draupadi, also known as Panchali. King Drupada of Panchala had promised his companion Drona that he would share his kingdom during their learning time together in the guru's ashram. However, when Dronacharya later visited Panchala and requested a portion of the kingdom, Drupada not only refused but also insulted him. In response, Drona, accompanied by Arjuna and other disciples, attacked Drupada and defeated him, taking half of his kingdom. To seek revenge on Drona, Drupada performed a Putrakameshti yagna to obtain a blessing. As a result, a boy named Dhrishtadyumna emerged from the sacrificial fire, followed by Draupadi, who appeared as a beautiful damsel.

When she emerged from fire, a heavenly voice (Akashvani) emanated that she would bring a big change in the future. In the arena of dharma and political affairs in Bharatvarsha, she would cause a lot of changes resulting in great battles, lakhs of killings & wounds and end of many monarchies and dynasties. Draupadi is portrayed as the most beautiful woman of her time, with dark complexion, lotus eyes, dark curly hair and an enchanting fragrance like that of a blue lotus.

Drupada wanted to get his daughter married. As per existing tradition, he organized a Swayamvara contest (self selection of husband contest or winner of the contest as husband) for Draupadi to choose her husband from the winner of the competitive contest. The module of contest was designed to test the efficiency of archery and for it to lift and string a bow and release the arrow to pierce the eye of a golden fish moving circularly by looking at its reflection in the water. All eligible princes, monarchs and others were invited to participate in the Swayamvara. They were unable to complete the test. Ultimately, Arjuna came and succeeded in the task who was dressed as Brahmin. Other attendees, including the Kauravas and Karna, both protected and attacked Arjuna and Draupadi. Arjuna and Bhima together defeated them all and returned home.

They returned home to find Kunti taking a bath. Thinking they had received good alms in the villages, she instructed them to share it equally among all the brothers. This misunderstanding, combined with motherly direction, led to an agreement that all five brothers would marry Draupadi.

She became the common wife of the five Pandava brothers, although she harbored intense love for Arjuna. A year was fixed for each Pandava brother, during which only that particular Pandava could enter Draupadi's private chamber.

During the time of the Mahabharata, such marriages or polyandry prevailed in society. In Draupadi's marriage, the principle that a woman was free to choose her husband and her choice was respected existed. However, at the same time, women were not treated equally, so Draupadi was compelled to marry five brothers without her will, love, and choice being considered even once.

She was won by the victor of the Swayamvara, but she was compelled to marry five brothers without her consent being sought. It shows that women were treated as mute spectators in the social system during the Mahabharata period.

Once Draupadi asked Krishhna why she had become the wife of five Pandavas. As per Hindu mythology, Krishna had a unique relationship with Draupadi. Even one of her names was Krishna. Krishna told her that she became the wife of all Pandavas not by accident, but by design. Lord Krishna disclosed to her that in her previous life, she prayed to Shiva to grant her a husband who would be honest, strong, skilled, handsome and intelligent. Instead of giving her one husband with all five qualities (in some version, Draupadi requested for a husband with fourteen qualities) Shiva gave her a boon of having five husbands, each with a unique quality, without taking into consideration the cultural taboo against polyandry, especially for women, as polyandry was prevalent among men, but rare for women. Upon receiving the boon of having five husbands, Draupadi doubted whether the boon was a blessing or a curse. Then Shiva gave boon to her that she would regain her virginity each morning when she took bath. Thus, she had the unique quality of remaining a virgin throughout her life. So, during the rotation of five Pandavas, all brothers were happy as well as satisfied with Draupadi. This conception might be incorrect and baseless. However, Draupadi made five Pandavas brothers united and she enjoyed a good marital life. Later she became a mother of five sons, one son each from the Pandava brothers. But Ashwathama killed her five sons during his ambush on the Pandava camp on the 18th day of the Mahabharata battle to avenge the death of his father, Drona.

As per Hindu mythology, there was an incident where Duryodhana fell into a pool that appeared to be a solid floor. Draupadi saw this from the balcony with amusement and commented "Andha Putra Andha"(blind son of the blind). Duryodhana felt insulted and as a result, the hatred and the agony caused a reason for the Mahabharat battle. Before the battle, in the game of dice, Yudhisdhthira lost everything and in continuation, he lost Draupadi also. She was brought into court forcefully. Dushasana dragged her to the court by the hair. Later on, her garments and attires were disrobed, but at the same time she was miraculously protected by Lord Krishna when she cried for help to Krishna in distress. Later she and five Pandavas were sent on exile for 13 years with the last one year being an incognito (secretly). Due to enmity, a great battle known as the Mahabharata took place, and ultimately the Pandavas were victorious.. After some years, Yudhishthira and his brothers chose to renounce worldly life. They embarked on their final journey towards the Himalayas and ultimately to heaven. Draupadi accompanied them, and she was the first to fall into a ravine in the Himalayas and die.

Bhima asked Yudhishthira why she had fallen and died first. He replied that although she was the wife of all five Pandavas, she had a great love and preference for Arjuna. So, she had to face the consequences of her actions. Thus, Draupadi who is also known as Panchali and Yajnaseni lost her life. She is referred to as a tragic heroine, one of central characters in the conflict of Kauravas s & Pandavas and an example of polyandry in the Mahabharata age

Shiva's boon to Arjuna:- According to the epic Mahabharata, Arjuna, also known as Partha and Dhananjaya, is the third brother among the five Pandava brothers. They are the five sons of Pandu, though not his biological sons, as his wife Kunti had three sons with the gods Yama, Vayu and Indra, and his second wife, Madri, had two sons with the twin Ashvini Kumaras. In the Mahabharata battle, Arjuna was an important warrior and skilled archer who led the Pandavas to victory by slaying many warriors, including Karna. Before the beginning of the war, God Krishna taught him the knowledge of Bhagavad Gita, the most sacred book of the Hindus

This is the story of when the Pandavas were in exile after losing their kingdom to the Kauravas. Vedvayasa suggested to Arjuna to please Lord Shiva to obtain the celestial weapon. To obtain it, Arjuna went to the banks of the Bhagirathi River to meditate and please Shiva. He began his severe penance for Shiva. Observing his penance over a long period, Shiva descended to Earth along with

Mother Parvati and his Ganas, appearing in the form of the Kirata tribe to test Arjuna's devotion.

Meanwhile his cousin Duryodhan sent a Boar to disturb Arjuna's penance. A demon named Mukasura came in disguise of a wild boar to attack Arjuna, but Arjuna and Kirata both shot arrows and killed him simultaneously. Now Kirata claimed that he killed the boar, but Arjuna denied and said that he killed the boar. Thus, the dispute between them resulted in the physical clashes. Arjuna's assault on Kirata was foiled by Kirata. In a sense of his futility, he used his fatal Gandiva, Shiva absorbed his Gandiva. Enraged, Arjuna took his hard sword and smashed it on the head of Kirata, but instead of wounding Kirata's head, the sword was broken into pieces. Still Arjuna had not realized that Kirat is not an ordinary tribal man, but he is some extraordinary hunter. Arjuna, frustrated, started fighting with trees, stones and boulders and finally with bare hands. Kirata was successful in averting all attacks attempted by Arjuna. On the other hand, Arjuna was badly beaten and injured in the fight. Ultimately, he fainted. Upon regaining consciousness, he recalled the purpose of his journey and the undertaking of his penance. With great pain and agony, he attempted to fashion a Shivalinga from the soil and began to pray to Shiva. And when he offered flowers and dried leaves to the Shivalinga, he was utterly surprised to find that he offered flowers and dried leaves falling on Kirata, then he realized that he was fighting none other than Shiva. Arjuna fell on the feet of Kirata (Shiva) and begged his pardon for his fighting with him. As Lord Bholebaba, Shiva was pleased and appeared in his true form along with Mother Parvati.

He gave Arjuna his most destructive and mighty Pashupataastra with all knowledge and techniques related to its launching, firing, withdrawing and others. Shiva also taught how to fire with eyes or mind using a bow. It distinctly shows that the weapon which was given by Shiva was automatically operated with virtual and mental direction. Shiva also gave boon to Arjuna that there would be no warrior /archer better than him on the Earth. After getting Pashupatastra, Arjuna was well equipped with the most fatal weapons.

At the end of the 13-year exile period, driven by jealousy and enmity, Duryodhana refused to return the territories of the Pandavas that they had discovered during their exile, claiming that no return of their kingdom had been agreed upon. The dispute and clash had reached its peak; the Kauravas were adamant about not compromising with the Pandavas. As a final attempt to uphold Rajdharma (the principles of righteous governance), Krishna went to Hastinapur to persuade the Kauravas to recognize reality, avoid the bloodshed of their kin, and embrace the path of peace.

Krishna appealed to the Kauravas to return Indraprastha to the Pandavas, but they refused to comply. Krishna proposed to give five villages to the Pandavas, one for each brother. However, Duryodhana rejected this proposal and declared that he would not part with even a piece of land as small as a needle's tip to the Pandavas. He ordered his soldiers to arrest Krishna, thus insulting him. Angered by this disrespect, Krishna cursed Duryodhana, foretelling his inevitable downfall, and then departed from Hastinapur. He informed the Pandavas of the situation and advised them to prepare for war, as war was now the only option left to settle the dispute and secure their rightful claims.

Ultimately, the Kurukshetra war was started between the Pandavas and Kauravas. During the war, various types of weapons were used by the prominent warriors as well as ordinary soldiers. It is believed that lakhs were badly injured and killed. The war lasted for 18 days and except for only 12 major warriors –five Pandavas, Krishna, Satyaki, Ashwatthama, Kripacharya, Yututs, Vrishaketu and Kritvarma, all were killed. The Kauravas were completely annihilated. The great war is famous as Mahabharat war and more importantly, before commencement of the Kurukshetra war. Arjuna was nervous and confused about what was right and what was wrong, He turned to Krishna for divine advice and teachings. Krishna, who was there as charioteer, advised him of performing his duty without worrying about the outcome of his duty and efforts. The conversation between Krishna and Arjun shaped the Bhagavad Gita, one of the most sacred and philosophical books of the Hindus. The

Bhagavad Gita contains the essence of life and solutions of all doubts regarding human life. This epic is not confined to only the Hindu, but also the people of other religions. Actually Gita is regarded as 'Human Shastra' or Anthropology'

No doubt, Arjuna was a key warrior in Pandava victory in the Kurukshshetra war. He killed many powerful and great warriors of the Kauravas' side. He was also successful in killing Karna with help of Krishna, as Karna was believed to be a more powerful and efficient warrior than Arjuna. By using Pashupatastra, given by Shiva, he killed Jayadratha and on the advice of Krishna, threw Jayadratha's head to the lap of his father who was in meditation far away from the Kurukshetra. Arjuna of course was the greater archer and fighter whose contribution to the Pandavas' victory in the Kurukshetra war was immense.

Shiva's boon to Jayadratha:- According to the epic Mahabharata, Jayadratha was king of Sindhu kingdom. He was son of Vriddhakshatra and husband of Dushala, the only sister of 100 kauravas brothers. Being a king and having good relations with the Kauravas, he gradually became arrogant and self-indulgent. Due to his intimacy with Duryodhana, he grew jealous and hostile towards the Pandavas, attempting to harm them

Moreover, his father after transfer of power to his son Jayadratha, led an ascetic life. Since Vriddhakshatra loved his son so deeply that he started performing difficult penance and obtained a boon for his son that he could be only killed by the greatest warrior on the earth and too with the universe's greatest weapon. Still, he was not satisfied with this boon, he continued his tapasya and was able to get another boon whatsoever would make his son Jayadratha's severed head fall on the earth, and would have had his head blown to pieces. Thus, by performing severe penance and in result getting two boons, Vriddhakshatra tried to protect his son Jayadratha from death as these boons made it impossible to kill Jayadratha. So, Jayadratha became a very arrogant and egoistic man.

When the Pandavas were in exile, the Pandavas went hunting to gather food. They left Draupadi alone at the ashram (hut). Meanwhile, Jayadratha went to Draupadi and initially she welcomed him as the Pandavas brother-in-law. But he, obsessed with her charm and beauty, proposed to marry her, Draupadi vehemently refused his proposal. Enraged, Jayadratha abducts Draupadi and starts moving towards his kingdom. On returning to their ashram, Pandavas did not find Draupadi there and searched for her but in vain. Later on, they came to know through their friend Dhaatreyika that Jayadratha had forcefully captured Draupadi and carried her away.

Yudhishthira ordered his younger brothers to rescue her from Jayadratha. The Pandavas brothers chased Jayadratha and his soldiers and they went on a rampage by killing Jayadrath's soldiers and seeing the killing of his army, Jayadratha left Draupadi and ran away. Draupadi was found safe, but Yudhisthira again ordered his brothers to capture and to fetch Jayadratha. Since Jayadratha was very far away and in order to catch him, Arjuna used his divine weapon to cut the horse of Jayadratha. Ultimately, Bhima seized him by his hair, slammed him on the ground and started to kick him on his head. But he was deterred, as Yudhishthira instructed them to bring Jayadratha back alive. Bhima managed to control his anger and shaved Jayadratha's head, then bound him in chains before presenting him to Yudhishthira. Draupadi was asked to decide his punishment, but she declared that Jayadratha had already been severely beaten and treated as a slave, so she chose to let him go free. Badly beaten and humiliated, Jayadratha returned to his kingdom.

After his humiliation and physical assault by the Pandavas, Jayadratha thought something different. He gave control of his kingdom to his wife and started severe penance to lord Shiva. Pleased with his rigorous penance, Shiva appeared and asked for boon. Jayadratha requested for a boon that he would be able to defeat all five Pandava brothers, Shiva said that because Krishna was a companion of Arjuna, Arjuna could not be defeated by him. Shiva, never letting his devotees despair, granted a boon to Jayadratha: the power to hold all the Pandava brothers at bay for one day in battle, except Arjuna.

In other words, lord Shiva granted a boon to Jayadratha that he would kill any one warrior of Pandavas except Arjuna's side in one day of battle.

Jayadratha, king of Sindhu and brother-in-law of the Kauravas sided with Duryodhana in the Kurukshetra war. On the first day of the Kurukshetra, at noon, Jayadratha defeated king Drupada, but spared him. The war progressed resulting in terrific bloodshed and killing of the warriors of both sides. On the 13th day of the Mahabharata war, after discussing and implementing their strategy, Dronacharya crafted the Chakravyuha. The Pandavas challenged themselves to enter and exit the Chakravyuha alive.

As part of Dronacharya's strategy, Arjuna and Krishna were compelled to battle with the Susharma and the Trigata army elsewhere, away from the Chakravyuha. In their absence, Abhimanyu, the young son of Arjuna who knew how to enter the Chakravyuha but not how to exit it, was unfortunately entrusted with the task of breaking through the formation. Abhimanyu managed to enter the formation intended for the Pandavas (without Arjuna) and led their forces, but meanwhile Jayadratha invoked tremendous strength using Shiva's boon.

He immediately moved to close the gap and successfully held all the Pandava brothers and their forces at bay. Consequently, the young warrior Abhimanyu had to fight within the Chakravyuha and wreaked havoc, but he did not know how to exit from it. He became deeply trapped and fought valiantly, but he was ultimately killed brutally in a combined attack by the Kaurava warriors. Jayadratha played an active role in trapping and killing Abhimanyu.

Arjuna arrived at the end of the 13th day of the Kurukshetra war and learned about the death of his son Abhimanyu and the brutal manner in which Jayadratha and other warriors of the Kaurava side had killed him.

It was found that Jayadratha was the main cause for Abhimanyu's death. Arjuna vowed to kill him the very next day before sunset, failing which he would kill himself by jumping into a pyre of fire. As per the prevailing war system, war lasted till sunset, and it started the next day after sunrise.

The Kauravas decided to save Jayadratha from Arjuna at any cost. So Dronacharya arranged a combination of 3 Vyuhas (triangular arms formations) in order to protect Jayadratha from Arjuna. The formations consisted of the cart formation (Shakata vyuha), Needle formation (Suchimukhi vyuha) and lotus formation (Padam vyuha). To destroy these arms formations was not so easy and a time consuming task. Although Bhima, Satyaki and Arjun tried to harm the Kaurava army, but Arjuna failed to destroy the formations and consequently he pledged to kill himself before the sunset. Krishna saw that there were thousand army and warriors between Jayadratha and Arjuna and it was not possible for Arjuna to kill Jayadratha, in result he would accept the death. To rescue Arjuna from a sad happening, Krishna did a ploy by sending his Sudarshan Chakra to cover the sun and created an illusion of the sunset. The Kaurava warriors rejoiced over Arjuna's defeat and were desirous of watching his imminent suicide. Jayadratha who was hiding, came out and laughed amusedly. Finding Jayadratha near Arjuna, Krishna at once freed the sun from the cover of Sudarshan Chakra and told Arjuna that the sun had still not set and was shining in the sky. He instructed Arjuna to cut Jayadratha's head with such force that his severed head would fall in the lap of Jayadratha's father who was very far away from the Kurukshetra battlefield. Arjuna quickly picked up his Gandiva and shot a Pashupatashatra at Jayadratha in such a way that Jayadratha 's head flew away very far and landed on the lap of his father Vridhakshatra. That time, his father was in the state of meditation, and suddenly his son's head dropped in his lap. He was horrified and hurriedly got up. The severed head fell on the ground and Vridhakshatra's head was burst into pieces. Thus, due to a boon requested by Vridhakshatra for punishment of a person who would kill his son Jayadratha, he was himself killed by throwing the severed head of his son on the ground.

Shiva 's boon to Jayadratha proved true that Jayadratha was killed by Arjuna who was of course the greatest warrior in the Dwapar age and with his divine weapons like Gandiva and Pashupatastra. This boon Jayadratha also implied that no one is immortal, and death is eternal reality. The reason for death may vary, and no boon or effort can prevent it. Since Shiva is the god of destruction, any boon he grants ultimately accelerates one's demise and leads to their destruction. Moreover, the two boons obtained by Jayadratha's father for his safety could not save him from death. It is a fact that everyone must complete the cycle of birth and death. Destruction ushers in new creation, and this process continues endlessly.

Shiva's boon to Lord Krishna:- God Krishna is a great deity in Hinduism and is widely worshiped not only by Hindus but also by others. He is believed to be an incarnation of Vishnu and possesses 16 kalas (qualities) that enhance his charismatic personality.

The anecdotes and narratives of his life are referred to as Krishna Leela. He possesses multi-faceted qualities: he is a true lover, a great warrior, the preacher of the Bhagavad Gita, and the charioteer to Arjuna in the Kurukshetra war. He helps Draupadi avoid being disrobed by the Kauravas, and he shows great respect for his poor friend Sudama. His life is full of diverse activities and incredible deeds. Krishna is often depicted in idols as having black or blue skin. He is also known by various other names, epithets, and titles that reflect his many associations, attributes, and roles, such as Giridhara, lifter of Govardhan Mountain; Banshidhar, flute player; Gopala, protector of cows; and so on.

The legends of Krishna's childhood and youth describe him as a cowherd and a mischievous boy known as Makhan Chor (butter thief). He is also portrayed as a determined boy who lifts the Govardhan Hill to protect the people from the fury of God Indra and the devastating rains and floods. Additionally, Krishna is described as an enchanter and playful lover of the Gopis of Vrindavan, especially Radha. The iconic and divine love stories and dances with the Gopis and Radha are regarded as Ras-Leela.

In his youth, Krishna, along with his elder brother Balarama, overthrows and kills the despotic king of Mathura, his own uncle Kansa (Mama), and reinstates Ugrasen, Kansa's father. After hearing a prophecy, Kansa imprisons his sister Devaki and her husband Vasudeva, and Krishna is born in the prison. After killing Kansa, Krishna, along with the Yadava army, starts living in the newly built city of Dwarka. Later, Krishna befriends Arjuna and supports the Pandavas against the Kauravas in the Kurukshetra War. Krishna plays a key role in the victory of the Pandavas in the Mahabharata War.

As far as Krishna's married life is concerned, according to the Bhagavata Purana, Krishna has eight wives: Rukmini, Satyabhama, Jambavati, Kalindi, Nagnajiti, Mitravinda, Lakshmana, and Bhadra. In the Dwapara Yuga, polygamous marriage was prevalent in society, and men were free to have more than one wife. Polygamous marriages were generally solemnized for the fulfillment of love, friendship, alliances with other kings (the fathers of the brides/bridegrooms), the extension of one's kingdom, and the outcome of Swayamvara (self-selection of a groom). This system was customary among the clans of deities, demons (daityas), humans, and others. Krishna married multiple wives for several reasons. Despite having eight wives, Krishna is most commonly depicted with Radha. According to Hindu scriptures, with Krishna, Radha is believed to be the supreme goddess. Krishna is only satisfied by devotional service in loving servitude to the supreme god, and Radha is the personification of devotional service. Many devotees worship her for her blessing as the only way to attain Krishna. Thus, uttering "Radha-Krishna" is an effective method for approaching the absolute reality (Radha) and the deity (Krishna) as a person first and foremost. Radha and Krishna are believed to be one, and their bond is considered the epitome of eternal love. Radha-Krishna represents the feminine and masculine realities of God.

The group of eight principal queen-consorts of Krishna is known as Ashtabharyas. According to Hindu mythology, Rukmini and Satyabhama are the main among the Ashtabharyas. Rukmini, the princess of Vidarbha, was Krishna's first wife and chief queen (Patrani). She is believed to be an avatar of the goddess Lakshmi. Satyabhama, Krishna's third wife, a Yadava princess, is considered to be Bhudevi, the goddess of the Earth.

Rukmini, a princess of the Vidarbha kingdom, loved Krishna deeply, and Krishna was very emotionally attached to her. However, her brother Rukmi was adamant that she marry Shishupala, the crown prince of Chedi and a cousin of Krishna. Rukmini was never ready to marry Shishupala because her love and affection for Krishna was enormous. She sent a message to Krishna, requesting him to prevent her unwanted marriage. In response, Krishna heroically carried her away. As per her wish, Krishna eloped with her and married Rukmini. Since she loved Krishna immensely, she was a devoted wife and humble in her service to him.

Satyabhama was the daughter of King Satrajit of the Yadava dynasty, who was the royal treasurer of Dwarka and the owner of the Syamantaka jewel. Satrajit had received the jewel from the god Surya Deva and was unwilling to part with it, even for Krishna. Once, Krishna requested that Satrajit give him the jewel, but Satrajit refused. Later, Satrajit's brother Prasenjit went hunting while wearing the jewel.

He was killed by a lion. Jambavan killed that lion and took the jewel. He gave it to his daughter, Jambavati. When Prasenjit did not return with the jewel, Satrajit falsely accused Krishna of killing Prasenjit in the forest to obtain the jewel. Knowing the false allegation that he had killed Prasenjit for the jewel, Krishna was upset. To clear his reputation, he went to the forest and reached the cave where Jambavan and his daughter Jambavati were living.

Jambavan attacked Krishna, thinking he was an intruder who had come to take the jewel. They fought fiercely for 28 days, during which Jambavan was severely injured by Krishna's sword. At last, Jambavan recognized Krishna as Rama, realizing that only a divine power could defeat him, and he surrendered to Krishna.

Regretting his mistaken fight with Krishna, Jambavan gave him the jewel and his daughter Jambavati in marriage. Krishna returned from the forest with the jewel and Jambavati as his wife.

As the practice of polygamy was prevalent, Krishna accepted Jambavati as his wife. He returned the jewel to Satrajit and narrated the whole episode. Satrajit apologized for his false accusation and promptly offered his daughter Satyabhama and the jewel to Krishna. In turn, Krishna accepted Satyabhama in marriage but refused the jewel.

The grand wedding ceremony of Krishna and Satyabhama was celebrated. She became a true and devoted wife to Krishna and often prided herself on being his favorite, believing that he loved her more than his other wives, especially Rukmini, because she had a special hold over his heart.

The other wife (sahpatni) was envious and the comparison between Rukmini and Satyabhama was massive and vocal. This was the charisma of Krishna, he loved each wife in such a way that each one of them thought she had control over his heart. Thus, both Rukmini and Satyabhama were under the illusion that he loved them the most and that they had a special hold over him. Both queens were very beautiful. They loved & adored Krishna very much. Since Satyabhama was an extrovert and egoist, she usually proclaimed her beauty and love for Krishna, whereas Rukmini was also gorgeous but at the same time she was introverted and consequently modest about her beauty and love for Krishna. In spite of non -utterance of Rukmini's beauty and love, Satyabhama used to complain that it was Rukmini who stole her glory. So, her vanity caused her ego to rise, leading to jealousy towards Rukmini and an inner envy that burned inside her.

It is interesting to refer to an episode which exhibits and distinguishes between the silent love of Rukmani and vocal love of Satyabhama. Once Satyabhama was boasting that Krishna loved her the most. Meanwhile Narada Muni appeared there and countered that Rukmini really loved Krishna by heart and Satyabhama's love was purely an illusion. Satyabhama challenged NaradaMuni to prove her wrong to which he agreed. He convinced her that if she offered herself to Krishna and then returned to him, she could keep Krishna all to herself. She agreed to that offer. Narada said the wife who paid the greater amount would win Krishna back. Satyabhama was happy and confident that she would win against Krishna as Rukmini did not have so much wealth. Narada decided that Krishna would be weighed. A large weighing balance was brought, and Satyabhama placed her wealth on one scale. On the other scale, Krishna was requested to stand.

After several attempts and placing her entire wealth, Krishna still outweighed Satyabhama's offerings. Thus, Satyabhama failed to reclaim Krishna. Upon seeing Krishna on the scale, Rukmini stepped in and plucked a Tulsi leaf, placing it on top of the piled wealth on the scale. Krishna was then outweighed by the Tulsi leaf. This demonstrated that God values true devotion from his devotees, not wealth and ostentation. Devotion leads to enlightenment, while ego and pride destroy one's devotion to God. Satyabhama was shocked by this revelation.

Still, jealousy and hostility arose at times, especially when Rukmini had a son named Pradyumna, who was exceptionally handsome, powerful, and courageous, loved by all. When Satyabhama saw everyone showering Pradyumna with love and affection, she became jealous, insecure, and frustrated. She wanted a son just like Pradyumna. Upon hearing Satyabhama's desire, Krishna was perplexed and asked her what could be done to have a son like Pradyumna. Although Krishna was an incarnation of God Vishnu and possessed divine power, he found himself unable to produce a desired son. He began to pray, but his efforts were in vain. Meanwhile, Satyabhama persisted in her desire to have a son like Pradyumna. Krishna then approached a spiritual master for blessings and advice in this matter. The spiritual Guru expressed his inability to help Krishna and advised him to seek help from Shiva, as only Lord Shiva could assist him.

Krishna started praying and continued for many years. Normally, Shiva does not take long to respond to the prayers of his devotees, but in this case, Shiva did not appear promptly. Krishna persisted in his prayers. After many years, Lord Shiva along with Maa Parvati appeared before Krishna and asked the purpose of his prayers. Krishna replied that he had been praying to Shiva for a desirable boon. Pleased, Shiva asked what boon Krishna desired. Krishna explained that his wife Satyabhama wished to have a son exactly like Pradyumna, who was his son with Rukmini. Satyabhama was determined to have a child like Pradyumna, so Krishna requested Shiva to grant this boon to fulfill her desire. Shiva granted the boon as requested by Krishna.

Krishna's prayer to Shiva illustrates that for a peaceful and harmonious married life, spouses must compromise and make efforts to satisfy each other. Sometimes, fulfilling a spouse's desires or wishes may not be easy, but it is crucial to avoid hostility and tension in the relationship. Satyabhama's strong desire to have a son like Pradyumna compelled Krishna to seek Shiva's help, despite Krishna being a god and capable of performing miracles. This demonstrates that an ideal husband should strive to fulfill his wife's needs and desires for a better married life, just as a wife should do for her husband. Flexibility, accommodation, and sharing of feelings are essential for maintaining a strong marital bond and avoiding difficult situations.

Krishna's prayer to Shiva for a boon highlights the distinctions between Shiva and Krishna, although both embody the same universal energy and consciousness. Shiva stands as the supreme deity of the Trimurti, the most powerful among them. He transcends birth and death, existing infinitely and eternally. Shiva is the creator and destroyer of the universe, perpetually renewing existence, as described in the Padma Purana. He is omnipotent, omnipresent, and omniscient.

In contrast, Krishna is also a powerful deity renowned for his divine plays (leelas) and extraordinary feats. His profound discourse with Arjuna during the Kurukshetra war resulted in the sacred scripture, the Bhagavad Gita. Born as an incarnation of Vishnu, Krishna entered the world through his mother's womb and later departed. When Satyabhama expressed her desire to have a son like Pradyumna, Krishna prayerfully turned to Shiva to fulfill her wish.

Shiva possesses the ability to alter destiny, demonstrating his timeless nature as Mahakaal, beyond the constraints of time (Kaal) that limit even gods and avatars like Krishna.

According to Vedic scriptures, there are numerous references where Shiva is depicted as the supreme god in some contexts, while in others, Krishna, an avatar of Vishnu, is revered as supreme. Faithful devotees do not distinguish which deity is greater. This reflects the merit of Hindu pluralism, where many gods are worshiped with utmost devotion and faith.

Shiva's boon to Ravana:- Ravana is well known as the king of Lanka, celebrated for his knowledge and scholarship, yet notorious for his evil deeds. He possessed many qualities that made him a learned scholar and was well-versed in the six Shastras and the four Vedas. Ravana was born to the great sage Vishrava and his wife Kaikesi, a demon princess. His grandfather was Rishi Pulastya, one of the mind-born sons (Manas putras) of Brahma. His maternal grandfather was Sumal (or Sumalaya), the king of the Rakshasas.

Kaikesi, Ravana's mother, preferred Vishrava, father of Kubera, over any other king or demon.

Ravana, Kubera, and their other brothers completed their education under Vishrava in the ashram. Ravana was brilliant and mastered the Vedas and other scriptures from childhood. Due to certain reasons, Ravana and his brothers were more attached to their maternal lineage. Consequently, they adopted certain demon qualities that were quite distinct from the qualities associated with deities. Demon culture, customs, and attitudes differed significantly from those of the deities. Although Ravana was the son of a sage and a Brahmin well-versed in the Vedas, he was influenced adversely by demon traits, habits, and attitudes, and as a result, he took pride in being a Rakshasa (demon).

Kuber and Ravana were half-brothers as they share the same father - Visravas. Kuber was the king of Lanka and also the deity of wealth whereas Ravana, along with his brothers, maternal grandfather, and uncles, lived a modest and isolated life. They harbored dreams of capturing Kubera and other noble kings to rule over their kingdoms. Ravana was a great warrior, brave, and a learned scholar with kingly qualities. His ambitions were grand.

To fulfill their dreams, Ravana, along with his two brothers Kumbhakarna and Vibhishana, began severe penances to Brahma on Mount Gokarna for 11, 000 years. Ultimately, Brahma was pleased and granted Ravana boons that made him invincible to creations except humans. Additionally, Brahma bestowed upon him weapons, a chariot, and the ability to shapeshift.

Subsequently, Ravana attacked Lanka with his army and seized it from his stepbrother Kubera. Kubera fled in fear and settled in Alkapuri, while Ravana also captured Kubera's Pushpak automatic aircraft. He appointed Shukracharya as his priest.

Ravana was very ambitious and aimed to rule over the world, including all deities and humans. He embarked on a grand mission to conquer kingdoms, often proclaiming "Yuddham Dehi" (give battle) or surrender. He conquered many kingdoms in Aryavarta, killing kings and others, and taking queens and other beautiful women captive. Atrocities and bloodshed were committed ruthlessly. If a king surrendered to Ravana, he showed some mild kindness before annexing their kingdom.

Eventually, he reached near Mount Kailash where he found no inhabitants or palaces, but encountered a sturdy and strong bull-like man moving cautiously like a warrior. Ravana inquired about the name of the kingdom and its king.

The soldier, Nandi, informed Ravana that his name was Nandi, and that the god Mahadeva, the god of all gods, resided atop Mount Kailash. Ravana was completely perplexed upon hearing about the greatness and importance of Mahadeva. He was surprised to find no palace, no security arrangements, and no royal activities, which are typically necessary and natural for a king. Therefore, Ravana took Nandi's response lightly and instructed him to convey to Mahadeva that Ravana challenged him to fight. Ravana cried out "Yuddham Dehi!" and declared himself as Ravana, the king of Lanka, son of sage Vishrava, and grandson of Rishi Pulastya.

Nandi warned Ravana not to think of fighting with the god Mahadeva, as he was insignificant and minuscule compared to Mahadeva and not permitted to do so. Enraged, Ravana pushed Nandi, and a fight ensued, and Nandi was defeated. Recognizing Ravana's strength, Nandi agreed to convey Ravana's message to Mahadeva. Nandi described Ravana and his intentions to Shiva, and Mahadeva agreed to accept Ravana's challenge.

When Ravana saw Mahadeva, he was completely bewildered and stunned by the uniqueness and extraordinariness of Mahadeva. The mendicant god was smeared with ash, dressed in animal hide, carrying a skull, sitting under the open sky, holding a trident and a damroo, with eyes shut or half-shut, a crescent moon and flowing river on his head, knotted hair, and a third eye.

Despite Ravana's determination to duel, he shouted "Yuddham dehi!" and the battle commenced. Ravana exerted his full strength and employed all his strategic moves against Mahadeva, but Mahadeva effortlessly subdued Ravana as if he were a child. Realizing his error, Ravana understood he must seek forgiveness from Mahadeva. He immediately bowed his head, grasped Mahadeva's feet, and pleaded, "Shivam Shivam, save me!"

Understanding Mahadeva's temperament—quick to anger yet also quick to forgive—Mahadeva pardoned Ravana and asked about his lineage. Ravana described his background and other details. However, Mahadeva's anger flared up again as he rebuked Ravana, condemning him for his notorious deeds: attacking and conquering kingdoms, killing kings and innocent people, imprisoning queens and other women, and dishonoring their dignity. Mahadeva portrayed Ravana as greedy, cruel, ambitious, a murderer, and barbaric.

Ravana listened quietly to Mahadeva and replied that he and his clan were not inherently evil, but were disliked by the deity clan due to continuous class conflicts and clashes between deities and demons. He explained that their cultures, traditions, and customs were different, and deities often viewed demons as mostly illiterate, tribal, jungle inhabitants, and poor.

Ravana referred to the episode of Samudra Manthan (Ocean churning), where both demons and deities had agreed to share equally any Ratnas (gems or objects) found during the churning of the ocean. However, a larger share of objects like elephants and Goddess Lakshmi were taken by the deity side. When the elixir (Amrit) was found, a conspiracy was devised to prevent the demons from tasting it, fearing their potential immortality. Rahu, a demon, managed to taste the elixir in disguise, but Vishnu swiftly decapitated him as punishment

What was his fault, and did the deities keep their word and honor the agreement of equal sharing? Ravana continued his argument that he and his family were not guilty of dishonoring women's dignity and pride. He pointed out that whenever someone began performing penance for a boon from the gods, Indra, the king of the deities, feared losing his empire and power. Indra often used Apsaras (nymphs) to disturb and disrupt their penance. For instance, Vishvamitra's severe penance was broken by Apsara Menaka sent by Indra.

Ravana argued that the deities were cunning, deceitful, and hypocritical. His logical and factual arguments convinced Shiva, who is impartial and free from prejudice or pre-assumptions. Consequently, Shiva's anger dissipated, and he blessed Ravana. Ravana then praised Shiva by singing and dancing in reverence.

Later on, Ravana proved himself to be a devout follower of Shiva, and he became very close to Shiva. After their marriage, Shiva and Parvati (Shakti) arrived at Mount Kailash. Upon realizing there was no dwelling for them to live in, Parvati expressed her desire for a house. Shiva, who typically lived in the open sky regardless of weather conditions, pondered the necessity of having a house.

When Parvati needed shelter from the winter cold, Shiva took her to a crematorium to warm themselves by the funeral pyre. When she inquired about rain, Shiva carried her in his arms above the clouds where it did not rain. Despite these gestures, Parvati remained unconvinced and disagreed with

Shiva, emphasizing the necessity of a house for a better married life.

Although Shiva viewed a house as a burden, an attachment, and a source of unhappiness, he agreed to build one to please Parvati. He asked Ravana to construct a house for her.

Ravana was overjoyed when Shiva asked him to build a house for Parvati. Using his knowledge of Vastu Shastra or the secret understanding of space, he constructed a grand palace that became the most magnificent on Earth. Over time, Ravana became attached to the palace and desired to possess it for himself. He was not just a simple and wise devotee of Shiva; he was also cunning and clever, devising a plan to acquire the palace.

When Shiva visited and was greatly pleased with the palace, he wished to reward Ravana for his excellent work and asked what boon he desired. Ravana promptly requested the palace itself as his reward, and Lord Shiva agreed, saying, "So be it" (tathastu). When Parvati learned that Shiva had returned the palace to Ravana as a reward, she understood Shiva's nature and did not become angry. Later, Ravana invited her to stay in the palace as his guest, attempting to please the divine couple.

This episode illustrates Shiva's simplicity, childlike qualities, and non-attachment to material things, juxtaposed with Ravana's craftiness, greed, and attachment to worldly possessions.

Once, Ravana conceived the idea of lifting Mount Kailasha along with the divine couple to his kingdom of Lanka. His intention was to be able to pray to Shiva without traveling from Lanka to Mount Kailasha. Moreover, he desired for Shiva to stay in Lanka, demonstrating his ambition to exert control even over divinity. Ravana uprooted Mount Kailasha, and Shiva neither minded nor objected to Ravana's action. However, Parvati (Shakti) was upset by Ravana's intention to move Mount Kailasha. She implored Ravana to cease lifting Kailasha, but he adamantly refused and confidently declared that he would carry Mount Kailasha, along with Shiva, her, and their belongings on his shoulders.

Upon hearing Ravana's arrogant response, Shiva pressed his big toe against the ground and created an intense force that crushed Ravana under the weight of Mount Kailash. According to the scriptures, Ravana remained pinned beneath the mountain for a thousand years, seeking forgiveness by singing hymns in praise of Shiva (Shiva Tandava Stotram). Pleased with Ravana's devotion, Shiva blessed him and allowed him to emerge from beneath Mount Kailasha. Shiva also granted him an invincible sword and a powerful linga (Atmalinga) for worship. To please Shiva, Ravana composed the immortal verse "Shiva Tandava Stotram, " which extols the beauty, valor, and power of Mahadeva. This stotram comprises highly intricate Sanskrit words, showcasing Ravana's scholarly knowledge. It remains one of the most effective and powerful Shiva mantras of all time.

This episode also underscores that while Shiva is omnipotent, Ravana's power pales in comparison. Ravana seeks greater power through pleasing Shiva, hoping to overcome fear, enjoy material wealth, and become more powerful. However, he never comprehends why Shiva, despite possessing divine power, chooses to lead an ascetic life.

Ravana, who was a devotee of Shiva, always tried to please Shiva for boons of immortality, prosperity, and power. According to legend, Ravana undertook intense penance to please God Shiva, which continued for a hundred years. During this severe penance, he chopped off his head ten times to demonstrate his devotion and dedication to Shiva. It is believed that each time he cut off his head, another one appeared, resulting in Ravana having ten heads.

Pleased with Ravana's steadfastness and severity, Shiva appeared and offered him a boon. Ravana requested immortality, but Shiva refused, stating that anyone who is born must eventually die.

Shiva gave Ravana a gem filled with the nectar of immortality. Pleased with Ravana, Shiva also granted him further boons. At Ravana's request, he was granted immunity and protection from gods, demons, and animals, though not from humans, as Ravana considered humans weak, incapable, and less powerful. Ironically, Rama, in human form, ultimately killed him.

The killing of Ravana illustrates that despite his immense power, possession of destructive weapons, and the nectar of immortality, everyone must eventually die. Shiva's boon to Ravana, despite being a god of destruction, only hastened the evil king's demise.

As per mythology, Ravana designed and made the "Rudra Veena, " a lute using one of his heads and one of his hands. His head served as the gourd of the veena, his hand as its beam, and his nerves as its strings. The Rudra Veena was then offered to Shiva and is also known as Ravan-haath (Hand of Ravana). Using the Veena, Ravana sang a song known as the Shiva Stotram, praising Shiva and thereby pleasing him. Ravana was blessed by Shiva as a result.

Ravana often tried to please him out of devotion. Ravana also understood the innocence and childlike nature of Shiva. Once, Ravana took advantage of Shiva's simple nature and expressed his desire to have goddess Parvati as his wife. Shiva neither became enraged nor displeased upon hearing Ravana's immoral and inexcusable request.

He simply stated that if Parvati wanted to go with Ravana, she was free to do so. Being Bholenath, Shiva could not grasp the importance of marital rights and the sanctity of conjugal relationships and loyalty.

To teach a lesson to the evil and cunning Ravana, Maa Parvati decided to take action. She transformed a frog (Manduka) into a beautiful damsel named Mandodari and placed her atop Mount Kailasha. When Ravana reached the summit of Kailasha and saw the beautiful and charming woman, he assumed she must be Parvati because only Parvati is allowed to sit there. Immediately, he picked her up, took her to Lanka, and made her his queen. Ravana and Mandodari lived together happily.

Shiva and Parvati watched with amusement as the demon king Ravana loved the frog-woman, believing her to be Parvati, and thought that he had tricked Shiva himself and exploited his simplicity and naivety. In reality, Ravana had deceived himself, as he perhaps did not understand the true nature of divine power.

There is another version of the above episode where, upon completing his austere penance, Ravana pleased Shiva who then offered him a boon. With malicious intent, Ravana requested Parvati as his wife. Astonished, Shiva warned Ravana that Parvati, being Adishakti and the mother of nature, could not be the wife of anyone else, including Ravana. Shiva suggested Ravana ask for another boon, but Ravana remained adamant and accused Shiva of not keeping his word. Eventually, Shiva reluctantly agreed to give Parvati to Ravana and instructed her to go with him.

As Parvati accompanied Ravana, they encountered the sage Muni Narada along the way. Narada persuaded Parvati to transform into Bhadrakali to be freed from Shiva's command. Parvati then manifested as Bhadrakali, fierce and violent. When Ravana saw the terrifying Bhadrakali, she told him that Shiva had sent her along, keeping Parvati for himself. Enraged, Ravana left Bhadrakali there and hurried to confront Shiva, accusing him of deception and vowing to find

Parvati at any cost. Bhadrakali returned to Mount Kailasha.

Meanwhile, as Ravana searched for Parvati, she transformed a frog (Manduka) into a beautiful and enchanting woman named Mandodari, placing her at the summit of Kailasha. When Ravana saw Mandodari, he immediately fell in love and, mistaking her for Parvati, took her to Lanka, married her, and they lived happily together. Ravana's malicious desire to have Parvati as his wife was thwarted by Parvati herself, demonstrating that Shiva (Purusha) and Parvati (Shakti, nature) are inseparable and complementary to each other.

Ravana was continuously in touch with his god Shiva. Whenever a chance comes up, he utilizes it and asks for a boon from Shiva, because Ravana has many desires to be fulfilled, so he is never content with one boon. Shiva never minds giving boons twice or thrice to a devotee if he is pleased with their severe penance. Ravana, being very cunning and ambitious, undertook rigorous penance to please Shiva and fulfill his desires. He began a tough penance with the intention of requesting Shiva to shift from Mount Kailash to Lanka.

Impressed by the severity of Ravana's penance, Shiva was pleased and asked Ravana for a boon. The shrewd Ravana requested Shiva to relocate himself from Kailasa to Lanka because he found it difficult to travel from Lanka to Kailasha to worship Shiva. However, Ravana had hidden intentions behind this request.

Shiva, suspecting Ravana's motives for wanting him to move, could not agree to such a request. Instead, he offered Ravana a Shivalinga, stating that it would be as good as his presence. Shiva also imposed a condition: Ravana must not place the linga down anywhere during its transportation. If he did, that place would become the site of the linga.

Ravana agreed to the condition, believing it to be an easy task to carry the linga from Kailasa to Lanka without any obstacles due to his enormous power. Taking the Shivalinga on his shoulders, Ravana departed for Lanka.

As Ravana journeyed towards Lanka, the gods feared the consequences of the linga being in Ravana's kingdom. They urgently approached god Vishnu and requested his intervention to prevent Ravana from successfully transporting the linga to Lanka.

God Vishnu instructed Varuna, the god of water, to enter Ravana's stomach and induce him to relieve himself immediately. Varuna complied and descended to the ground, where he looked for someone to hold the linga while Ravana attended to his needs. Spotting a Brahmin (who was actually Vishnu in disguise), Ravana requested him to hold the linga temporarily.

The Brahmin was willing to hold the linga for a few minutes but was in a hurry to reach his destination. He shouted that he wanted to leave. He said that If Ravana delayed, he would place the linga on the ground. Ravana rushed to relieve himself, but due to Varuna's influence, he took longer than expected. The Brahmin (who was actually God Vishnu) shouted for Ravana to hurry, but Ravana's delay led the Brahmin to place the linga on the ground and disappear.

Upon returning, Ravana found the linga firmly rooted in the ground. Despite his attempts to uproot it with all his strength, he failed miserably. Eventually, he prayed to the linga. The place where the linga became fixed is now well known as Deoghar (the home of God).

The episode of the linga being grounded at Deoghar illustrates that Ravana never succeeded in fulfilling his malicious desire to shift the linga to Lanka and gain control over it for more power. Divine power thwarted the demon's ambitions.

Ravana acquired a vast empire on earth and amassed many dangerous weapons and arms. His army consisted of brave and aggressive fighters, committed soldiers, and hundreds of thousands of well-decorated elephants and horses. His brothers, sons, and relatives were great warriors capable of leading and winning difficult battles. Ravana ruled with mighty power over gods, humans, and demons. According to Valmiki's Ramayana, Ravana, a tyrant of great power, held the gods at ransom and even captured planets like Saturn (Shanidev). However, he was also a devout follower of the god Shiva, a great scholar, a capable ruler, and a master of the Veena, known as Ravanahattha.

To please Shiva, Ravana undertook severe penances from time to time in order to gain more boons, seeking increased strength, victory, and the coveted immortality. Thus, Ravana became the emperor over all the earth and attained supremacy over gods, demons, humans, and animals alike. He tortured gods and other races, fueling anger and hatred among the deities against him. However, due to their weakness and helplessness, they were not in a position to confront and fight against Ravana.

They appealed to Vishnu to help them in such a critical situation. Vishnu pondered that Ravana had received a boon for protection from deities, demons, and others, but not from human beings and monkeys. Ravana had not considered any threat from humans and monkeys; therefore, he did not seek protection from them. Vishnu then incarnated as Rama to King Dashratha, and along with Rama, Dashratha's other sons — Laxmana, Bharata, and

Shatrughna — were also born. As Rama and his brothers grew up and were married, Rama married Sita, the daughter of King Janaka, by breaking Shiva's bow in the Swayamvara.

When King Dashratha decided to crown his eldest son, Rama, as the king, he was compelled by two boons granted to Kaikeyi to banish Rama from the kingdom for fourteen years and make Bharata the king of Ayodhya. Dashratha, helplessly, had to honor the promises he had made to Queen Kaikeyi. As a result, Rama, along with Sita and his younger brother Lakshmana, left the palace. They discarded their royal garments and donned the attire of hermits. After several days of travel, they reached Dandakaranya and decided to settle there.

During their banishment in the Dandakaranya forest, Rama and his brother Lakshmana fought and defeated many demons. One day, Surpanakha, the sister of Ravana, came to Rama's hut and proposed marriage to him. Rama declined, explaining that he was already married to Sita, and suggested that Surpanakha should approach Lakshmana instead. However, Lakshmana also refused her proposal.

Surpanakha, persistent in her desire, continued to pursue him. In demon culture, it was customary for a female demon to choose her husband, but Lakshmana remained opposed to accepting her. In a fit of rage during their argument, Lakshmana cut off her nose and ears. With her disfigured face, Surpanakha returned to Lanka to show Ravana what Lakshmana had done.

Upon seeing Surpnakha's injuries, Ravana became furious and decided to seek revenge. He abducted Sita from her hut in Dandakaranya and took her to Lanka, where he confined her in the Ashoka grove.

To free Sita from Ravana's captivity, Rama, along with Laxmana and a vast army of warriors and monkeys, attacked Lanka. A furious battle ensued, resulting in the death and injury of many of Ravana's relatives and soldiers. In the final confrontation between Rama and Ravana, both used various weapons in their attempts to kill each other. Ultimately, Rama unleashed a divine arrow infused with the power of the gods, which pierced Ravana's heart and killed him. Thus, Ravana, a powerful emperor, great scholar, fortified with boons, and deeply ambitious, lay dead on the battlefield.

In spite of being a devotee of Shiva, Ravana was defeated and killed by Rama, and Shiva did not intervene to help his devotee in the battle. Proud Ravana never sought advice or help from Shiva, believing he could not be defeated by a mortal man like Rama, forgetting that Rama was the incarnation of Lord Vishnu. Although Ravana was a great devotee of Shiva, who embodies the principle of Vairagya (absolute detachment), Ravana did not learn from Shiva's life nor follow his path. Instead, he misused the boons he received from Shiva.

During his penance and praise of Shiva, Ravana received the mighty sword Chandrahas, which could kill any enemy with each strike, but with the condition that it must be used for righteous purposes; otherwise, it would return to Shiva. When Ravana used the sword against Jatayu, who tried to save Sita from him, the sword Chandrahas returned to Shiva. Thus, Ravana lost the destructive sword due to its immoral use; otherwise, Shiva's sword might have been used against Rama.

Similarly, God Shiva grants boons and weapons to Ravana but does not condone his involvement in anti-dharma activities. When Sita is abducted by Ravana, his end draws near. It is a fact that Shiva's boons to devotees involved in nefarious deeds accelerate their destruction, as Shiva is the god of destruction, and the destruction of old things and wicked individuals is inevitable.

It is very strange that all demons and others who pleased Shiva with their severe penances requested boons for worldly enjoyment, power, kingdoms, and victory. They failed to consider that Shiva himself lives as a hermit, under the open sky, on the top of Mount Kailash, bearing no clothes but animal skins, and without any worldly amenities or attachments. Despite this, Shiva, the hermit, happily grants boons to his devotees as they desire. As a result, those devotees who receive boons of prosperity, power, wealth, and supremacy often meet pitiable ends.

It is relevant to mention that Shiva is a hermit who lives an austere life, whereas his devotees are generally well-to-do and pray for worldly prosperity. On the other hand, Lord Vishnu, the god of preservation, is adorned with gems and jewelry and lives lavishly. He usually rests on the Sheshnag, while Lakshmi, the goddess of wealth, presses his legs. In contrast, Vishnu's devotees live ascetic lives, are pure vegetarians, and are Vaishnavas, which means they lead simple and hard lives. They often suffer in the world, and it is believed that this suffering and ascetic life are tests of their devotion to Vishnu. Ultimately, the devotees of Vishnu are believed to be brought to Vaikunthdham for his blessings and salvation.

The above reality can also be observed in other religious sects. For example, in Jainism, Jain saints (sadhus) lead very strict lives without any physical amenities. Some (Digambara saints) do not wear clothes, while others(Swetamba wear simple white cloth. Even on shivering winter nights, they move on foot, rarely taking food, which is offered once a day on their palms by Jain followers. Additionally, the hair on their heads and beards is removed by hand.

The life of the Jain sadhu (saint) contrasts sharply with that of most Jain followers, who are often businessmen, wealthy, and prosperous, enjoying all worldly facilities. While the saint lives in poverty, his followers are rich. In Hinduism, Mahantas (monks) often own mathas (monasteries) and are wealthy, while their followers are generally poor. This phenomenon also applies to other religions, such as Islam, where Islamic moulvis (clerics) are often very rich and have control over mosques and Islamic institutions.

Therefore, it can be easily said that the outcome of the Shiva-Ravana episode reflects a universal truth that remains relevant even today.

Shiva 's boon to river Narmada : Shiva bestows boons not only upon demons and humans but also on non-living things. The River Narmada is a prime example, as Shiva granted it the boon to flow continuously and to form Shiva Lingam stones from the pebbles in its flowing waters. There are different versions of the River Narmada's origin. According to one version, for the welfare of the public, Shiva went to the Maikal Hills (Amarkantaka) to perform penance. After some time, a pool was formed on the hill from the drops of sweat that emanated from his body during his severe penance

According to mythology, a girl was born from the pool of Shiva's sweat. Shiva opened his eyes and found the girl there. He decreed that she would flow like a river, covering a large area of the country. That river has been called Narmada and also Shankari, the daughter of Lord Shankar. The Narmada, being the daughter of Shiva, flows with "Rav" (voice), so it is also known as Rewa.

According to another version, King Hiranya Teja of the Chandra dynasty realized that the souls of his ancestors would wander on the earth as their ashes had not been immersed in any holy river. To ensure the salvation of their souls, he started performing penance to Lord Shiva, who then incarnated Narmada on the earth as a boon to King Hiranya Teja. The water of Narmada was offered to King Hiranyateja's ancestors for the salvation of their souls.

There is another legend that states two teardrops from the god Brahma, who is believed to be the first god and the creator of the universe, fell to the earth, giving rise to two rivers—the Narmada and the Brahmaputra (according to some, the Sone River).

Shiva instructed Narmada to flow continuously for the welfare of mankind and other creatures. Since then, Narmada has been flowing with great force from Amarkantak to the Arabian Sea, covering vast stretches of Madhya Pradesh, Maharashtra, and Gujarat, and nourishing these regions. It is believed that Narmada is the daughter of Shiva, and as such, he blessed that every stone carried by Narmada would be worshiped as a Shivalinga. The Shivalinga stones found in the Narmada are formed from coarse stone pieces due to the continuous friction of the river's streams along its rocky path.

Shiva also granted a boon that the Narmada River is so holy that merely catching a glimpse of it is enough for people to attain virtue and be absolved of their sins. Therefore, on Narmada Jayanti (Magh Shukla Saptami, believed to be the day when the Narmada began to flow), lakhs of devotees gather on its banks at various places like Jabalpur, Mandla, Amarkantak, Hoshangabad, and Omkareshwar to behold the river. This illustrates the great reverence accorded to the Narmada River.

There are different stories regarding the origin of the Narmada River, and it is believed that Narmada is still unmarried, which is why she is also known as the Angry Maiden. She flows with great force and sometimes causes havoc. According to the scriptures, King Maikal set a condition that his daughter Narmada would marry only the prince who could present her with a Gulbakavli, a rare flower. Prince Sonbhadra, who understood Narmada's beauty and charm, offered the Gulbakavli flower to her father.

The marriage between Narmada and Sonbhadra was arranged. Although Narmada had not yet met Sonbhadra, upon hearing of his bravery, handsomeness, and other qualities, she fell in love with him. The wedding date was still some time away, but due to the intensity of her love, she became restless. Consequently, she decided to send a message to Sonbhadra through her servant Johila, who was also a beautiful woman. However, Johila had different intentions and requested Narmada to lend her dresses and jewelry. Johila then went to Sonbhadra dressed in Narmada's princely attire and jewelry. Mistaking her for Narmada, Sonbhadra treated Johila as if she were Narmada herself. Instead of revealing her true identity, Johila continued to pose as Narmada.

Narmada accepts his love and enjoys her time with Sonbhadra. When Johila does not return for a long time, Narmada decides to go to Sonbhadra herself. There, she finds both of them together, deeply involved. Feeling humiliated and insulted by Sonbhadra's infidelity, she decides to end any relationship with him. Shocked by this discovery, she changes her course, flowing westward from east to west, until she merges into the Arabian Sea. Narmada is regarded as an icon of self-esteem and rebellion.

According to Hindu mythology, Narmada remains an eternal spinster, flowing through hills, green forests, ravines, and rocky paths with a tumultuous roar. Even today, during the pilgrimage around the Narmada River, pilgrims often hear its murmurs. Narmada is considered the most sacred river among all sanctified rivers in India, even more holy than the Ganga. It is believed that even the Ganga comes to Narmada to take a dip and purify itself. According to the Matsya Purana, the Ganga is sacred in the area of Kankhal and the Saraswati river in Kurukshetra, but Narmada is holy throughout its course because Shiva granted it the boon of perpetual sanctity and continuous flow without ever drying up.

According to mythology, the waters of the Yamuna are blessed in a week, the Saraswati in three days, the Ganga in a single day, and the Narmada in a single moment.

The Narmada is always regarded as Maa Narmada, although it is the only unmarried river among all others. It is a specialty of Hinduism that all rivers, mountains, and seas are personified as male or female and addressed as mothers, especially rivers; the Brahmaputra is an exception as it is considered male. Therefore, Narmada, Ganga, and other rivers are referred to as Maa (Mother). The greatness of the Narmada can be understood from the fact that the Purana "Narmada Purana" is dedicated solely to this river, guiding people with various stories and mythological episodes regarding its origin, flow, temperament, and experiences of love and hate.

Regarding the descent of Narmada, there is a famous story that once Yudhisthira, accompanied by Draupadi, arrived at the bank of the river Narmada where sage Markandeya was resting. Yudhisthira asked Markandeya about the reason he had chosen the bank of Narmada as a resting place, given the many other holy places of great significance. Rishi Markandeya then narrated the story of how some sages had requested King Pururva to bring the river Narmada to the earth so that the world could be liberated from sins. The sages asked Pururva to find out how the river Narmada descends to the earth.

To fulfill the request of the Rishis, Pururva began a severe penance to please Lord Shiva, knowing that only Shiva could fulfill his longing. Pleased with Pururva's rigorous penance, Shiva appeared and asked him to choose a boon. Pururva expressed his wish for the descent of the Narmada River on earth, and Shiva granted him that boon. Shiva then instructed Narmada to descend to the earth, but Narmada expressed her concern that she needed a solid base; otherwise, she might pierce the ground and flow underground, similar to the story of the Ganga's descent. Shiva then instructed Paryanka, the son of the Vindhyachal Mountain, to hold Narmada as she descended to the earth. Paryanka held the descending Narmada, and thus the Narmada River came into existence. Narmada blessed Pururva and instructed him to perform tarpan rituals in the names of his ancestors to liberate them from their sins. Pururva performed the rituals and thereby liberated all his ancestors.

Having completed his tale, Markandeya told Yudhishthira that anyone who takes a holy plunge in the Narmada will attain virtues equivalent to those gained from performing an Ashwamedha Yagna.

It is widely believed that Narmada is Chirkumari (eternally virgin). According to another version, after Pururva's ancestors attained liberation from all their sins through his rituals of tarpan, other people also started performing tarpan in the names of their ancestors. However, since Narmada was a virgin, she did not allow her divine touch to others and deities. All the deities requested Narmada to marry King Purukutsa. She agreed to become the consort of King Purukutsa, who was actually Samudra Deva (sea god), but had been cursed by Brahma to become a human being.

After their marriage, King Purukutsa learned from Narmada about the rituals needed to liberate his ancestors. Because of this, the Narmada River is considered a very holy river, believed to be the daughter of Shiva, and is worshiped by Hindus as a goddess (Narmada Maiya). Narmada Jayanti is a significant festival in India, celebrated with great reverence. The Narmada River is unique as it is the only river around which devotees perform a parikrama (circumambulation), traveling more than 2, 600 kilometers.

The parikrama may begin at the origin of the Narmada, proceed to its confluence, and then return to the starting point. However, this is not a strict rule; the parikrama can start and end at any point, as long as it is performed clockwise. It is believed that the Narmada parikrama is an ancient tradition; according to Hindu mythology, Rishi Markandeya himself performed it. The Narmada is considered a source of positive energy, and circling around it during the parikrama is believed to imbue pilgrims with this positivity, transforming negativity into a positive life force. The Narmada parikrama holds immense significance among Hindus and is seen as a sacred act capable of purifying and spiritually uplifting pilgrims. It is believed that completing the parikrama of the holy Narmada River washes away all the sins of the devotees.

The Narmada is associated with numerous episodes regarding its origin, life, and holiness. Of particular importance is Shiva's boon to the Narmada, ensuring its longevity, continuous flow through rocky hills, the ability to create natural Banalingas (Shivalingas) in its waters, and its sacredness. Narmada is renowned as the daughter of Shiva and also as Chirkumari (the Eternal Spinster).

Shiva's boon to Narmada is immensely beneficial to mankind, vegetation, and living creatures in the Vindhyachal region. The Narmada is the lifeblood for millions of inhabitants in Madhya Pradesh and Gujarat.

Shiva's boon to Nandi:- It is well known that in most Shiva temples, there is a statue of a seated bull positioned in front of the Shiva Lingam. When worshippers finish their prayers or offerings to Shiva, they whisper their wishes and desires into the ears of the seated bull. According to Hindu mythology, it is essential for a Shivalaya (Shiva temple) to have a bull in front of the Shiva Lingam. This bull is Nandi, a steadfast and austere devotee of Shiva who also serves as his mount.

It is believed that Shiva, pleased with Nandi's devotion, service, and sincerity, blessed him and declared him as the medium between devotees and Shiva himself. Devotees whisper their wishes into Nandi's ears, which are believed to reach Shiva through him. This tradition of worshiping Shiva alongside Nandi can be traced back to the ancient Indus Valley Civilization. The famous "Pashupati

Seal" depicts a seated figure, often identified as Shiva, and "Bull Seals" have been found in Mohenjo-Daro and Harappa. These archaeological findings have led researchers to conclude that the worship of Shiva with Nandi has been a longstanding tradition for thousands of years.

Generally, Nandi is visualized as a strong bull, symbolizing untamed power. An ox, on the other hand, is a domesticated bull that has been castrated and is therefore unable to reproduce. After castration, a bull becomes an ox and serves society as a gentle bullock, pulling plows and carts. Oxen play a crucial role in agriculture and transportation, serving as helpers of Shiva. They are considered friends of farmers and steadfast assistants to villagers. However, oxen cannot sire calves. For breeding, an intact bull is necessary, but such bulls are wild and aggressive, making them unsuitable for plowing or pulling carts.

An intact bull mates with cows, enabling them to give birth to calves and provide milk. Moreover, an intact bull cannot be restrained and is allowed to roam freely for the sake of human prosperity. Even today, some Hindus feel devoted to offering fodder and water to bulls, never harming them, as they are considered mounts of Shiva. When a well-built bull is seen, it evokes a sanctified feeling for Lord Shiva.

Shiva uses an intact and undomesticated bull, Nandi, as his mount, symbolizing Shiva's self-sufficiency and competence. Even though Parvati sits beside Shiva on the bull, Nandi cannot be fully domesticated. Shiva, naturally a hermit and wild like Nandi, who mates with cows, cannot be tamed or domesticated. While Parvati (Shakti) compels Shiva to engage with the world, he never fully embraces it.

According to some religious scriptures and the book *Vayam Rakshamah* by Acharya Chatursen, Nandi is depicted as a man—very strong, faithful, and a warrior. He is described as the son of the sage Shilada, who had no children due to his celibacy and abstention from marriage. When someone informed him that without a son, he could not repay the debt (Pitra-rin) owed to his ancestors who gave him life, it became essential to discharge this debt during funeral ceremonies by offering balls of mashed rice (pinda) to the ancestors. This repayment of Pitra-rin is crucial for attaining the subtle body (sukshma sharira) and departing from the world.

To rectify this, Shilada undertook severe penance to please god Indra for a boon to have a child. After some time, Indra appeared before the sage and advised him to perform penance to Lord Shiva instead. Shilada then engaged in rigorous penance to Lord Shiva, seeking a son blessed with immortality. Shiva granted his wish, and Shilada named the child "Nandi."

There is another account in which Nandi was born from a yagna performed by sage Shilada, and his body was adorned with armor made of diamonds. Celestial dancers and singers performed on this auspicious occasion, and the deities showered flowers on the child. The boy was named 'Nandi,' meaning "one who brings joy." However, upon returning home, Nandi lost his divine appearance and transformed into an ordinary boy. Sage Shilada was troubled by this sudden change but made every effort to ensure that Nandi received a good education. By the age of seven, Nandi was well-versed in the Vedas and all sacred texts.

One day, the deities Varuna and Mitra visited Sage Shilada and observed auspicious signs indicating that Nandi had a very short lifespan; he would not live beyond the age of eight. Sage Shilada was deeply distressed upon learning of Nandi's fate. Nandi himself accepted this destiny with composure but was concerned about his father's sorrow over his premature death. Consequently, he began to pray to Shiva with devotion and faith.

Seeing Nandi's austere devotion, Shiva appeared before him and blessed him. Shiva adorned Nandi with a necklace and granted him immortality.

In addition, Shiva declared that Nandi would be worshiped alongside him and become his vahana (mount). Immediately, Nandi gained all divine powers and transformed into a half-bull, half-human form. According to another version, Nandi grew as a devoted follower of Shiva. On the banks of the river Narmada, near Tripur Tirth Kshetra (present-day Nandikeshwar temple in Jabalpur, M. P.), he performed penance to become Shiva's Gana and mount. Shiva appeared before him and granted his boon. Nandi expressed his desires, and Shiva blessed him, granting that he would be a Gana and Shiva's mount forever.

Nandi is not only the vahana of Shiva but also possesses divine knowledge of "Agamic" and "Tantric" teachings imparted by Shiva himself. He passed this divine knowledge to his eight disciples, instructing them to spread it in eight different directions of the world. According to the Tamil *Thiruvilaiyadal Puranam*, Nandi once incarnated as a whale to reunite Parvati with Shiva.

It is believed that Shiva, who typically remains in meditation and does not speak, would reveal all the secrets and mysteries of life and the universe when Parvati requested. Shiva would disclose these secrets attentively, with complete concentration and closed eyes. Initially, Parvati would listen keenly, but later she often fell into a deep sleep. During these times, creatures such as pigeons at Amarnath and crows (Kakbhundi) would mimic Parvati's voice, allowing Shiva to continue imparting His teachings uninterrupted.

Similarly, one day Parvati requested Shiva to explain the meaning of the Vedas. Shiva started to explain and elaborate on the Vedas' meaning and importance. As usual, Parvati fell asleep during the discourse. When Shiva noticed her sleeping, he became upset and opened his eyes. Suddenly angry, he cursed her to be reborn as the daughter of a fisherman. Parvati then had to incarnate as a fisherwoman to atone for her curse.

Nandi knew the entire story and, to reunite his master and beloved wife, took the form of a whale. He began causing harm to people, especially the fishing community. The father of the fisherwoman, Parvati, declared that anyone who killed the whale would marry his beautiful daughter. Many fishermen and others attempted to capture and kill the whale, but all their efforts were in vain, and panic spread throughout the community.

Seeing the plight of the fishermen, Shiva disguised himself as a fisherman and arrived. He promised to kill the dangerous whale and soon fulfilled his promise by slaying the whale. He then asked for the hand of the fisherman's daughter in marriage. Her parents happily accepted Shiva as their son-in-law, and the marriage was solemnized. After that, Parvati returned to her previous form.

Thus, Nandi was successful in reuniting Shiva and Parvati, demonstrating his profound devotion to the divine couple. There is also another story explaining why people who visit a Shiva temple whisper their wishes into the ears of the Nandi bull after praying or offering to Shiva. It is believed that whatever wishes are whispered into Nandi's ears reach Shiva.

There is a mythological story behind this belief. Once, Shiva was meditating with Parvati. Seeing them in meditation, Nandi decided to join them. He sat in front of Shiva, much like how the statue of the bull Nandi is placed before Shiva in temples. While they were meditating, Jalandhar, who considered Shiva as his enemy, arrived and abducted Parvati.

Shiva, deeply engrossed in meditation, was unaware of this. Meanwhile, the gods were terrified and unsure how to inform Shiva without disrupting his meditation and potentially incurring his wrath. They turned to Ganesha for help in communicating

Parvati's abduction to Shiva. Ganesha attempted to rouse Shiva from his meditation but was unsuccessful.

Thinking quickly, Ganesha whispered all the details of Parvati's abduction by Jalandhar into Nandi's ears. Nandi, startled by the news, immediately relayed everything he had heard to Shiva. Upon hearing this, Shiva swiftly emerged from his deep meditation without any disturbance.

Since that time, the tradition of whispering wishes into Nandi's ears has continued. It is believed that when wishes are whispered into the bull's ears, they are communicated to Shiva, who listens to all wishes and fulfills them accordingly. It is also strongly believed that worship of Shiva remains incomplete without also worshiping Nandi alongside him.

Nandi, according to mythology, is an embodiment of Shiva in animal form and cannot be separated from him, serving as his mount and gatekeeper of Mount Kailasha, Shiva's heavenly abode. He is also an important Gana of Shiva. Whenever Shiva engages in battle, Nandi participates valiantly. It is believed that Nandi is an incarnation of Shiva, born to fulfill the boon given to Rishi Shilada, who, unmarried and practicing celibacy, undertook severe penance to Shiva to have a son capable of repaying the Pitra-Rin (ancestors' debts).

The fact that a mount of Shiva receives such importance and respect distinctly demonstrates Shiva's greatness and impartiality. It shows that any creature, whether animal, ghost, goblin, demon, or deity, finds refuge and importance from Shiva without prejudice or segregation. All are treated equally. It is believed that Shiva sees only emotional attachment, feeling, and devotion, disregarding shape, race, creed, or the type of offering. All devotees are equally considered, and their worship is readily accepted by Shiva, who is regarded as the god of all living and nonliving beings.

Shiva's boon to Markandeya:- In ancient times, there was a sage named Mrikanda who was married but childless. He decided to perform a rigorous penance (tapa) to propitiate Lord Shiva and started his arduous devotion to seek a boon. Ultimately, Lord

Shiva was pleased with Mrikanda's hard penance and appeared before the sage, offering him a boon. Sage Mrikanda requested a son from Shiva. Shiva then gave the sage a choice: a wise son who would live for sixteen years or a foolish son who would live for one hundred years. The sage chose the wise son, believing that a wise son with a shorter lifespan is better than a foolish son who lives longer.

A son was born, and the rishi named him Markandeya. He was blessed and grew up to be an exemplary son, destined to die at the age of sixteen. Markandeya mastered the Vedas and shastras and became a devoted worshiper of Shiva. His parents, worried about his fate, kept the secret of his destiny from him until just before his sixteenth year to prevent him from becoming disheartened. When Markandeya turned sixteen, he began severe austerities and continued his worship of the Shiva linga. On the fateful day of his death, the messengers of Yama, the god of death, came for him. However, finding him absorbed in the worship of Shiva, they were unable to take his life, as they had no power over a devotee of Shiva. They returned empty-handed.

When Yama, the god of death, came to take Markandeya's life and found him still worshiping the Shiva linga, Markandeya said to Yama, "Let me finish my prayers, and then I am ready to die." According to mythology and religious texts, Yama never waits for prayers or pleas. Dispassionately, he threw his noose and began dragging Markandeya towards Yamloka, the land of death. Markandeya clung to the Shiva linga, crying for help and resisting Yama's forceful pull. In another version of the story, Yama threw his noose around the young sage's neck, but it also encircled the Shiva linga. Angered by this, Shiva emerged from the linga and attacked Yama to save his devotee.

After slaying Yama, Shiva resurrected him at the request of the deities. If Yama were not revived, who would fulfill the role of Dharmaraj, making judgments on beings' deeds after death? Markandeya remained an immortal sage and declared that Shiva is Yamantaka, the destroyer of Yama. Shiva is also known as Kalantaka, the destroyer of time and death, and has acquired the epithet Mahakal, signifying his transcendence beyond time. Ujjain is renowned for the Mahakal temple, drawing pilgrims from all over the world who come to pray and pay respects to Shiva as Mahakal. The incident where Lord Shiva saved Markandeya from the clutches of Yama and slew Yama is said to have taken place on the banks of the Markanda River flowing in Kurukshetra, Haryana. The ancient Markandeyeshwar Mahadeva Temple was built at this site, which has been renovated into a magnificent and modern temple in the present age.

Since then, Hindus believe that Markandeya is one of the immortals, like Hanuman, Ashwathama, Mahabali and others. It is said that he is a great Chiranjivi, living with his body forever. His body always appears young and never succumbs to old age or decay, attributed to his yogic powers. It is believed that he resides somewhere in the Himalayan terrain, engaged in deep meditation, Vedic studies, or yogic activities.

Sage Markandeya was a scholarly and learned sage who composed the 'Markandeya Purana', which is likely one of the oldest Puranas. This Purana consists of 137 chapters, with chapters 81 through 93 dedicated to the Devi Mahatmya The text begins with Jaimini, the founder of Mimansa, seeking answers from Markandeya for questions raised in the Mahabharata but left unanswered. Markandeya, stating his need to perform Vedic rituals, advises Jaimini to seek out four wise birds dwelling in the Vindhya range.

Sage Jaimini meets the birds and poses his questions, which form chapters 4 to 45 of the Markandeya Purana. This discussion intertwines moral instructions with mythology, theories of Karma, Samsara, Dharma, and verses from texts such as the Mahabharata and the Gautama Dharmasutras. Additionally, several chapters in the Bhagavata Purana are dedicated to his conversations and prayers, and he is also mentioned in the Mahabharata

Presently, there is a Markandeya Tirtha located on the trekking route to the Yamunotri Shrine in the Uttarkashi district, Uttarakhand, where it is believed the sage composed the Markandeya Purana.

The legend of Shiva saving Markandeya is said to have taken place on the banks of the river Gomati in Kaithi, Varanasi, where an ancient temple, known as the Markandeya Mahadeva Temple, now stands. However, another version of the story is associated with Kerala, where at the site of the Triprangode Shiva Temple, Markandeya clung to the Shiva linga to escape from Yama. Additionally, a third version suggests that the event of Shiva saving Markandeya from Yama's clutch occurred at the Parli Vaidyanath Jyotirlinga in the Beed district of Maharashtra.

According to the Bhagavata Purana, there is an episode involving Markandeya where he had been continuously worshiping Lord Vishnu for six manvantaras (an age of Manu). Alarmed by the sage's immense ability and power, Indra feared losing his kingdom and being overthrown. Consequently, he assigned numerous Apsaras, Gandharvas, and Kamadeva, the god of love and desire, to disrupt the sage's ascetic penance and prayers. It is notable in various mythological events that Indra consistently feared losing his kingdom to other sages and demons engaged in penance and prayers. Therefore, he swiftly engaged in destructive activities to disturb or end their penances and prayers, ensuring they would not gain control over his kingdom.

The celestial beings traveled to the sage's hermitage, located in the Himalayas along the banks of the river Pushpabhadra. Despite their songs, dances, and attempts at seduction, the sage remained undisturbed. Failing to disrupt his penance, they returned empty-handed and admired Sage Markandeya's unwavering and steadfast devotion.

Lord Vishnu then appeared before Markandeya in the guise of the sage brothers Nara-Narayana. The sage praised the brothers and requested a vision of Vishnu's Maya (illusion), which was granted. In Indian philosophies, Maya has different meanings depending on the context. In later Vedic texts, Maya refers to a magical illusion where things appear to be real but are not what they seem. In the Advaita

Vedanta school of Hindu philosophy, Maya is the powerful force that creates the cosmic illusion, making the phenomenal world appear real.

One evening, while Markandeya was praying, he experienced a vision of the Pralaya (deluge), the dissolution of the universe. A great deluge submerged the earth, destroying all living beings, and the sage found himself as the only creature left alive, floating on the waters. As the deluge propelled him, the sage observed a banyan tree, upon whose branch he saw a dazzling baby on a leaf. Markandeya was amazed at the sight of its wondrous form. Entering the form of the baby, he witnessed the entire universe, the passage of the ages, all living beings, and a vision of his own hermitage. Leaving the baby's form and returning to the vision of the deluge, the sage tried to hug the baby, knowing it to be Vishnu himself. The baby disappeared, and the Maya was subsequently dispersed, returning Markandeya to the real world and his hermitage.

Even though Markandeya praised Vishnu, Shiva and Parvati appeared before the sage, and he sang the praise of Shiva and Parvati. Pleased by the sage, Shiva offered him a boon. The sage requested to remain a devotee of Vishnu, and Shiva granted this boon to Markandeya. Additionally, Shiva declared that the sage would be immortal, become a great religious saint, and author a Purana. This story demonstrates the greatness of Shiva, who is also pleased with the devotees of Vishnu and grants them boons.

According to the Sati Purana, a confidential segment of the Markandeya Purana, Goddess Durga granted Markandeya a boon to write a text on 'Veera Charitra' (Brave Character), describing her valor and gallantry. This text is famously known as "Durga Saptashati, " a revered portion of the Markandeya Purana. The place where Goddess Durga granted this boon is known as Yamkeshwar. The Devi Mahatmya, which is also called Saptasati, Chandi-mahatmya, or Chandi Patha, is the first bhakti text for those who worship Durga or Chandi as Shakti. Reciting the Chandi Path is very popular in West Bengal and Odisha, especially during Navratri and Durga Puja.

The text includes its Yoga philosophy in chapters 39 to 43, emphasizing it as the path to gain self-knowledge and liberation (moksha), overcoming past karma. The Markandeya Purana also includes discussions on Yoga, featuring the portrayal and teachings of Dattatreya, which, according to Rigopoulos, are primarily centered around Jnana Yoga. This emphasis on jnana is within a nondual (Advaita Vedanta) framework.

In simpler terms, the Markandeya Purana, along with the Vishnu, Yayu, Narada, and Kurma Puranas, according to Sahasra-budhe, unmistakably places Advaita (nonduality) concepts likely reflecting Advaita before the time of Adi Shankaracharya.

The text of the Markandeya Purana covers a diverse range of topics, including society, religion, and mythology. Its chapters contain information on family, marriage, social life, social conventions, food, customs, ceremonies, the position of women, geographic structures, flora, and fauna prevalent in ancient Indian society during the time of Sage Markandeya. Essentially, the Markandeya Purana serves as a comprehensive treatise on geography, social science, moral science, as well as mythology and theology.

Incarnation of Shiva:- In Hinduism and many other religions, the concept and mythological story of the incarnation of the gods exist. In Hinduism, the incarnations of Vishnu are particularly well-known and widely described. According to the Bhagavad Gita, chapter 4, verse 7, the concept of the incarnation (Avatar) of God is proclaimed at Kurukshetra in the Mahabharata. Srikrishna declared:

"Whenever there is a decline in Dharma and an increase in Adharma, then I incarnate myself."

This means that "for the protection of the good and for the destruction of the wicked and the establishment of Dharma and peace, I (God) manifest myself from age to age."

The entire universe is created, protected, and destroyed by the three gods of the Trinity family: Brahma, Vishnu, and Shiva. Vishnu is the Preserver of the universe, Brahma is the Creator, and Shiva is the Destroyer. Vishnu, who protects and sustains the world and maintains order in it, is called the Saviour. There is a continuous cycle of creation, maintenance, and destruction of the universe, and from time to time, there are disturbances, conflicts, and threats to mankind and Dharma. Vishnu, as the preserver of peace and Dharma, must incarnate or take an avatar to punish the wicked and establish peace in the world.

On earth, there are two groups: the good and the evil, and there are continuous conflicts and struggles between them. When the good is in a dominant position, there is peace, Dharma, harmony, and progress. Conversely, when the evil acquires supremacy over the good, there is unrest, Adharma, crime, killing, and torture, causing deities and mankind to be harassed and agonized. This poses a danger to Dharma, culture, and humanity. Since Vishnu is the protector of the universe along with Dharma and humanity, the protection and maintenance of the world against evil and threats is his continuous duty. When Dharma on earth and the creation of the universe face threats from evil or hostile situations, Vishnu must take avatars in different forms and sizes to defeat or destroy the evil and save humanity, Dharma, and culture in the world.

According to Hindu scriptures and literature, there are ten main avatars of Vishnu. All nine avatars have appeared except for one, Kalki, who is believed to appear at the end of the Kali Yuga. According to the Puranic descriptions, the existing universe has four yugas: Satya Yuga, Treta Yuga, Dwapara Yuga, and the last, Kali Yuga. Three yugas have passed, and now Kali Yuga exists. At the end of Kali Yuga, there will be severe unrest, destruction, conflicts, crimes, corruption, and all evil things at their zenith. As a result, dharma, culture, and humanity will be in peril. Vishnu's tenth incarnation as Kalki will be born to establish dharma, rule, and order on earth. The entire world will be annihilated, making way for the formation of a new universe.

God Vishnu has taken nine avatars to date, and his 10th avatar will be Kalki at the end of the Kali Yuga. The Garuda Purana recounts a detailed description of these ten avatars (Dashavatar). The ten avatars of Vishnu are Matsya (the fish), Kurma (the tortoise), Varaha (the boar), Narasimha (the half-man and half-lion), Vamana (the dwarf), Parashurama (the Brahmin warrior), Rama (the avatar of morality and truth), Krishna (the diplomat), Buddha (the social reformer), and Kalki (yet to come). The stories of all nine avatars of Vishnu are well-known, particularly the episodes of Rama and Krishna, which hold great significance for Hindus and others. Even an illiterate person may describe the greatness of Rama and Krishna. The Ramayana and the Mahabharata are two major epics in Hinduism. The Ramayana narrates the story of Rama, while the Mahabharata recounts the story of Krishna, offering detailed accounts of the struggle between the law of the jungle and the code of civilization, and the ultimate triumph of truth over falsehood. Rama and Krishna are revered gods, and the dialogue between Krishna and Arjuna is recorded in the Bhagavad Gita, which is a treatise on motivation, karma without desire, and ways of life. Hindus hold these gods in great respect and devotion, as both have profoundly influenced Indian life and culture.

Buddha is also considered the 9th avatar of Vishnu. The Buddha attained enlightenment and introduced a new path known as Buddhism, which emphasized social justice, fraternity, and equality. This path spread to China, Japan, Korea, Sri Lanka, Vietnam, Cambodia, and other countries. Some of Vishnu's avatars, like Vamana and Narasimha, had very brief periods to accomplish their purposes, while one avatar, Parashurama, had a prolonged presence on earth and is believed to be immortal and in perpetual penance. Parashurama was a warrior with an ax (Parshu) and is known for having eliminated the Kshatriyas from the earth 21 times.

The Matsya avatar, the first avatar of Vishnu, saves mankind and all other creatures from the great Pralaya (deluge). Before the deluge, Manu was asked to collect all creatures, grains, and spices and keep them on a boat. Vishnu appears as a vast fish with a horn, to which Manu ties the boat, leading them to safety. Manu is believed to be the first man on earth, and naturally, all of mankind are his offspring, hence terms like Manav, Manushya, and even Man originate from the word Manu. Manu wrote the "Manu Smriti, which outlines the rules and regulations of Hinduism and describes the framework of society, life, and the caste system. It is considered the first ancient legal text and constitution among the many Dharmashastras of Hinduism. In fact, the Manu Smriti is a manual of Hinduism. However, some contents of Manu Smriti have created controversy for advocating the caste system, inhumane treatment of lower castes, and the secondary position of women in society.

Interestingly, the great Pralaya (deluge) is also mentioned in the Old Testament of the Bible, which is regarded as a sacred text by Christians, Jews, and Muslims. In this version, God instructed Noah to build an ark and bring every kind of species of creature aboard, along with his family. When a great flood occurred, everything was destroyed except for Noah's ark. Thus, Noah saved all species from the catastrophe of the deluge, and a new world was established. The similarity between the story of the great Pralaya in Hinduism and that in the Old

Testament suggests that Hinduism is one of the most ancient religions and has a scientifically accurate account. Similar episodes, with slight variations, are repeated in other world religions.

In modern times, all avatars from Matsya (the fish) to Rama, Krishna, and Buddha are very popular and revered in India, except for Varaha (the boar or pig). Following the arrival and dominance of Muslims in India, the boar/pig was looked down upon because, in Islam, the boar/pig is considered Naapak (unholy) and Haram (forbidden), and not suitable for keeping like other animals such as cows or horses. As a result, the Varaha avatar has been sidelined and is not commonly worshiped or depicted in temples or elsewhere.

It is quite surprising that Vishnu's ten avatars, in ascending order from Matsya (the fish) to Buddha, reflect the modern theory of evolution. This interpretation was first proposed by the saint Bhaktivinoda Thakur in his 1873 book *Krishna-samhita*. Other theosophists have also supported the idea that the avatars in Hindu texts symbolize Darwinian evolution. The ten avatars (Dashavatars) represent the ascending order of the evolution of species: Matsya (fish – Paleozoic era), Kurma (amphibious tortoise), Varaha (boar – Cenozoic era), Narasimha (man-lion, the last animal and semi-human avatar), Vamana (growing dwarf, the first step toward the human form), Parashurama (human form, but violent), Rama (a perfect human with high moral values), Krishna (a human with high intellect), Buddha (a social reformer and founder of Buddhism), and Kalki (the final avatar yet to be born). The Dashavatars progress from the lowest forms of life, starting with the fish and tortoise, to developed humanity, mirroring the modern theory of evolution.

One scholar wrote, "Indeed, the concept of Dash avatars in Hinduism is centuries before the birth of Darwin and the doctrine of evolution, and before any word like evolution existed in any language of the world. Truthfully speaking, the Dashavatars provide rough ideas of vertebrate evolution: a fish, a tortoise, a boar, a man-lion, a dwarf, and then four men (with Kalki still unborn)." This striking similarity between Darwin's theory and the Dashavatara suggests that Charles Darwin might have been inspired by or had some knowledge of the Dashavatars before formulating the theory of evolution, which is based on the idea that all species are related and gradually change, taking on more developed forms over time. Genetic variation in populations affects the physical characteristics of organisms.

As for the avatars of Shiva, he does not take avatars like Vishnu or other gods. While Vishnu leaves his abode and appears in various human or other forms on earth, Shiva, as the supreme deity, is beyond the limitations of time, form, and space; he is omnipresent. Moreover, Shiva is the god of constructive destruction, as his destruction paves the way for new construction and development in the world. Whenever evil predominates, encroachments on nature and humanity occur, and violations of Dharma are committed, Shiva assumes the form of Rudra and performs the fearsome Tandav dance to annihilate the evil. Therefore, he does not need to take an avatar on earth or be born from the womb of a woman to combat evil.

According to the Puranas, the avatars of Shiva are entities born from his Ansha (part or emanation) rather than direct manifestations like the Dashavatars of Vishnu. Shiva has granted boons to certain beings to be born from his Ansha and power, and these beings are known as Shiva's avatars. For example, Hanuman, the vanara god who helped Rama, possesses an element of Rudra's Ansha and is regarded as a Rudravatar because he was born from Shiva's seed shed at the sight of Mohini.

Although Puranic scriptures occasionally mention avatars of Shiva, the avatar principle is neither universally accepted nor commonly adopted in Shaivism. There is a difference of views on the doctrine of incarnation between Vaishnavism and Shaivism. Shiva is the supreme soul who does not engage in the cycle of life and death. He is Anadi (without beginning) and Anant (without end). He is Nirakar (formless) and also Sakar (with form). Additionally, he is Trikaldarshi (one who sees the past, present, and future). Shiva does not need to take avatars to play a role in the world drama, but avatars born from elements (Ansha) of Shiva have appeared. Like Vishnu, some avatars with elements of Shiva were born on earth to fulfill the duty of destroying evil and relieving mankind from threats.

The number of Shiva's avatars is disputed; some Puranas mention 24 avatars, while others confirm only 19. This diversity is characteristic of Hinduism, where different versions exist for every mythological episode. Hinduism is ancient and is believed to have begun with the creation of the universe and the arrival of the Trinity family. Many rishis and scholars compiled 18 Puranas and various Brahmanic texts, resulting in different interpretations of stories linked to deities, particularly Vishnu and Shiva. Most Puranas support the idea of 19 avatars of Shiva, including Piplaad, Nandi, Virbhadra, Bhairava, Ashwatthama, Sharabha, Grihapati, Durvasa, Rishabha, Yatinath, Hanuman, Krishna Darshan, Bhikshuvarya, Sureshwar, Keerat, Sunat Nartak, Brahmachari, Yaksheshwar, and Avadhut.

Piplaad Avatar: According to mythology, there was a great Rishi named Dadhichi and his wife Swarcha, who lived in a jungle and were devoted to

Lord Shiva. Despite many years of marriage, they remained childless. Rishi Dadhichi performed intense penance to Shiva for a son, and Shiva granted him this boon. During his wife's pregnancy, Indra and other gods approached Rishi Dadhichi and requested his bones to create a weapon capable of defeating the Asura, Vritra, who could only be killed by a weapon made from Dadhichi's bones. Generous Dadhichi willingly sacrificed his life to donate his bones to Indra.

Upon learning of her husband's self-sacrifice, Swarcha placed her infant under a pipal tree, hence the child was named Piplaad. She then went away and ended her life to reunite with her husband. Piplaad was cared for by Dadhichi's sister, Dadhimati. As Piplaad grew older and learned about the circumstances of his father's death, he harbored resentment towards Shani Dev (Saturn) for causing troubles during his lifetime. As a result of his curse, Shani fell from the heavens. However, due to intervention by the gods, Piplaad forgave Shani on the condition that Shani would not trouble anyone before the age of sixteen. Additionally, worshiping

Piplaad would alleviate troubles caused by Shani and eliminate Shani Dosha.

Piplaad also learned how his parents had died and how Indra had maneuvered to obtain bones from his living father. To teach Indra a lesson, Piplaad performed severe penance to Shiva and obtained a demon to kill all the deities. Frightened, Indra and the other gods sought protection from Shiva. Shiva summoned Piplaad and made him realize that killing Indra and the gods would not bring his parents back. It would be better to forgive them, and Piplaad did so.

Later, Piplaad authored the "Prashna Upanishad, " one of the ten main Upanishads, which discusses the purpose of life through questions and answers. He became a renowned Vedic sage and philosopher in Hindu tradition, founding the Pippalada School of thought, which analyzes the Atharvaveda.

Nandi Avatar: Nandi is one of the most well-known avatars of Shiva, revered as the protector of herds. Born as the son of Rishi Shilada through a boon from Shiva, Nandi possessed an element of

Shiva's divine essence. He served as both the gatekeeper and the mount of Shiva. In Shiva temples, a statue of Nandi, the bull, is placed in front of Shiva, and worshiping Nandi is considered an integral part of worshiping Shiva. It is believed that whispering a wish into Nandi's ears will ensure it reaches Shiva. As a devout devotee, Nandi always resides with Shiva.

Virabhadra Avatar: After their marriage, Sati lived with Shiva on Mount Kailasha and proved to be a faithful and obedient wife. Out of love, she defied her father Prajapati Daksha and chose to follow Shiva without any demands, demonstrating unconditional love for him. Sati became synonymous with "an ideal wife" who would sacrifice her life for her husband. Despite her continuous and resolute efforts, the situation remained at a standstill, as Shiva refused to open his eyes and embrace her. He preferred to remain a hermit rather than a householder, but Sati remained hopeful and steadfast in her faith in Shiva.

When Sati learned that her father, Daksha, was performing the Ashwamedha Yagna to gain power and supremacy—a status tarnished by her rebellion and marriage to Shiva, whom Daksha disrespected—she was deeply troubled. Daksha disapproved of Shiva because, as Rudra, Shiva did not adhere to Vedic customs and rituals. Furthermore, Daksha harbored ambitions of ruling over mankind and lusted for power. He was drawn to physical pleasures, attachment, and a luxurious life, while Shiva, as an ascetic, had no interest in worldly comforts, wealth, or pleasure. Shiva lived under the open sky, wore animal hides, smeared himself with ashes, and had no worldly attachments. As the first yogi, he prioritized inner happiness, consciousness, and mental peace. In contrast, Daksha sought worldly enjoyment, power, popularity, and control over humanity.

Daksha invited all the gods and their wives to the Yagna, excluding Shiva. However, Sati, driven by her affection for her parents, insisted on attending the event, despite the breach of social etiquette involved in going to an uninvited ceremony. Shiva refused to accompany her without an invitation but did not stop her from going. At the

Yagna, all the gods had assembled to receive the offerings, but there was no seat reserved for Shiva. Sati realized that her father had deliberately excluded Shiva and herself. Angered, she confronted Daksha about his actions. Daksha insulted her for attending without an invitation, loudly proclaiming that Shiva did not follow Vedic and social traditions, wore animal hides instead of clothes, smeared himself with ashes, sat in crematoriums, and associated with ghosts, goblins, dogs, and other creatures. He declared Shiva unfit for any offering.

Sati was shocked that her father did not understand who Shiva truly was. Distraught and furious, she leaped into the sacred fire of the Yagna to stop it. However, Agni Dev, the god of fire, refused to touch her and burn her, so she immolated herself through tapa, sacrificing her life. Her sacrifice interrupted the Yagna.

The unexpected death of Sati resulted from the violent conflict between the world-renouncing Shiva and the worldly Daksha. Upon hearing the news of Sati's death, Shiva's heart broke, and his calm demeanor shattered. He was overcome with grief and rage. While Sati was alive, Shiva had been indifferent to her; her presence did not affect his meditation. However, her absence filled him with regret and unleashed his fury. In his anguish, he pulled out his hair and created a fearsome warrior called Virabhadra. Virabhadra, along with a horde of ghosts, goblins, and other wild creatures, rushed to Daksha's house and destroyed the Yagna site. The assembled deities, who had not intervened to save Sati, were severely beaten, and Daksha's followers were killed. Daksha's army could not withstand Virabhadra's ferocity and mighty onslaught. Some soldiers were wounded or killed, and the rest fled and hid. Even Daksha, the son of Brahma, could not withstand Virabhadra and was forced to flee the sacrificial hall, hiding in fear. Urine, blood, vomit, and saliva desecrated the pots and pans, and all the holy offerings were defiled. Chaos, cries, and horrifying scenes ensued. Virabhadra finally found Daksha hiding behind the altar and beheaded him.

According to the Padma Purana, Virabhadra is identified as the fierce form of Mangala (the planet

Mars). He was born when Shiva was consumed by anger and agony due to Sati's sudden death, and his sweat falling to the earth gave rise to the ferocious Virabhadra, who beheaded Daksha and destroyed the Yagna. Shiva later pacified Virabhadra and calmed him down, and he became the planet Agaraka (Mars).

According to the Skanda Purana, there was a fierce battle between Virabhadra and Vishnu.

When Vishnu learned that Virabhadra had arisen from Shiva's disheveled hair and was on his way to Daksha's house, Vishnu tried to stop him, but Virabhadra refused.

Vishnu wielded a mace against Virabhadra, who charged at Vishnu and pierced his chest with a trident. Vishnu fell to the ground but soon stood up and used various weapons against Virabhadra, who thwarted them all. Virabhadra showered Vishnu with powerful weapons, and Vishnu retaliated with equal might. Eventually, Vishnu realized that he could not defeat Virabhadra through ordinary means. He hurled his fatal Sudarshan Chakra at Virabhadra to kill him. Virabhadra attempted to stop Vishnu by casting a spell, causing the Sudarshan Chakra to halt in mid-air and immobilizing Vishnu. However, Vishnu broke the spell. Realizing the danger of his defeat, Vishnu hastily departed for Vaikuntha, leaving Daksha to face Virabhadra.

Veerabhadra is a violent form of Shiva associated with anger and retribution. He is depicted with dogs and ghosts and holds a severed head, either Brahma's or Daksha's, in his hand. He is a great warrior and symbolizes the destruction of ego and ignorance, born to annihilate Daksha, who embodied ego and ignorance.

There are two very important temples dedicated to Virabhadra in India, one at Lepakshi in Anantapur, Andhra Pradesh, and another at Yadur in Belgaum, Karnataka. Both temples are very ancient. The Virabhadra temple at Lepakshi was built by the governors of the Vijayanagar Empire and is famous for having one pillar that does not touch the ground. The Virabhadra temple at Yadur, situated on the bank of the Krishna River, was founded by the Veerashaiva sect of Karnataka in the 12th century.

There is another temple named as the Veerabhadra Temple, dedicated to Lord Shiva, which is located in Virbhadra Town near Rishikesh, Uttarakhand. This ancient temple, which is over 1,300 years old, is a revered site where Virbhadra, a fierce avatar of Lord Shiva, is worshiped. During the auspicious occasions of Shivratri and Sawan, special poojas and all-night jagrans are held to honor the deity.

The creation of the fierce warrior Virabhadra arose from the conflict between Shiva, Pashupati, and Daksha, Prajapati. Shiva, as a yogi and hermit, seeks inner happiness and satisfaction, whereas Daksha, as a king, seeks external pleasures and displays. Shiva, Pashupati, controls and conquers basic instincts such as anger, greed, sex, envy, and delusions possessed by animals. Shiva, an ascetic hermit, lacks desires and ambitions for worldly attachments. In contrast, Daksha, Prajapati, yearns for physical enjoyment and power to rule over his subjects. To prove his superiority, Daksha adheres to customs, rituals, and engages in Yagnas. Daksha dislikes Shiva, who does not accept Daksha's way of life. Daksha fails to understand Shiva and his philosophy, as Shiva gazes inwardly while Daksha's gaze is outward. Daksha seeks control over nature to feel secure, always fearful of his superiority and plagued by pride, ambition, and ego.

The beheading of Daksha resulted from his overwhelming ego, ambition, and pride, finite characteristics of a man who looks outward for material enjoyment instead of inward spirituality. Shiva, as an ascetic, has no interest in physical happiness, wealth, or health. He prefers inner happiness over external happiness, believing inner satisfaction lasts longer than outer happiness.

Bhairava Avatar: According to the Shiva Mahapurana, there was a conversation between Vishnu and Brahma in which Vishnu asked Brahma who the true creator of the universe was. Brahma, in his arrogance, claimed that he was the supreme creator and that Vishnu should worship him. He further believed that he could accomplish anything that Shiva could. As his pride and ego grew, Brahma forgot the importance and supremacy of Shiva, the true creator of the universe. He began to interfere in Shiva's work, asserting that he was the creator of the entire universe and that both Vishnu and Shiva were subordinate to him.

One day, Shiva became enraged and irritated by Brahma's erratic behavior. In his fury, Shiva pulled out a strand of hair from his head and threw it away, from which the fearsome Bhairava was born. Bhairava immediately rushed to Brahma and cut off one of his five heads. Since then, Bhairava has been depicted holding the skull (Kapala) of Brahma in his hand. With the severing of one of his heads, Brahma's ego was shattered, and he was enlightened to the reality of his ignorance. He felt immense gratitude towards Shiva for helping him realize his delusions.

There is another version in which Shiva himself created Bhairava. According to this version, there was a demon named Dahurasuran who performed severe penance and obtained a boon that made him invincible, except by Parvati. With this boon, Dahurasuran conquered the kingdoms of the deities, and his tyranny and oppression grew day by day, posing a grave threat to all the gods. In desperation, the deities pleaded with Parvati, who then transformed into Kali to kill Dahurasuran. Fueled by her rage, Kali successfully slew the demon. However, after the battle, her intense anger manifested as a child, whom Kali nursed with her milk.

Upon witnessing this, Shiva merged both Kali and the child into himself. From this merged form of Shiva, Bhairava emerged in his eight forms, known as the Ashtanga Bhairavas. Because Bhairava was born from this merged form of Shiva and Kali, he is considered a son of Shiva.

There is yet another version of Bhairava's birth according to some Puranas. It is characteristic of Hinduism to have many versions of mythological episodes due to its ancient origins. In ancient times, rishis, sages, and scholars often narrated the same mythological stories in different ways.

In this version, during a war between the deities and demons, the demons began to overpower the deities. Faced with imminent peril, the deities turned to Shiva and prayed for salvation from the demons, fearing annihilation. Shiva assured them of their safety and vowed to destroy the demons. To eliminate them, Shiva created Kala Bhairava, who successfully defeated the demons and rescued the deities.

It is said that from Kala Bhairava, the Ashtanga (eight) Bhairavas were further created. These Ashtanga Bhairavas married the Ashta Matrikas, and together they manifest in formidable and awe-inspiring forms. The Ashtanga Bhairavas are believed to govern the eight directions of the universe. From these Ashtanga Bhairavas and Ashta Matrikas, 64 Yoginis were also created.

It is believed that Shiva, in the form of Bhairava, guides each of the Shakti Peethas (Shakti Temples). Each Shakti Peeth is accompanied by a temple dedicated to Bhairava. Thus, Bhairava is commonly regarded as the guardian (Kotwal) of the Shakti Peeth temple and the locality where the Shakti Peeth is situated. In his form as Bhairava, Shiva protects the town from external dangers. Bhairava is both feared and appeased by travelers seeking entry into the city; without his permission, none can enter.

It is worth noting that the role of doorkeeper and guardian is typically performed by celibate and warrior gods. Temples dedicated to goddesses often have images of two Bhairavas: the white (Gora) Bhairava and the black (Kala) Bhairava. Kala Bhairava, who rides a dog, is the destroyer of malevolent spirits, while Gora Bhairava is fond of drinking bhang and enjoys the company of ghosts.

In addition to Shakti Peethas, idols of Bhairava are found in Shiva temples, typically facing the western direction, as it is believed that a west-facing Bhairava brings benefits and rewards. He is revered as Kshetrapala, the guardian of the territory. In Shiva temples, rituals begin with worship of Surya (the Sun) and conclude with Bhairava for auspiciousness. Devotees offer ghee baths (abhisheka), red flowers, ghee lamps, unbroken coconuts, honey, fibrous fruits, and other offerings to Bhairava to seek his blessings.

It is also believed that midnight, especially on Fridays, is an auspicious time to pray to Bhairava, as

Bhairava and his consort Bhairavi visit the worship spot (pujasthala) to bless devotees. Shaivites regard Bhairava as a protector who guards the eight directions, as well as women and travelers, especially at night.

Bhairava is worshiped by Hindus in India, Nepal, and Sri Lanka, and also by Tibetan Buddhists. In India, Bhairava temples are often located near Jyotirlinga temples in various parts of the country. For example, Bhairava temples can be found alongside Jyotirlinga temples such as Kal Bhairava, Patal Bhairava, and Vikram Bhairava temples at Ujjain, as well as the Bhairava temple at Kashi, where Bhairava is considered the guardian (Kotwal) or policeman of Kashi. Some famous Bhairava temples include Lord Kaalabhairaveshwara, Sri Kaala Bhairava Nath, and Bhairava temples at Sri Adichunchanagiri Math (Karnataka), in Madhya Pradesh, and at Maa Vaishno Devi Dham.

In Nepal, Bhairava is one of the predominant deities among the Newars, and there is a Bhairava temple in the Kathmandu Valley, where most inhabitants are Newars. These Bhairava temples in Nepal are mostly maintained by Newar priests. Buddhism has also been influenced by Bhairava, and consequently, in Buddhism, Bhairava is revered as a deity, Dharmapala, or dharma protector. Various Buddhist forms of Bhairava are known as Herukas, Vajrabhairava, and Mahakala. In the Vajrayana branch of Buddhism, Bhairava is a central deity in tantric rituals.

Bhairava is a fierce manifestation of Shiva, associated with annihilation and total destruction. Also known as Dandapati, he wields a rod (Danda) to punish sinners and evildoers. It is believed that worshiping Bhairava brings prosperity, success, good children, protection from premature death, and freedom from debts and liabilities. Bhairava has greatly influenced various aspects of Indian culture, including literature, religious rituals, and classical music. For example, Raga Bhairava, sung during the daytime, is believed to have originated from Shiva's own mouth and features powerful variations based on different note combinations and emotional qualities.

Through Bhairava, Shiva, the supreme god of destruction, demonstrates the necessity of total annihilation to eradicate evil, uncontrolled ego, prejudices, and threats, thereby establishing peace and dharma. Kala Bhairava also destroys time and space to initiate new cycles of life and universes. As an aspect of Shiva, Bhairava serves as the guardian and Kotwal (protector) of towns, cities, Shakti Peethas, and Shiva temples. Given the numerous Shakti Peethas and Shiva temples, there are correspondingly many Bhairavas tasked with their protection.

Bhairavas are potent creations of Shiva, entrusted with the duties of destruction, temple guarding, and city protection. Their presence evokes fear, terror, and caution among people, discouraging them from committing misdeeds and offenses. Thus, Bhairava, as an incarnation of Shiva, embodies Mahakala, the destroyer and protector against human suffering.

Ashwathama Avatar: According to the Mahabharata, the Hindu epic, Ashwathama is the son of Dronacharya and the grandson of Rishi

Bharadwaja. He was a great warrior who fought against the Pandavas on the side of the Kauravas in the Kurukshetra War.

Dronacharya was married to Kripi, the sister of Kripacharya. Despite many years of marriage, they remained childless. Desiring a son as valiant as Shiva, Drona undertook severe penance (tapasya) to Lord Shiva for many years. Pleased with his devotion, Shiva appeared and granted Drona a boon, promising him an immortal son. Ashwathama was born with a gem on his forehead that endowed him with superpowers and immense strength, making him invincible.

Drona lived a simple and difficult life due to his lack of success in his profession and faced acute scarcity of money. Consequently, Ashwathama had a challenging childhood, and his parents could not even afford milk for him. A poignant incident from their poverty-stricken life was when Ashwathama, crying for food, was given water mixed with flour instead of milk. There was the zenith of poverty and misery of Drona's family.

According to the Manu Smriti, as a Brahmin, Drona was expected to engage in priesthood, study the Vedas and religious texts, serve as a minister to the king, teach disciples, or become a sage. The main source of income for a Brahmin came from Dakshina (offerings) and Dan (gifts). However, due to compulsion, poverty, humiliation, or revenge, sometimes a Brahmin might sometimes adopt occupations beyond these traditional roles. Such deviations in archaic Hindu mythology often led to exceptional events that profoundly impacted mankind, giving rise to epic narratives.

For example, Parashurama, driven by honor and revenge, took up an ax (Parashu) and first slew his own mother and then the culprit Kartavirya Arjuna. He went on to annihilate the Kshatriya warriors twenty-one times over, challenging their abuse of power, unlawful seizure of property, and oppression of people. By eliminating the Kshatriyas, he restored cosmic balance on earth. Thus, Parashurama's legends are renowned for their violence, cycles of Kshatriya annihilation, and the fiery impulses of anger.

Another example is Ravana, the king of Lanka, who was born to Rishi Vishrava and the demoness Kaikesi, a demon princess. His grandfather was Rishi Pulastya. Although Ravana was born as a Brahmin and was a learned scholar well-versed in the six Shastras and four Vedas, he was more inclined toward his maternal demon ancestry. Preferring demon culture and customs over the Deity/Aryan culture, he took up warfare rather than adhering to Brahminical duties and responsibilities. He wielded arms and led armies to conquer other kingdoms, kill their rulers, and capture their queens and other beautiful women. Ultimately, he abducted Sita, the wife of Rama, an incarnation of Vishnu. This act led to a series of heinous and deadly events, culminating in the burning of Lanka to ashes, the death of Ravana and his kin, and the desolation of the splendid kingdom of Lanka.

The great epic Ramayana narrates the misdeeds of Ravana, the abduction of Sita, the war between Rama and Ravana, and the tragic demise of Ravana. The Ramayana also teaches that, in the end, truth always triumphs over falsehood.

Dronacharya, due to poverty and other reasons, adopted the occupation of a Kshatriya and became an expert in warfare, particularly archery. Struggling for the betterment of his family's life, he approached the Panchala king Drupada, his former classmate and friend. Drupada promised to assist Drona, but when Drona sought his help, King Drupada refused and insulted him by declaring that a king and a beggar could not be friends. Humiliated, Drona returned empty-handed but resolved to teach a lesson to the deceitful Drupada.

Later on, Drona became the guru of both the Pandavas and the Kauravas in Hastinapur. Ashwathama was also trained in the art of warfare along with them and did not get a chance to perform Brahminical work. Drona trained Arjuna to become the best archer in the world. After their warfare training, Drona instructed his disciples to defeat Drupada and bring him captive before him. Initially, the Kauravas attacked but failed to defeat Drupada. Subsequently, the Pandavas defeated Drupada, captured him, and presented him before Drona. Drona reprimanded Drupada and appointed his son

Ashwathama as the king of the southern part of Panchala.

Dronacharya typically favored Arjuna over his other disciples. It is often criticized that Dronacharya, in order to maintain Arjuna's status as the best archer, demanded that Ekalavya, a tribal archer who had learned archery by practicing in front of an idol of Dronacharya, gave his thumb as guru dakshina (teacher's fee). Ekalavya, though poor, cut off his right thumb and offered it to Drona.

Additionally, a competition was once organized in Hastinapur to test the proficiency of princes in the art of warfare. Karna, the son of Kunti (the mother of the Pandavas) by the sun god Surya, who was raised by a charioteer, participated and challenged Arjuna in archery. However, Dronacharya unfairly questioned Karna about his lineage. When Karna did not respond, Drona denied him the opportunity to compete with Arjuna, despite knowing who Karna was. Drona's biased behavior and questionable motives led to many unpleasant events in the future, stemming from his improper adaptation to the role of a

Brahmin. Similarly, Ashwathama also committed some unpardonable offenses later on as a warrior.

Due to ongoing conflicts arising from a dynastic succession struggle between two groups of cousins, the Kauravas and the Pandavas, for the throne of Hastinapur, along with various rivalries, conspiracies, insults, partialities, and favoritism, a great war known as the Mahabharata was fought in Kurukshetra. The epic is also replete with intrigue, politics, and philosophy. Several kingdoms from around the world participated as allies of the rival groups.

The Kurukshetra war began between the Kaurava and Pandava factions. Interestingly, Krishna's Yadu army sided with the Kauravas, while Krishna himself joined the Pandavas as Arjuna's charioteer. The Kaurava army was initially led by Bhisma, who was invincible due to a boon that allowed him to choose the time of his death. Krishna devised a plan to defeat Bhisma by placing Shikhandi on Arjuna's chariot. Shikhandi, who was transgender, was perceived by Bhisma as a woman rather than a man. When Shikhandi confronted him, Bhisma, not wanting to harm a woman, refused to shoot arrows at him. Seizing this moment of hesitation, Arjuna was instructed to shoot a hundred arrows through Bhisma's body. Thus, Bhisma was forced to lie on a bed of arrows and willingly accept his death.

After Bhisma's fall, the Kaurava army was led by Drona, a formidable and invincible warrior deeply attached to his son, Ashwathama. Krishna informed the Pandavas that defeating Drona in battle was impossible through conventional means, as "everything is fair in war and love." Krishna devised a plan in which Yudhishthira, known for his honesty and never speaking lies, would loudly announce that "Ashwathama is killed," while softly adding, "whether it's a man or an elephant."(aśvatthāmā hata iti kuñjare vinipātite) Upon hearing that Ashwathama was dead, Drona, stricken with grief and shock, lowered his weapons. Seizing the opportunity, Draupadi's brother, Dhrishtadyumna, beheaded Drona. Though this act was against the norms of civilized warfare, it was justified on the principle that everything is fair in war.

Upon learning of his father's deceptive death, Ashwathama became enraged and invoked the celestial weapon Narayanastra against the Pandavas. As the weapon was launched, it moved swiftly with thunderous sounds, causing great fear among the Pandava soldiers and warriors, who felt as though arrows were targeting them. Krishna, understanding the unique nature of the Narayanastra, which only targeted armed individuals, ordered all soldiers and warriors to disarm and leave their chariots. Consequently, the Narayanastra passed harmlessly by them, ensuring the safety of the Pandavas and their forces. Realizing the weapon's failure, Duryodhana urged Ashwathama to use it again, but Ashwathama despondently replied that the Narayanastra could not be used twice; if attempted, it would backfire on the user.

After Drona's death, Ashwathama was appointed as the commander of the Kaurava forces. Alongside Kripacharya and Kritavarma, he launched an attack at night on the Pandava camp. Attacking at night was against the ethics of warfare and was seen as a cowardly act. However,

Ashwathama was driven by intense stress and a desire for revenge over his father's deceitful killing.

Ashwathama, in a fit of rage and vengeance, first kicked and seized the half-awake Dhrishtadyumna, the killer of his father, and mercilessly killed him. He then proceeded to slaughter the Upapandavas—Shikhandi, Yudhamanyu, Uttamaujas—and many other warriors of the Pandava army. Anger and revenge clouded his rational thinking, wisdom, and conscience. Despite being a Brahmin, Ashwathama succumbed to the fiery passions of vengeance and anger. Traditionally, Brahmins were expected to maintain composure, but financial anxiety and a deprived quality of life could sometimes lead to hot-headedness or ill temper, as was the case with Ashwathama.

During that fateful night, the Pandavas and Krishna were away. Upon their return, when they learned of the brutal murders of their sons and warriors, they confronted Ashwathama at Sage Vyasa's ashram. Both Ashwathama and Arjuna invoked their Brahmastras to destroy each other.

Sage Vyasa intervened, preventing their weapons from colliding, and urged them to withdraw their lethal powers. Arjuna complied and withdrew his Brahmastra, but Ashwathama struggled to retract his. In a fit of rage and desperation, Ashwathama redirected the Brahmastra toward the womb of Uttara, the pregnant wife of Abhimanyu. However, the unborn child was miraculously saved by Krishna at the fervent request of Draupadi and Subhadra. This child came to be known as Parikshit, meaning "the tested one."

Enraged, the Pandavas attempted to kill Ashwathama but failed, as he was deemed immortal. Krishna intervened, forcefully removing the divine gemstone from Ashwathama's forehead, and cursed him to suffer from incessant bleeding, incurable wounds, and melting skin. Krishna decreed that Ashwathama would live as a leper, enduring perpetual agony without the relief of death or aid from others. Due to his immortality, he would bear these afflictions for eternity, until the end of Kaliyuga.

After Krishna's curse, Ashwathama left Kurukshetra for a remote and isolated place, far from human habitation. He lived in complete solitude, cut off from all physical contact with mankind and society. The wound inflicted by the removal of the gem on his forehead would neither heal nor be treated, causing his body to suffer from incurable diseases, festering sores, and ulcers for the rest of his life. It is believed that Ashwathama still roams the earth, residing alone in mountains and forests, devotedly worshiping Lord Shiva.

However, there is another version of the story that goes as follows. Ashwathama supposedly sought refuge with Parshurama, beseeching him to lift Krishna's curse. Ashwathama, who possessed an aspect of Shiva intended to eradicate evil from the world, had committed killings that were deemed heinous crimes. Parshurama accepted him as his disciple and, along with Sage Durvasa, initiated him into Shakti worship, which is considered the supreme form of worship for overcoming any adversity. Through this, Ashwathama is said to have circumvented Krishna's curse.

The tragic tale of Ashwathama underscores that immortality for a human is unnatural and goes against the laws of nature, where the cycle of birth, life, and death is inevitable for every creature on earth. Creation, evolution, and destruction are inherent aspects of nature. Humans are born, live, propagate future generations, and eventually die due to various causes such as old age, disease, accidents, murder, suicide, or sacrifice. If a human does not meet their timely end, old age, disease, injury, and despair will mar their existence. Death becomes the ultimate solace, offering release from all of life's hardships. Due to his immortality, Ashwathama is condemned to endure perpetual injury, pain, bleeding, and insufferable agony. For him, every breath is more tormenting than death itself. Thus, the desire for immortality is against nature and worse than any curse.

Sharabh Avatar: According to Hindu mythology, Narasimha, a ferocious avatar of Lord Vishnu, incarnated as a half-lion, half-human to slay the demon king Hiranyakashyap. Hiranyakashyap had gained special powers through a boon that made him nearly invincible: he could not be killed during the day or night, inside or outside of any dwelling, on earth, in the sky, in heaven, or in the netherworld; nor by any type of weapon, nor by man, god, demon, or animal. These conditions made him tyrannical, and he proclaimed himself to be a god. He forced all his subjects to worship him, but his son Prahlada, a staunch devotee of Vishnu, refused to do so.

Hiranyakashyap continuously tortured Prahlada to abandon his devotion to Vishnu and worship him instead, but Prahlada remained steadfast in his faith. In anger and frustration, Hiranyakashyap tied Prahlada to a pillar and attempted to kill him. He demanded to know the whereabouts of Vishnu from Prahlada, who insisted that Vishnu was omnipresent, even within the pillar. Enraged, Hiranyakashyap struck the pillar, and at that moment, Vishnu appeared in the form of Narasimha from within the broken pillar.

Narasimha swiftly attacked Hiranyakashyap, carrying him to the threshold of the palace where the pillar had been broken. There, Narasimha tore open Hiranyakashyap's abdomen with his terrifying claws, fulfilling all the conditions of the boon that protected him. The killing occurred at twilight, neither day nor night; the pillar was positioned neither inside nor outside the palace; Hiranyakashyap was killed with Narasimha's fearsome claws rather than a weapon; and Narasimha was seated on the threshold, thus not in the sky nor on the land while slaying the demon.

After slaying the demon king, Narasimha could not control his own wrath and became like an unstoppable force, wreaking havoc and burning the universe. His terrible roar created a dreadful situation throughout the cosmos. Even Vishnu himself could not pacify Narasimha or bring him under control. Concerned by this calamity, the deities approached Shiva and beseech him to intervene and stop Narasimha's rampage.

Shiva then assumed the form of Sharabha, a mythical creature depicted as a combination of human, lion, and bird (known as Sarabha in Sanskrit literature). According to the Kalika Purana, Sharabha is described as black in color, with four feet pointing downward and four feet pointing upward, and a massive body. It has a long face and nose, sharp claws, eight legs, eight tusks, a mane, and a long tail. Sharabha is known for its ability to leap high and emit a thunderous cry, striking fear into other creatures inhabiting hills and forests.

Sharabha possessed enormous strength, manifested specifically to pacify Vishnu's ferocious avatar, Narasimha (the human-lion). It had many hands, claws, and legs, resembling a huge dragon. With well-spread wings, a large mouth lined with sharp incisors, and formidable claws, Sharabha emitted a thunderous roar. Truly gigantic and fearsome, Sharabha had unique features that distinguished it. Various mythological accounts depict Sharabha differently, yet all agree on its extraordinary and distinctive form.

Sharabha was far superior to Narasimha in both bodily features and power. Using its long tail, Sharabha lifted the wrathful Narasimha with the intention of subduing him. Realizing his impending fate, Narasimha prayed to Sharabha, addressing him with beautiful epithets as the victorious Lord.

Narasimha then removed his lion's skin and presented it to Sharabha. In doing so, Sharabha liberated Narasimha, an incarnation of Vishnu, from his ferocious nature and animal form.

Although Sharabha is not widely known, especially in North India, many temples, deities, painted images, and scriptures depict Shiva in his Sharabha form. Interestingly, while there is no reference to Sharabha in the Narasimha Purana, the Atharva Veda mentions Maheshwara assuming the form of Sharabha and slaying Narasimha.

Sharabha temples are predominantly found in South India, with the Kampaheswarar temple at Thirubhuvanam being particularly renowned. Sharabheshwara, also known as Sri Pakshiraja, is commonly worshiped in Tantric rituals, believed to offer protection and dispel the effects of black magic and spirits (preta). Devotees believe that worshiping Sharabha on Vaishakha Purnima (full moon day) brings great benefits.

Shiva's incarnation in the form of Sharabha possesses very unique features, blending human, animal, and bird traits with massive strength, specifically to pacify and subdue Narasimha, an incarnation of Vishnu. As Shiva is the god of destruction, his purpose is to pave the way for new generations, constructions, and, more importantly, to establish peace and order in the world by destroying evil. Narasimha incarnated to defeat the tyrannical and oppressive Hiranyakashyap. However, after fulfilling this task, Narasimha, instead of returning, became a threat to humanity and the world's existence. Even Vishnu failed to persuade him to calm down and return to Vaikuntha (Vishnu's abode). At the request of the deities, Shiva, in the form of the fierce and unique Sharabha, destroyed the defiant and fearsome Narasimha, thus ensuring a new lease on the world. Therefore, Shiva is not only a destroyer but also a protector god.

Grihapati Avatar: According to Hindu mythology, Shiva is portrayed as Grihapati, born due to a boon given by Shiva to a sage. Grihpati is perceived as the child form of Shiva. It is believed that there was a sage named Vishwanar who, along with his wife Suchismati, lived near the banks of the river Narmada. Even after a long period of married life, they remained childless, causing them great distress and sadness. Suchismati frequently criticized her husband Vishvanar for not finding a solution to their problem.

The sage, being a devotee of Shiva and regularly worshiping him, felt deeply guilty about their childlessness. He decided to go to Kashi, Shiva's town, and perform penance to seek a boon from Shiva for a child. In his austere penance, Vishvanara prayed to Shiva earnestly. Pleased with Vishvanara's severe penance, Shiva, known for his benevolence, appeared before him, blessed him, and granted him a boon. Vishvanara requested Shiva for a son who would be like him. Shiva agreed and granted the boon.

In due course, Shuchismati gave birth to a son. At the child's naming ceremony, numerous deities, including Shiva with Parvati and Brahma, were present. Brahma named the child Grihapati, and all the deities bestowed their blessings upon him. Raised with the Vedas and other sacred texts,

Grihapati's brilliance and intelligence enabled him to master all the Vedas and religious scriptures.

When Grihapati turned nine, Narada, the wandering sage and son of Brahma, arrived. Upon seeing Grihapati, Narada foretold that he might face a fiery death in the future. Alarmed by this grim prophecy, Grihapati's parents were distressed, but he reassured them and resolved to perform penance in Kashi to avert this dire fate. In Kashi, he chose a sacred spot and installed a Shivalinga there. Facing the Shivalinga, he began his intense penance with fervent prayers.

During his austere penance, Lord Indra noticed Grihapati and arrived to bless him. Indra offered to grant him any wish as a boon. However, Grihapati, being a devoted follower of Shiva, politely refused to accept anything from Indra, stating that he would only seek blessings from Shiva himself. Indra, displeased by Grihapati's refusal, became furious and attempted to attack him with his Vajrayudha. Filled with fear, Grihapati prayed to Shiva for protection.

Upon Grihapati's desperate cry, Shiva appeared instantly. Seeing Shiva, Indra hurriedly departed. Shiva blessed Grihapati and assured him that he need not fear Indra's Vajra, as no weapon could harm him. Grihapati was deeply grateful to Shiva. The Shivalinga installed by Grihapati later became renowned as the "Agnisvaralinga," and worshiping it ensured protection from thunder, lightning, and fire. Shiva also appointed Grihapati as the lord of all directions.

In another version of the story, when Grihapati was nine years old, Narada visited and warned about the threat of fire. Vishvanara immediately went to Kashi and performed penance to appease Shiva. He received a boon from Shiva that his son would possess the qualities of fire, rendering him immune to harm from fire. Grihapati then installed a Shivalinga at Kashi and named it Agniswar Shivalinga.

The story of Grihapati, born as a result of Shiva's boon to a childless sage who performed rigorous tapasya (penance) for a son like Shiva, illustrates Shiva's nature as a god who is easily pleased and extremely generous. Shiva did not hesitate to grant Vishvanara's request for a son like himself. Moreover, Shiva always aids Grihapati whenever he prays and is in need. This story exemplifies Shiva's benevolent nature, showing that despite being known as a god of destruction, he is also a protector and patron to his devotees. Thus, Shiva, in the form of Grihapati, is considered the most compassionate and benign deity.

Durvasa Avatar: Durvasa is a prominent figure in Hindu mythology, recognized as an incarnation of Shiva, the god of destruction. He is renowned for his fiery temper and unpredictable nature, often acting impulsively. His name is derived from the Sanskrit word "dūrvā," which refers to a type of sacred grass used in Hindu rituals.

According to Hindu mythology, Durvasa was a renowned Rishi, the son of sage Atri and Anasuya. Despite being a devoted follower of Lord Shiva and Maa Parvati, he was notorious for his short temper. Durvasa had a habit of traveling widely, and upon finding even the slightest mistake or negligence by his hosts, he would immediately curse them without consideration. Indra, Saraswati, Rukmini, Shakuntala, and others fell victim to his curses. His name, "Durvasa, " combines "Dur" (difficult or bad in Sanskrit) and "Vasa" (to live), reflecting his reputation for anger and curses. Due to his volatile temper and thoughtless curses, all deities, humans, and demons feared him and sought to avoid him. Consequently, he was often an unwelcome guest. However, during times of contentment, he also bestowed blessings and granted boons, as seen in his interactions with Krishna and Kunti.

His quick temper and tendency to curse in anger are characteristic of someone who lives in an imagined world where they believe they are highly revered and deserving of respect from everyone. When this respect is not given for any reason, his mood can swing dramatically from low to high, resulting in fury and unpleasant curses. These fluctuations in energy levels and focus greatly influence his behavior, work, relationships, and other aspects of life. In a good mood, Durvasa is more sociable, talkative, and creative. This psychological syndrome suggests that Durvasa Rishi may have suffered from a bipolar disorder, which led him to frequently curse but rarely bless.

According to the Brahmanda Purana, there was once a fierce clash between Brahma and Shiva. In a fit of rage, Shiva became violently furious, causing the deities to flee in fear. Even Parvati complained that living with an enraged Shiva was unbearable. Realizing the harmful consequences of his anger, Shiva transferred his fury into the womb of Anasuya, the wife of sage Atri. Later, a child named Durvasa was born to Anasuya, meaning "difficult to live with, " as he was born from Shiva's anger. Durvasa had an irritable nature and suffered from mental disorders. His short temper and tendency to curse in anger caused misery for many individuals, prompting both humans and deities to receive him with great reverence whenever he visited, out of fear.

In Hindu mythology, Durvasa would curse deities and humans if he felt insulted or disrespected. According to a story in the Vishnu Purana, Durvasa was offered a garland by Vidyadhari, a nymph of the air. While wandering, he encountered Indra riding his elephant Airavata, attended by other gods. Durvasa threw the garland at Indra, who caught it and placed it on the elephant's head. However, the elephant was disturbed by the strong fragrance of the flowers and threw the garland to the ground, crushing it. Seeing his garland treated so callously, Durvasa became immediately enraged and cursed Indra to lose all his powers and be cast down from his position, much like the garland. Indra realized his mistake and begged Durvasa for forgiveness to mitigate the curse, but the sage flatly refused. As a result of the curse, Indra's powers and strength diminished, leading to the loss of control over his kingdom. Taking advantage of this weakened state, Bali, the demon king, waged war against the deities and emerged victorious.

According to various Puranas, Durvasa's curse on Indra indirectly led to the churning of the ocean (Samudra Manthan). Indra needed Amrit (nectar) to regain his lost powers and strength. After consuming the Amrit, Indra regained his powers and strength and was able to defeat the demons.

Thus, Durvasa's curse triggered the churning of the ocean, plunging Indra and the deities into a period of hardship.

The story of Shakuntala begins with her being the daughter of sage Vishvamitra and Menaka, a nymph. Due to various reasons, Vishvamitra left Menaka, who subsequently left the baby near Rishi Kanva's hermitage before returning to heaven. The baby was discovered and raised by Rishi Kanva, who named her Shakuntala (as she was surrounded by Shakunta birds). Shakuntala grew up in the forest near Kanva's hermitage.

One day, while King Dushyanta was hunting in the forest near Kanva's ashram, he encountered Shakuntala. They fell in love at first sight, and their love deepened quickly. They married according to the Gandharva marriage system, which was prevalent in ancient times and allowed young individuals to choose their life partners without barriers of caste, creed, or community. Before returning to his kingdom, Dushyanta gave Shakuntala his personal ring as a token of his promise to bring her to his palace.

Shakuntala's love and marriage with Dushyanta became so significant to her that she spent her days daydreaming about him, often forgetting her surroundings and daily routines. The intensity of their love led her to live in a dreamlike state.

One day, the irascible sage Durvasa visited the ashram. Shakuntala, lost in her dreams of Dushyanta, failed to greet Durvasa properly. Enraged, Durvasa cursed Shakuntala, proclaiming that the person she was dreaming of would forget her. At the urging of her companions, Durvasa advised Shakuntala to show Dushyanta the signet ring he had given her, which would nullify the curse.

Later, Shakuntala set out to meet Dushyanta. During her journey, she had to cross a river by boat. While on the boat, she absentmindedly put her hand in the water, causing the ring to slip off her finger without her noticing. Upon arriving at Dushyanta's court and presenting herself as his wife, she was dismayed to find that he did not recognize her and had no recollection of their love and marriage. Humiliated, she returned to Kanva's ashram.

Shakuntala later gave birth to a son, whom she named Bharat. It is widely believed that the country was named "Bharat" after Shakuntala's son.

Fortunately, a fisherman was surprised to find a royal ring in the belly of a fish caught in his net. He took the ring to the palace and presented it to King Dushyanta. Upon seeing the ring, Dushyanta immediately remembered his love, marriage, and promises to Shakuntala. He hurried to Rishi Kanva's ashram but could not find her there. Eventually, he located Shakuntala and their brave son Bharata. Thus, after enduring much suffering due to Durvasa's curse, the family was finally reunited. Shakuntala had faced hardships raising her son alone and lived like a hermit (sannyasin) despite being a queen.

According to Hindu mythology, Goddess Saraswati, the deity of knowledge, wisdom, arts, music, and mental prowess, was seated in Brahma's court among many sages, including the choleric sage Durvasa, who was chanting the Vedas. Saraswati noticed that Durvasa was reciting Vedic shlokas incorrectly with discordant tones, which made her laugh. Enraged by Saraswati's laughter, Durvasa cursed her to be born on Earth as a human being. Everyone was shocked, and Saraswati was deeply anguished by Durvasa's curse. She repented, wept, and begged for forgiveness, expressing utmost respect for him. After several pleas, Durvasa informed Saraswati that she would be liberated from the curse upon meeting the sannyasin Adi Shankara, an incarnation of Shiva.

Thus, Saraswati was born as Bharati in a Brahmin family on the banks of the River Sone. From a young age, she mastered the Vedas and Shastras. She married the renowned scholar and pandit Mandana Mishra and became famous as Ubhaya Bharati. A famous intellectual debate ensued between Adi Shankaracharya, who propagated the doctrine of Advaita Vedanta, and Pandit Mandana Mishra, a great scholar of Mimamsa. It was held in Bihar. When the question arose of who would judge the debate's winner between Adi Shankaracharya and Pandit Mandana Mishra, Ubhaya Bharati declared herself the judge, asserting her superiority over both contestants.

After an intense debate, Mandana Mishra conceded defeat, but Ubhaya Bharati argued that since a wife is part of her husband, Adi Shankaracharya had to defeat her as well to be considered the winner. Shankaracharya agreed and engaged in a debate with her. Ultimately, she was defeated.

Realizing that Adi Shankaracharya was none other than Shiva and in accordance with Durvasa's curse, Bharati knew her time on Earth had come to an end. However, it is believed that at Adi Shankaracharya's request, she chose to remain in Sringeri as Sharda. The Sringeri Sharadamba Temple in Sringeri is a renowned temple dedicated to Saraswati.

Once, Krishna and Rukmini visited Durvasa's ashram and invited him to their palace for dinner. Instead of accepting their invitation graciously, Durvasa imposed a unique and insulting condition: they had to yank his chariot. While pulling the chariot, Rukmini, fatigued and thirsty from the sunlight, asked Krishna for water. Krishna, by striking his foot on the ground, brought forth water, and Rukmini quench her thirst. Short-tempered

Durvasa became enraged that Rukmini had not sought his permission before drinking water. He cursed her to endure twelve years of separation from Krishna. Anger often clouds rational thinking and conscience, leading to improper conclusions and erroneous decisions in its impulsive grip. Durvasa frequently made wrong decisions in fits of anger, resulting in harsh curses. His curse on Rukmini was indeed severe; though she accepted it, she suffered emotional sorrow and lamentation. Rukmini performed penance for twelve years at that very spot to lift the curse, and finally, pleased with her sincere prayers, Lord Vishnu appeared and dissolved the curse. Thus, after twelve years of separation, Rukmini and Krishna reunited and lived happily together.

Durvasa also cursed that the water of Dwarka's land would become salty and unsuitable for human consumption. Dwarka, situated near the sea, naturally has salty water due to continuous evaporation, salt accumulation, and lack of drainage of seawater. The saltiness of the seawater around Dwarka could be attributed to Durvasa's curse.

Many natural occurrences or creations are often attributed to acts of gods or god-like personalities in various religions.

According to the Brahma Vaivarta Purana, Durvasa married Kandali, the daughter of sage Aurva. It seemed as though fate had ensured that Kandali possessed a temperament similar to Durvasa's—short-tempered, arrogant, rude, and impolite. When both husband and wife are short-tempered and arrogant, marital life becomes endangered and filled with misery, as a successful marriage depends on mutual understanding, cooperation, support, adjustment, and tolerance. The absence of these elements leads to marital failure and discord. Durvasa, being a sage of an enraged nature, could not tolerate his wife's unpleasant behavior for long. Thus, Durvasa's short temper and aggressiveness did not spare even his wife, Kandali. Once, in a heated exchange, he cursed her to be reduced to a heap of dust. His own curse thus destroyed his married life, illustrating that a terrible nature and habits harm not only others but also oneself.

At that moment, Sage Aurva, Kandali's father, arrived and inquired about his daughter's whereabouts. Upon learning of her death due to Durvasa's curse, Aurva became furious and cursed Durvasa to be insulted by the entire world for his anger and arrogance. Thus, Durvasa became a victim of a curse, and the one who cursed him became cursed himself. This illustrates the balancing act of nature.

Durvasa sometimes behaves irrationally and ridiculously due to his infatuated mind and thoughts. He was an unpredictable sage who could harm anyone without reason. Such an incident occurred when Durvasa was eating kheer (rice pudding) and Krishna was present. Suddenly, Durvasa ordered Krishna to smear the leftover kheer on his body with the intention to bless him with invulnerability. However, Krishna applied the kheer over his entire body except his feet (talvas). Upon seeing this, Durvasa became angry and cursed Krishna, stating that because he did not fully obey his order by not applying the kheer to his feet, they would remain penetrable and could cause his death.

Durvasa's intention to bless Krishna thus turned into a curse.

According to the Bhagavata Purana, a hunter named Jara shot an arrow at Krishna's feet by mistake while he was resting under a tree. Krishna's left foot, partly visible like a deer to the hunter, was struck, leading to his ordinary death. This death of Krishna was the result of both Durvasa's curse and Gandhari's curse. After the end of the Kurukshetra war and the loss of all her sons, Gandhari blamed Krishna for their deaths and cursed him to perish alone as an ordinary man. Krishna, who played a crucial role and exhibited charismatic leadership in the Mahabharata war, met his end at the hands of an ordinary hunter in solitude.

<u>Death is the ultimate step of life. Life completes after death. Life is a cycle of birth, survival and death that has been rotating infinitely. All have to rotate in this cycle, and it is an axiom.</u>

It is a psychological fact that a person with a short temper sometimes tries to be kind and do favors for others when they are calm and composed. This behavioral change is also observed in Durvasa.

He would grant boons to those who pleased him, particularly when he had been well served as an honorable guest. When Kunti was a young girl, Durvasa visited her, and she served him so well that he taught her a mantra capable of summoning any deity and having a son by that deity through another man if her husband was unable to do so due to health issues or other reasons. This practice, known as **Niyoga,** permitted the wife to bear a child who would be regarded as equal to any other child, without any stigma or discrimination. For example, Pandu and his elder brother Dhritarashtra were born through this practice. **Niyoga** was recognized in ancient texts like the Manusmriti, which outlined the conditions under which it could be practiced. The child born through **Niyoga** was considered the legitimate offspring of the couple, referred to as a Kshetraja child.

Curious and unsure, Kunti decided to test the mantra. She recited it to call upon Surya, the Sun God. To her astonishment, he appeared before her and made her pregnant, even though she was unmarried. She bore her first son, Karna, but fearing the consequences and disgrace of being an unmarried mother, she placed her son in a basket and set it afloat in a river. Later, her son was found in the Anga kingdom by a charioteer of Angaraj, who raised him with his wife.

Kunti later married Pandu, the prince of the Hastinapur kingdom. Unfortunately, due to a curse, Pandu was incapable of fathering children with her or his other wife, Madri. With his permission, Kunti used her mantra to invoke Yama, Vayu, and Indra, and as a result, she bore sons by them, including Yudhishthira from Yama, Bhim from Vayu and Arjun from Indra. Pandu told Kunti to give the mantra to his second wife Madri to have sons; Kunti gave the mantra to Madri who called upon the Ashwini twins, the celestial physicians, to get pregnant. She gave birth to two sons Nakul and Sahadeva. Thus, Pandu became a father of 5 sons who became famous as the five Pandavas.

Durvasa's boon to Kunti led to the births of Karna and the five Pandavas. The continuous conflicts and enmity between the Kauravas and the Pandavas culminated in the Kurukshetra War, which involved kings from almost the entire known world. The great epic, the Mahabharata, describes these conflicts, the greed and misery, the warfare, and the deaths of countless warriors, ultimately ending with the victory of the Pandavas and the annihilation of the Kauravas. It was on the battlefield of Kurukshetra that Krishna delivered the Bhagavad Gita, now revered as one of the most sacred texts of Hinduism. If not for Durvasa's boon to Kunti, the Mahabharata and the Bhagavad Gita might not have come into existence, as the Pandavas and Karna would not have been born. In this sense, Durvasa's boon to Kunti can be seen as the catalyst for the events that led to the creation of the Mahabharata.

According to the Shiva Purana, there is another story involving Durvasa and Draupadi. Once, while Durvasa was bathing in a river, his clothes were swept away by the strong currents, leaving him in a difficult situation. Draupadi, who was nearby, offered him her own clothes. Grateful for her kindness, Durvasa blessed her, ensuring that she would never lack clothing in times of dire need. This blessing later protected Draupadi when the Kauravas attempted to disrobe her after winning her in a gamble. Despite their efforts, they were unable to strip her of her clothes in the assembly hall, and her modesty and dignity were preserved. This incident suggests that Durvasa was not only a powerful sage but also a seer or scholar of astrology, as he foresaw the necessity of such a blessing.

Additionally, the Uttara Khanda of Valmiki's Ramayana recounts another episode involving Durvasa. Once, Rama had a conversation with Yama, the god of death, who was disguised as an ascetic sage. Yama instructed that their discussion was to remain strictly confidential, and anyone who entered the room during their discourse was to be executed. Rama agreed and entrusted Lakshmana with the task of guarding the door, ensuring that no one would enter under any circumstances.

Meanwhile, Durvasa appeared at Rama's doorstep and demanded to enter the room. Lakshmana, following Rama's orders, politely asked the sage to wait until Rama had finished his meeting. However, Durvasa became furious at being denied entry and threatened to curse all of Ayodhya if Lakshmana did not immediately inform Rama of his arrival. Lakshmana was deeply troubled and found himself in a dilemma. He decided it was better for him alone to face death than to risk the destruction of Ayodhya. He interrupted Rama's meeting to inform him of Durvasa's arrival and his desire to meet. Rama quickly concluded his meeting with Yama and welcomed Durvasa with due respect. Durvasa expressed his wish for food, and Rama fed him. Satisfied, Durvasa went on his way.

However, since Lakshmana had disobeyed Rama's promise to Yama, he was bound to be executed. Rama was anguished at the thought of killing his beloved brother, who had always stood by him through every trial. Seeking counsel, Rama turned to his advisers to resolve this agonizing dilemma. Sage Vasishta suggested that instead of execution, Lakshmana could be exiled permanently, as abandonment was considered equivalent to death. Following this advice, Rama ordered Lakshmana to leave forever. Lakshmana, heartbroken, left the palace and went to the banks of the Sarayu River, where he decided to end his life. He drowned himself in the river. After Lakshmana's death, Rama, too, took Jalsamadhi (water burial) in the Sarayu, marking the end of the Ramayana era and the most idealistic incarnation of Lord Vishnu.

Durvasa's sudden arrival and his insistence on meeting Rama immediately led to the tragic and unexpected death of Lakshmana and eventually, Rama's own departure from the world. This series of events brought an end to the Ramayana era.

In the Mahabharata, Durvasa ultimately met his end at the hands of Arjuna on the battlefield of Kurukshetra. His anger and short temper were his downfall, but his curses and blessings had profound impacts on the lives of those who encountered him. His impulsive and often mindless actions, driven by anger, brought misery and pain to many. He cursed deities, demons, and humans alike, often without considering the severity of his actions. Durvasa, who embodied an element of Lord Shiva, became notorious for his wrathful curses, which were often not deserved by the victims. His short temper and lack of calm judgment serve as a cautionary tale of how uncontrolled anger can create chaos and suffering in the lives of others and in society as a whole. Sage Durvasa was indeed a manifestation of Shiva's wrathful aspect, and his life exemplifies how a person with a short temper and an unsound mind can bring about unpleasant situations and disrupt harmony.

Rishabha Avatar:- The Rishabha avatar of Shiva is a complex subject, as some scholars believe that Rishabha is an incarnation of Vishnu according to the Bhagavat Purana, while others assert that Rishabha is the first Tirthankara of Jainism. In Jainism, a Tirthankara is an omniscient being who attains Kevala Jnana (absolute knowledge) and serves as a spiritual teacher of Dharma. A Tirthankara is a guru who has conquered samsara, the cycle of death and rebirth, and has paved a path for others to follow. There are 24 Tirthankaras in Jainism, with Rishabhadeva being the first and Mahavira Swami being the last and most significant Tirthankara.

However, according to Shiva texts like the Linga Purana, Tirthankara Rishabhadeva is actually an avatar of Shiva, who was later adopted as the first Tirthankara Rishabhadeva in Jainism. In Vedic literature, Rishabha is described as a "bull, " a nickname for Shiva. The identical name, "Rishabha, " has led to confusion regarding the identity of Rishabha as an avatar of different gods. It is possible that there is only one Rishabha, who has been described differently as an avatar of Shiva, Vishnu, or as Rishabhadeva, the Tirthankara. On the other hand, there might be three distinct figures: Rishabha as an avatar of Shiva, another as an avatar of Vishnu, and a third as the Tirthankara, each born in different periods.

According to Hindu mythology, during the churning of the ocean, a pot filled with nectar emerged from the ocean. All participants, both deities and demons, assembled to obtain the nectar. It is believed that just one drop of the nectar grants immortality. According to mutual agreement, everything that emerged from the churning of the ocean would be equally distributed among the deities and demons. However, Vishnu realized that if the demons consumed the nectar and became immortal, they would be invincible and could wreak havoc on the deities and humanity. To prevent this, Vishnu created many beautiful nymphs, and the demons were immediately captivated by them, forgetting about the nectar. The demons forcibly took the nymphs to Patala Lok (the underworld).

While the demons were preoccupied with the nymphs, the deities consumed all the nectar. However, one demon, Rahu, disguised himself as a deity and managed to taste the elixir. When his deception was discovered, Vishnu swiftly decapitated him, but because he had already tasted the nectar, Rahu became immortal. His head and body became two separate entities known as Rahu and Ketu.

When the demons realized they had been tricked by the deities, they attacked them. However, since the deities had become immortal after consuming the nectar, the demons were ultimately defeated and fled back to Patala Lok to hide. Vishnu then pursued the demons to Patala Lok and completely destroyed them, freeing the captive nymphs. Upon seeing the handsome and attractive

Vishnu, the nymphs fell in love with him. They prayed to Lord Shiva for a boon, asking that Vishnu become their husband. Shiva, who is easily pleased, granted their wish. Using his Maya (supernatural power), Shiva then compelled Vishnu to live with the nymphs in Patala Lok, forsaking his duties and responsibilities toward the universe.

Vishnu lived with the nymphs in Patala Lok, and over time, some of the nymphs bore sons by him. However, due to the environment and conditions of Patala Lok, these sons developed demonic dispositions. They attacked all the lokas (according to Hindu mythology, there are three lokas in the universe: Akash Lok, Bhu Lok, and Patala Lok) and wreaked havoc. They tortured, killed, and injured the deities. Victimized by their oppression, the deities approached Shiva, informed him of the dire situation, and pleaded with him to annihilate Vishnu's sons.

To free the deities from the tyranny of Vishnu's sons, Shiva incarnated in the form of "Vrishabha" (an ox) and descended to Patala Lok, where he destroyed all of Vishnu's sons with his horns. Upon witnessing the destruction of his progeny, Vishnu became enraged and attacked Vrishabha, the ox form of Shiva. However, all of Vishnu's attacks were thwarted.

It is believed that the battle between Vishnu and Vrishabha was prolonged and ended in a stalemate, with neither side achieving victory nor suffering defeat. During this time, some Apsaras (nymphs) who had earlier ensnared Vishnu, using the power of their boons, released him from their influence. Vishnu then regained his original memory and realized his mistake. It is said that he praised Lord Shiva, and at Shiva's request, Vishnu returned to Vishnu-lok. However, he forgot to retrieve his Sudarshan Chakra from Patala Lok. In Vishnu-lok, Vishnu received another Sudarshan Chakra from Shiva.

Shiva, in the form of Vrishabha, destroyed Vishnu's sons in Patala Lok, not out of a desire to destroy creation, but to eradicate the intrinsic negative human traits, imperfections, and illusions. Shiva is the destroyer of all evil, wrong systems, decaying customs, oppressive social injustices, and fears. In essence, he is a constructive destroyer. When Vishnu's sons caused disasters in the world, Shiva did not hesitate to kill them to uphold law and order and to protect the honor and respect of the deities. Truly, Shiva in the form of Vrishabha is the protector of humanity.

On the other hand, the Rishabha avatar episode illustrates the deep bond of affection between Shiva and Vishnu. Both are equal, important, and victorious, complementing each other. Together, they ensure the existence and functioning of the entire universe and its systems.

YathinathAvatar:- In Hindu mythology, there was a Bhil named Aahuk who lived on the hill of the Arbudachal mountain. Aahuk was a poor tribesman who lived with his wife, Aahuka, in a small hut. Both he and his wife were devoted followers of Lord Shiva. Their days began and ended with prayers to Shiva, and their devotion became renowned far and wide.

One day, Lord Shiva, also known as Bholenath, decided to test their devotion. He appeared before them disguised as a hermit named Yatinath.

"Yatinath" means "Master of Ascetics, " as "Yati" refers to a sannyasi (hermit) and "Nath" means master. It is believed that Shiva, in the form of Yatinath, is closely associated with the Master of the hermit kingdom.

Aahuk and his wife welcomed Yatinath with the utmost respect and treated him very well. Yatinath then requested shelter for the night. Aahuk was unsure how he could accommodate his guest because he had a small hut that could hold no more than two people at a time. However, his wife suggested that Aahuk sleep outside the hut with his weapons, as it would be unfortunate to miss the opportunity to extend their hospitality to the guest.

Shiva, in the form of Yatinath, slept inside the hut, while Aahuk slept outside. Unfortunately, at midnight, while Aahuk was in deep sleep, a wild animal attacked and killed him. In the morning, when Yatinath found that Aahuk was dead, his heart was filled with grief. However, Aahuka consoled Yatinath and decided to give up her life on her husband's pyre. Moved by this tragic situation, Shiva revealed his true form and blessed her, saying that in her next birth, her husband would be born into a royal family as Nala, and she would be born as Damayanti. Shiva also promised that he would appear as a swan to help them reunite.

With these words, Lord Shiva manifested as the immovable Achaleshwar Linga, a sacred symbol of divine blessings granted to Aahuk and Aahuka, ensuring their destined reunion in their next lives as Nala and Damayanti.

In the form of Yatinath, Shiva emphasized the importance of hospitality as a noble virtue. Guests are always treated as gods, as expressed in the saying "Atithi Devo Bhava. " Welcoming a guest is seen as a reflection of a person's good character. As Yatinath, Shiva tested the hospitality of the Bhil spouses, who sacrificed their lives to provide shelter to an unknown visitor. Recognizing the exceptional hospitality of the Bhil spouses, Shiva, in the form of a swan, reunited them after their rebirth as Nala and Damayanti.

It is believed that Aahuka was reborn as Damayanti, the Yadava princess of the Vidarbha kingdom, while Aahuk was reborn as Nala, the prince who later became the king of the Nishadha kingdom. One day, a beautiful swan came to Damayanti and told her about Nala. The swan had been sent by Nala after hearing of her beauty and desire. Impressed by the swan's description of Nala's qualities and nature, Damayanti fell in love with him. The swan, which was actually Shiva in disguise, acted as a messenger between them. Thanks to its skillful communication, Nala and Damayanti fell in love and eventually married. Thus, Shiva, in the form of a swan, united them. Shiva's blessings are always fruitful, and his devotees are forever graced by them.

Krishna Darshan Avatar:- According to the Shiva Purana, in ancient times, there was a prince named Nabhag, the son of Shradhadeva, who belonged to the Ikshvaku dynasty. During his childhood, he was sent to a gurukul for education. He took more time than usual to master the subjects. In his absence, and without waiting for his return, his brothers divided the kingdom's wealth among themselves.

After completion of his education at gurukul he returned home and found that all the wealth of the kingdom was distributed and owned by them. He demanded his share of the wealth from his brothers. His brothers intimated that the whole wealth and properties of the kingdom were divided among his brothers forgetting to fix his share, so no wealth remained for him. They told him to go and meet their father Shradhadeva for his share.

Nabhag went to his father and requested his share of the kingdom's wealth and properties. Instead of resolving the dispute and distributing the wealth among all the brothers, his father advised him to visit Sage Angiras, who was struggling to complete a Yajna due to his worldly attachments. His father suggested that Nabhag use his knowledge and discussion to help Angiras overcome these attachments. If Sage Angiras was pleased with him, he would give Nabhag all the wealth that remained unused after the completion of the Yajna.

Nabhag went to the place where Sage Angiras was performing the Yajna. He introduced himself to the sage and explained that material attachments and desires are significant obstacles to successfully performing a Yajna. He then discoursed on the virtues of religiousness. As a result, Sage Angiras was able to free himself from all attachments and gratifications, and the Yajna was successfully completed.

Sage Angiras was very pleased with the young scholar Nabhag for his deep knowledge of various aspects of religion (dharma). As a reward, the sage gave Nabhag all the remaining wealth from the Yajna and then departed for heaven. Shortly after, Lord Shiva, in the form of Krishna Darshan, arrived and claimed the wealth that had been donated to Nabhag by Angiras.

Nabhag opposed Krishna Darshan's claim, asserting that the wealth had been gifted to him by Angiras. Krishna Darshan then suggested that Nabhag seek his father Shradhadeva's opinion on the matter. Nabhag went to his father, explained the dispute, and asked for his advice. Shradhadeva revealed that the one staking a claim on the wealth was none other than Lord Shiva in the form of Krishna Darshan. He explained that, according to tradition, whatever remains after the completion of a Yajna rightfully belongs to Shiva.

Upon learning the true identity of Krishna Darshan and understanding that Shiva was the rightful owner of the remaining wealth, Nabhag felt content and joyful. He returned to Krishna Darshan and recounted what his father had revealed. Nabhag then praised and worshiped Shiva, ultimately attaining salvation (Moksha) through Shiva's blessings.

In the form of Krishna Darshan, Shiva emphasized the importance of detachment from material possessions and pleasures, reminding us that attachment to worldly properties is fleeting and not the true purpose of life.

Detachment leads to spirituality, bringing a sense of peace, wholeness, and satisfaction. Even Shiva lives an ascetic life, indifferent to all physical attachments. He teaches Nabhag the importance of asceticism, urging him to refrain from the lure of external glitters and the lust for possession and power. Shiva staked his claim on the remaining wealth of Sage Angiras to help Nabhag realize the insignificance of wealth and property in achieving inner satisfaction and attaining salvation.

Since Nabhag was learned and possessed deep knowledge of religious texts, Shiva sought to teach him that wisdom is meaningless if it does not lead to liberation from the lust for power, the tendency for possession, the desire for physical gratification, and the fear of loss and death. True wisdom should guide one toward detachment, ultimately leading to Moksha (salvation). Shiva also emphasized the importance of Yajna for human beings, as Yajna is central to human activity.

Yajna involves the domestication of humans through rules, regulations, and rituals that are suitable for society. In exchange for this domestication, Yajna grants abundance, security, and protection from fear. Additionally, Yajna purifies the heart and the environment, enabling the fulfillment of desires.

Bhikshuvarya Avatar:- The Bhikshuvarya avatar is connected to the story of King Satyaratha of Vidarbha, his queen, and their son. After the Mahabharata, the surviving kings returned to their respective kingdoms. The Kalyuga began following the end of the Dwapar Yuga on Earth. As Kalyuga took hold, the distinction between Dharma (righteousness) and Adharma (unrighteousness) blurred, with Adharma becoming more dominant. Crimes such as robbery, theft, and harassment became rampant, and kings were increasingly involved in attacking, killing, and capturing other kingdoms. Enmity, violence, conspiracy and terror spread widely.

In this turbulent time, King Satyaratha was attacked by an enemy king and killed on the battlefield. His pregnant wife fled the kingdom and hid in a forest. There, in solitude, she gave birth to a son. Near the forest was a pond, and to quench her thirst, the queen carried her infant to the pond. She laid her child down near the water's edge and went to drink, but she was suddenly caught and killed by a crocodile. After some time, the infant began to cry out from thirst and hunger.

The child's continuous cries echoed through the forest, yet there was no one to care for the hungry, orphaned infant. However, Lord Shiva, who is omnipresent, could not bear the suffering of the helpless child. In his compassion, Shiva decided to rescue the child from this dire situation. Inspired by Shiva, a poor woman was drawn to the crying child. Shiva then took the form of a monk and appeared before her. He advised the woman to adopt the child, to raise him with love, affection, and care as if he were her own son, and to take full responsibility for him.

The woman was initially hesitant, fearing that someone might come to claim the child as their own. The monk then revealed that the child was no ordinary infant but the son of King Satyaratha of Vidarbha. In his previous life, King Satyaratha, then named Pandya, had been a great devotee of Shiva. However, his devotion was driven by fear of enemy kings and hostile kingdoms. Because his prayers were motivated by self-preservation rather than pure devotion, Satyaratha was destined to be killed by an enemy king in his current life.

Similarly, the child's mother, who had used deceitful means to eliminate her husband's other wife, was killed by a crocodile as a consequence of her past sins. The child was left an orphan due to the untimely deaths of his parents, both of whom were suffering the consequences of their past actions. The monk urged the woman to care for the orphaned child, and she accepted him as her own.

Pleased with her willingness to adopt the child, Shiva revealed his true form to the woman and blessed her. This compassionate manifestation of Shiva as a monk is known as Bhikshuvarya.

The woman adopted the child, naming him Dharma Gupta. He grew up, married a Gandharva girl, and gathered enough forces and weapons to reclaim his father's lost kingdom. He successfully conquered it and declared himself the king.

The form of Shiva as Bhikshuvarya illustrates that Shiva is indeed the supreme deity of the trinity. As an omnipresent and omniscient being, Shiva exists in every atom of the universe and is aware of every activity within it. He is the protector of all creatures and the universe. Whenever someone is in distress and helpless, Shiva arrives to offer assistance and provides the strength needed to overcome their problems. He continually showers grace upon his devotees. When the orphaned child was crying from hunger in the forest, Shiva was deeply moved by the child's plight and took action to help him, saving him from grief and starvation. Thus, he assumed the form of Bhikshuvarya to ensure the child's safety and find a foster caregiver.

The episode of Bhikshuvarya also underscores that our sins and misdeeds not only affect us but also impact the future of our children. Our actions in this life influence our destiny, determining whether we experience heaven or hell, which in essence exist on earth. The consequences of our sins and mistakes will affect both ourselves and our offspring, both in this life and in future lives. For example, King Satyaratha and his wife were killed in their current lives due to sins committed in their previous lives. Similarly, their son became an orphan and suffered because of his parents' past misdeeds.

Therefore, it is crucial to make good decisions and act with dedication and a righteous mindset to ensure a safe and obstacle-free future for ourselves and our children. A life free from enmity, greed, crime, theft, and illegal activities is essential for eligibility for heaven and a prosperous future.

Sureshwar Avatar:- The story of Sureshwar's incarnation narrates the tale of a young boy named Upamanyu, the son of the sage Vyaghrapaad, who lived in a hut near a forest. One day, Upamanyu wanted to drink milk, but his mother informed him that there was no milk available at that moment. However, he persisted in his request and began to weep. Concerned, his mother suggested that he worship Lord Shiva, as Shiva is known to be a kindhearted god who might provide milk for him. She likely mentioned this to distract him from his desire for milk. However, Upamanyu took her words seriously and set off for the Himalayas. In the dense forest of the Himalayas, he began performing a penance to please Shiva. His penance was so intense that it generated immense heat, causing all three worlds to start burning.

Seeing the three worlds burn and wanting to test his devotion, Shiva and Goddess Parvati appeared before Upamanyu, disguised as Indra and Indrani. They told Upamanyu to stop his penance, claiming that they, Indra and Indrani, were pleased with his devotion and penance. They also urged him to stop worshiping Shiva and asked him to state his desires, promising to fulfill them. However, Upamanyu remained unmoved and continued his penance.

In response, they began to abuse and curse Shiva. Hearing these insulting words against Shiva, Upamanyu became furious, for he had learned from his mother that Shiva was omnipotent. Enraged, he prepared to attack the disguised Indra.

Shiva and Parvati were pleased to see his unwavering dedication and devotion. They then revealed their true identities and blessed him. Shiva promised Upamanyu that he, along with Parvati, would always be present in the vicinity of his hermitage. Upamanyu returned home and narrated the entire story to his family. Shiva earned the name "Sureshwar" because he had appeared in the disguise of Indra (a synonym for Suresh).

The Sureshwar avatar exemplifies the greatness of Shiva, showing that he watches over all his devotees and seeks to help them. When Upamanyu was performing penance to Shiva, the god kept a close watch on his young devotee. In a playful mood, Shiva decided to test the boy to see if Upamanyu truly knew him. Disguised as Indra, with Parvati as Indrani, they appeared before the child devotees. Both tried to convince Upamanyu that they were Shiva and Parvati, but through his unwavering faith and devotion, he successfully recognized them. Shiva then blessed his devotee.

This episode also illustrates that Shiva is easily pleased by his devotees, regardless of their status, manner of worship, or type of offering. There are many stories of Shiva and Parvati visiting the earth. Whenever they see any creature in hardship, they try to alleviate the problem. These stories highlight Shiva's greatness, compassion, helpfulness, and omnipresence.

Keerat Avatar:- As mentioned in one episode of the Mahabharata, during the dice game between the Pandavas and the Kauravas, a new round was initiated after the Pandavas had lost some earlier rounds. In this round, if the Pandavas won, the Kauravas would return all the items they had lost in the previous gambling sessions. However, if the Pandavas lost, they would have to go into exile in the forest for twelve years and live incognito for an additional year. Despite the objections of his four brothers, Yudhisthira decided to play the dice game again. Unfortunately, Yudhisthira lost the game because of Shakuni's deceit.

As a result, the Pandavas, even losing Draupadi, gave up their royal clothes and left for the forest.

During their exile, Krishna advised Arjuna to perform penance to Lord Shiva to strengthen themselves and obtain Shiva's Pashupata weapon. Arjuna began his penance to appease Shiva. When Duryodhana learned of Arjuna's penance, he sent a powerful demon named Mūka (sometimes referred to as Mudh) to kill him. The demon took the form of a wild boar and approached the place where Arjuna was deep in penance. The demon could not be killed by an ordinary arrow.

Sensing the critical situation, Lord Shiva, whose presence and vision encompassed all, took the form of a Keerat, a tribal hunter, and arrived at the scene. Arjuna was absorbed in his meditation.

When his concentration was disturbed by a loud noise, he opened his eyes and saw a boar being chased by the Keerat. As the wild boar approached Arjuna, he immediately shot an arrow at it. At the same time, Shiva, disguised as the Keerat, also struck the demon-turned-boar with a fatal arrow. Due to Shiva's illusion, Arjuna did not recognize him and mistook him for an ordinary hunter. Arjuna claimed that he had killed the boar with his arrow, but Shiva, in disguise, objected and insisted that he was the one who had killed it. This led to a dispute between them, resulting in a physical clash.

During the duel, Arjuna used all his weapons against the Keerat, but the Keerat effortlessly deflected his attacks. Arjuna exhausted all his weapons in vain. When Keerat launched an assault, Arjuna was unable to defend himself and fell to the ground with the first strike. Facing imminent defeat, Arjuna quickly made a Shivalinga and prayed to Shiva, placing a garland on the Shivalinga and then around the neck of the Keerat. Arjuna instantly realized that the hunter was no ordinary being; he suspected he might be Shiva. He stopped fighting and bowed before the Keerat.

Lord Shiva, pleased by Arjuna's valor and devotion, revealed his true form. Arjuna, ashamed of having fought with Shiva, was consoled by the god. Shiva blessed Arjuna with victory over the Kauravas and bestowed upon him the invincible Pashupata weapon.

On Krishna's advice, Arjuna had begun a severe penance to Shiva with the goal of obtaining the powerful and deadly Pashupata weapon, which would be crucial in defeating the enemy warriors in battle. It is believed that after witnessing Arjuna's penance, a group of sages approached Shiva and requested his assistance for Arjuna. Shiva, taking the form of the Keerat, tested Arjuna's valor and ability to determine if he was worthy of wielding the Pashupata. Shiva always ensures that his devotees are deserving of the gifts they seek. Thus, in the guise of the Keerat, Shiva fought with Arjuna, who bravely faced the challenge. When Arjuna was overpowered, he made a Shivalinga and worshiped it, demonstrating his unwavering devotion even in peril. Arjuna's display of both warrior skill and total devotion to Shiva pleased Bholenath, who then granted him the formidable Pashupata weapon.

Later, during the Kurukshetra war, Arjuna, following Krishna's advice, used the Pashupata against the great warrior Karna, ultimately killing him. Karna's death played a pivotal role in securing the victory of the Pandavas over the Kauravas.

Sunatnartak Avatar:- After the death of Sati, and at the request of the Devas to replace Daksha's head with that of a male goat, Shiva withdrew to his snowy mountain beneath the Pole Star and retreated into a cave. Sati, the goddess, had opened Shiva's heart, allowing him to feel her presence and devotion. Shiva experienced loss and reacted with intense emotion. The goddess desired Shiva's engagement with the world so that he could become Shankara (Shiva as a householder). To fulfill this purpose, the goddess was reborn as Parvati, the daughter of Himavan, the king of mountains.

To assist Parvati in awakening Shiva, the Devas enlisted the help of Kama, the god of carnal desire. Kama, using his arrows of sensual sensation, attempted to rouse Shiva from his deep meditative state. However, Shiva, being no ordinary ascetic and the Lord of Beasts (Pashupati), remained unaffected. Yet, sensing an unusual disturbance, he merely opened his third eye. From it, a blazing missile emerged, setting Kama ablaze, while Shiva remained as tranquil as ever.

Parvati decides to undertake tapasya to awaken the Tapasvin. She gives up wearing jewelry, royal garments, cosmetics, and the comforts of a luxurious life, embracing the life of a Sanyasin. With single-minded devotion, she prays to Shiva and performs a severe penance. According to the Shiva Purana, Parvati's intense vrata eventually rouses Shiva. He opens his eyes and approaches her.

Shiva asks if she truly wishes to marry a wandering mendicant and hermit who has no home. Parvati firmly expresses that she desires him in any form and anywhere. Her devotion is so intense that Shiva finally agrees to be her bridegroom. She then asks him to come to her home, meet her father, and formally request her hand in marriage. Shiva readily agrees.

There are two versions of how Shiva meets Himavat(Himavan), father of Parvati. The more famous version describes how Shiva arrives on a bull, accompanied by his Ganas, at Himavat's abode to ask for Parvati's hand in marriage. Shiva is clad in animal hide, smeared with ash, adorned with garlands of serpents, and holds a trident and Damroo. He is accompanied by demons, Ganas, ghosts, and Yakshas and is in a state of intoxication from bhang and narcotic hemp. This appearance frightens and surprises everyone, including Parvati's mother, sisters, and other relatives. Maina, Parvati's mother, is shocked by Shiva's uncivilized form, and her sisters and other relatives mock him. Even Parvati's father is disturbed by his daughter's choice of such a wild, eccentric, and hermit-like husband.

Seeing the tension between her father and her suitor, Parvati realizes the unusual situation. She approaches Shiva, falls at his feet, and prays to him to change his appearance. She explains that her family is not enlightened enough to understand his true nature and greatness, while he, being enlightened, should understand their limitations.

Shiva is moved by her devotion and transforms himself into Somasundara (beautiful as the moon), becoming the most handsome man on earth. Seeing Shiva now as a graceful and handsome figure, her father agrees to the marriage. Everyone rejoices at the wedding of Shiva and Parvati (Shakti). It is a rare occasion where perpetual enemies, demons, deities, Ganas, ghosts, Yakshas, and others come together in celebration.

The second version relates to Shiva's appearance as Sunat Nartak. Moved by Parvati's severe and continuous penance, and after a brief conversation with her about her determination to marry him, Shiva agreed to go to her residence to meet her father and seek her hand in marriage.

Shiva, known for his diverse qualities and passions, decided to surprise Parvati and her family. He took on the form of Sunat Nartak, a performer with a Damroo (rattle drum) in hand, and presented himself as a "Nat" (a dancer known for entertaining onlookers and earning money). Shiva performed a dance in the court of Himavat, Parvati's father. His dance was so captivating and spectacular that King

Himavat was greatly charmed and wished to reward Nat. When Himavat asked what could be given to him, Natraj requested Parvati as his reward. This request enraged Himavat, who ordered the Nat to leave the court immediately or face prosecution. Nat departed, but later, Shiva, in his true form as Natraj, met Parvati, revealed his identity, and told her the entire story before leaving.

Eventually, Parvati's parents realized that the Nat was none other than Shiva. They regretted not recognizing him earlier and requested him to return to their palace. They agreed to give Parvati's hand in marriage to Shiva. The marriage between Shiva and Parvati was solemnized, and Shiva took her to his abode on Mount Kailasha.

Shiva's appearance as Sunat Nartak before Parvati's parents showcases another aspect of his nature. While he is a serious tapasvi whose meditation cannot be disrupted by external stimuli (even Kama, the god of desire, could not affect his meditation, resulting in Kama being reduced to ashes), he is also Bholenath, kindhearted and simple. As Sunat Nartak, he danced with love and festivity.

Shiva is the first god to master all forms of dance. As Natraj, the Lord of Dance, his dance emanates cosmic rays and vibrations of joy throughout the universe. All creation is enchanted by it. The "Natya Shastra, " written by Bharata Muni, is a famous and ancient encyclopedic treatise on the arts of dance, music, and dramatic compositions. Natraj Shiva served as an inspiration for Bharata Muni to write this book, as Shiva embodies the essence and evolution of dance.

When Shiva dances in joy, he is known as Natraj. However, when he dances in anger, this violent dance is referred to as "Tandava. " During Tandava, cosmic and fiery rays spread throughout the universe to destroy everything, including the universe itself and all sins that hinder dharma. This destruction paves the way for the creation of a new universe. When ego, sins, and adharma dominate over dharma, the order of things, and culture, Shiva performs the Rudra (fretful) Tandava to eliminate these obstacles and create a new world.

As Sunat Nartak, Shiva performed the "Anand Tandava, " a dance of joy and gratification, and asked Parvati's father for her hand in marriage. Her father was unable to recognize who he was. Humans often fail to perceive divine acts and realize the presence of the divine. However, later, he comes to understand his inability to recognize divine power and actions.

Brahmachari Avatar:- It is believed that Sati was reborn as Parvati, the daughter of King Himavan and Queen Maina. From a young age, Parvati exhibited intense devotion to Lord Shiva, who resided in a cave in the Himalayas. She began performing severe penance to win Shiva's favor. Despite her continuous and intense tapasya, Shiva remained unmoved. Parvati, undeterred, lived as a sanyasin, relinquishing all luxuries.

Ultimately, Shiva decided to test Parvati's devotion and reverence. While she was performing penance by a riverbank, Shiva appeared before her in the form of a Brahmachari. He inquired about the purpose of her penance, to which she replied that she sought Shiva as her husband. The Brahmachari began to criticize Shiva, describing him as a mendicant smeared with ash, with matted hair, dressed in animal hide, adorned with snake garlands, and homeless. He warned her that such a Shiva would not be a suitable husband, predicting a life of no happiness, luxury, home, food, or comfort. He suggested that her marriage would be disastrous, given Shiva's lifestyle as a wanderer living in crematoriums and forests.

Despite these warnings, Parvati remained resolute. She was determined to marry Shiva and live with him no matter where. Impressed by her unwavering devotion, Shiva, in the guise of the Brahmachari, revealed his true form and blessed her. He agreed to accept her as his wife.

After the self-immolation of Sati, Shiva withdrew into a cave on the mountain, detaching himself from Prakriti (nature). For the new generation, the union of Purusha (Shiva) and Prakriti (nature) is essential. Thus, Prakriti (Sati) was reborn as Parvati, the daughter of Himavan, the king of the mountains. Shiva's abode, Kailasha, is located in Himavan's kingdom. Just as Sati had, Parvati resolved that Shiva would be her husband. She aimed to make Shiva a householder to restart the creation of the new generation. She sought to engage him with the world and transform him from a hermit into Shankara (a householder).

Parvati undertook severe penance and prayer to marry Shiva. Despite being a princess, she lived as a sanyasin, forsaking royal clothes, jewelry, cosmetics, and regal comforts. Her actions eventually stirred Shiva. To test her devotion, he appeared as a Brahmachari and criticized Shiva's lifestyle. However, Parvati's determination and devotion shone through, and Shiva revealed his true form, promising to marry her.

Shiva, being omniscient, understood the depth and purpose of Parvati's birth and her penance. His act of appearing as a Brahmachari was part of his divine play to test her determination. Shiva had already foreseen that Parvati, embodying nature (Prakriti), would be his bride, and that for the world's renewal, he, as Purusha, would need to marry her.

Yaksheshewar Avavatr:- Once, Sage Durvasa visited Indra, the king of the gods, and gifted him a fragrant garland. However, in a state of intoxication,

Indra tossed the garland onto the trunk of his elephant. The garland fell to the ground and was crushed under the elephant's feet. Angered by this disrespect, Durvasa cursed Indra, declaring that he would lose all his splendor. As a result, Lakshmi, the goddess of prosperity, immediately disappeared, and gloom spread everywhere, bringing misery to all.

To restore their former glory and bring Lakshmi back, the Devas planned to churn the ocean. They sought the help of the Asuras, and despite their previous differences, they came together to start the Samudra Manthan (churning of the ocean). The ocean frothed and fumed for eons until, eventually, the waters coagulated and yielded a wealth of treasures. Among these treasures, Lakshmi emerged and was accepted by Vishnu.

Later on, a viscous mass called Halahala, or poison, emerged from the ocean. The deities and the demons were terrified by the tremendous heat and poisonous vapor it generated. The substance was so toxic that it could not be safely contained on Earth; it threatened to burn everything and annihilate all living creatures.

To ensure the safety of all beings, the demons and deities turned to Lord Shiva for help. Although Shiva was neither involved in the churning of the ocean nor a beneficiary of the treasures it produced, he was the only one with the power to handle such a dire situation due to his mastery over Yoga. Despite his indifference to worldly matters, he agreed to help.

Shiva began to drink the Halahala to protect the world from its harmful effects. Meanwhile, Parvati, seeing the danger, immediately clasped his neck tightly to prevent the poison from reaching his abdomen. As a result, the poison collected in Shiva's throat, turning it blue due to its toxic effects. Consequently, Shiva is known as "Neelkantha," or "the blue-throated one."

Like a protective and concerned wife, Parvati (Shakti) was angry at how Shiva was being treated. She did not want Shiva to consume the poison, as he was not responsible for its creation. Those who created the poison should bear the responsibility for it. However, Shiva, as Bholenath, cares deeply for his devotees' prayers and willingly took on the task.

After the poison, Nectar (Amrita) emerged from the ocean. The deities deceitfully consumed the nectar without sharing it with the demons. However, Rahu, one of the demons, drank the nectar in disguise as a deity and became immortal. When Vishnu discovered that Rahu had consumed the nectar, he became enraged and severed Rahu's head with his Sudarshan chakra. Despite this, because Rahu was immortal, his head and body became the celestial entities Rahu and Ketu in Hindu mythology.

Since the demons did not receive any nectar, they remained Asuras (mortals) while the deities who drank the nectar became Suras (gods of light) and attained immortality. The Suras, or Devas, were thus illuminated by the nectar.

According to the ethics of the joint venture, the demons were entitled to drink the nectar. However, due to deceit and a lack of respect for these ethics, the deities consumed the nectar without sharing it with the demons. Additionally, Rahu's head was severed by the Sudarshan Chakra for drinking the nectar. The demons were enraged by the deities' betrayal, leading to a tremendous battle. The deities emerged victorious because they were immortal due to the effects of the Amrita, while the mortal demons were defeated.

The victory led the deities to become arrogant and egotistical. They grew unkind and autocratic. As the god of destruction, Shiva is responsible for removing anything that disrupts social harmony, human nature, the flourishing of nature, and the order of things, thereby paving the way for social equality, humility, and a peaceful society.

Seeing the deities' arrogance, Shiva decided to teach them a lesson to highlight their powerlessness. He approached them disguised as a Yaksha. He inquired about the source of their arrogance, to which the deities proudly attributed their pride to their victory over the demons.

Shiva, in his Yaksha form (known as Yaksheshwar), responded that their pride and arrogance were misplaced, as their victory was due to the grace and blessing of others. The deities disagreed. Shiva then placed a grass leaf before them and challenged them to cut it if they were truly powerful. Each deity attempted to cut the grass with their weapons but failed miserably. They were astonished and demoralized by their inability to cut such a simple object and began to question why they had failed.

A heavenly voice then revealed from the sky that the Yaksha was actually Shiva. The deities recognized their mistakes and delusions. They apologized to Lord Shiva and sought his blessing. After diminishing their false pride and arrogance, Shiva disappeared.

Shiva's form as Yaksheshwar demonstrates that he destroys evil, including lust, desires, arrogance, ego, greed, and ignorance. The world should be peaceful, non-violent, non-intrusive, and harmonious. When there is any disturbance in the natural order or inhumane activities, Shiva does not hesitate to eradicate it.

Avdhut Avatar:- According to the Vishnu Purana, the position of Indra, king of the deities, changes in every Manvantara—a cyclic period of time in Hindu cosmology. Indra is also depicted in Buddhist and Jain mythologies. He wields the weapon Vajra, which is a thunderbolt, and rides a white elephant named Airavata.

According to Hindu mythology and religious literature, Indra is the king of the Devas and ruler of Swarga (Heaven). He is associated with lightning, thunder, storms, rain, rivers, and war, and is frequently mentioned as a deity in the Rigveda. Indra is depicted as a powerful deity who leads a luxurious life, with a splendid court adorned by beautiful apsaras (celestial nymphs) such as Menaka, Urvashi, and Rambha. However, he is also notorious for his indulgence in drinking, hedonism, and adultery. Indra is always fearful of losing his kingdom and position, so whenever a sage performs penance, he often tries to disturb them using unfair means, such as sending apsaras to distract them.

Despite having immense power as the king of the deities and leading a royal life, Indra was always insecure, dissatisfied, and suffered from feelings of inferiority. He noticed that he was not given the same respect and importance as the gods of the Trimurti—Brahma, Vishnu, and especially Shiva. Indra could not comprehend why Shiva, the god of destruction, was so widely worshiped, with temples dedicated to him everywhere. He observed that all beings—deities, demons, and humans alike—prayed and worshiped Lord Shiva. Even the demons, who were natural rivals to the deities, sought refuge in Shiva and performed rigorous penance for his favor. Everyone revered Shiva and called him "Mahadeva," the god of gods, despite the fact that Shiva lived under the open sky, had no palace, no luxury, and wandered in forests and mountains as a hermit.

The more Indra thought about Shiva's significance, the more puzzled he became. He lacked the wisdom and insight to understand that Shiva's destruction meant the eradication of all evils, lusts, and desires, leading to ultimate dissolution. Moreover, Shiva was not just a dogmatic destroyer, but a constructive one—destroying only to pave the way for the creation, construction, and development of new and better things.

Indra once devised a plan to prove to the world that he was greater than Lord Shiva. Consequently, he, along with Guru Vrihaspati, went to Kailasha to meet Shiva. Shiva, the *trikala darshi* (one who knows the past, present, and future), saw that Indra and Vrihaspati were approaching him. To test their arrogance, Shiva took the form of an Avadhut, a wandering ascetic, and blocked their path. When Indra and Vrihaspati encountered this unkempt, semi-nude ascetic with long hair, they were enraged and demanded that the Avadhut move out of their way. They failed to recognize that the Avadhut was actually Lord Shiva in disguise. To their utter shock, the Avadhut remained unmoved. Angry and humiliated, Indra asserted his identity as the king of the deities and warned the Avadhut that blocking his way would come at a great cost. Yet, the Avadhut remained silent and did not move.

Feeling insulted that an ordinary sage would ignore him, Indra decided to teach the Avadhut a lesson. He raised his Vajra, the deadly weapon, to strike the sage. However, before he could attack, his hands were paralyzed by Shiva's divine power. Realizing the severity of his mistake, Indra watched in terror as Avadhut opened his third eye, which had the power to kill him instantly. At that moment, both Indra and Vrihaspati realized that the Avadhut was actually Lord Shiva. They immediately began to pray for forgiveness for their disrespect and ignorance.

As is his nature, Shiva's anger subsided as quickly as it arose. He calmed down and forgave Indra. However, since his third eye had been opened, the energy from it needed to be released. Instead of directing this energy toward Indra, Shiva diverted it into the ocean, where it gave birth to Jalandhar.

Shiva assumed the Avadhut avatar to crush the arrogance and ego of Indra, the king of the deities. Indra was accustomed to judging the capability and worth of individuals based on their outer appearance and status. He believed that power and wealth were inherently linked to affluence, luxury, nobility, and ego. Proud of his position as king of the deities, Indra compared himself to Shiva, viewing him merely as a hermit and ascetic. However, he failed to realize that inner strength and power are far superior to outer appearances. His underestimation of Shiva's capabilities, based solely on Shiva's external disposition and clothing, ultimately compelled Indra to bow before him. This story serves as a reminder that a person's true strength and worth should be judged not by their position or post, but by their qualities and abilities.

Hanuman Avatar:- Lord Hanuman is considered the eleventh avatar of Lord Shiva and was born to Mata Anjani and Kesari.

Hanuman, the mighty monkey god of Hinduism, is renowned for his devotion, humility, celibacy, and strength. He is widely worshiped across India, with numerous Hanuman temples found in every region of the country. Tuesday is considered Hanuman's day, and large crowds of devotees visit Hanuman temples on this day. Hanuman is especially revered by athletes, particularly wrestlers, who pray to him for strength, success, and overcoming obstacles. Merely remembering Hanuman's name can infuse anyone, especially wrestlers and combatants, with confidence, energy, and a fighting spirit.

Hanuman is regarded as a Rudra-Avatar, an incarnation of Rudra (Shiva). He is also known as

Pawan-Sut (son of Vayu, the wind god), Keshari-Nandan (son of Keshari), and Anjani-Putra (son of Anjani). The belief in Hanuman as a Rudra-Avatar is supported by a story mentioned in the Shiva Purana.

According to this story, a demon named Bhasmasura performed severe penance to please Shiva. When Shiva was pleased, Bhasmasura requested a boon that would grant him the power to turn anyone to ashes by touching their head with his hand. After receiving this unique boon, Bhasmasura immediately attempted to touch Shiva's head, intending to burn him to ashes and possess Goddess Parvati. Shiva, realizing the danger, fled, with Bhasmasura in pursuit. Desperate and frightened, Shiva sought the help of Vishnu.

Vishnu, in response, took the form of Mohini, an enchantress of extraordinary beauty and sensuality. Enchanted by Mohini's ravishing appearance, Bhasmasura stopped chasing Shiva and instead asked Mohini to marry him. Mohini agreed, but with a condition: Bhasmasura had to dance with her and imitate her every move perfectly. The dance began, and Bhasmasura tried to mimic Mohini's various postures. At one point, Mohini placed her hand on her head, and Bhasmasura, eager to imitate her, did the same. In doing so, he forgot about the boon he had received. As soon as he touched his own head, Bhasmasura was immediately burned to ashes, destroyed by his own power.

Shiva was running continuously, but sometime later he found out that Bhasmasura was no longer chasing him. Shiva retreated and found Vishnu there, also there were ashes nearby. Vishnu told how Bhasmasura turned into ashes. Shiva wanted to see Mohini, and Vishnu took the form of Mohani. She had such beauty that even Shiva was enchanted. He embraced her, and from this union, a divine essence was created. Vishnu carefully preserved this essence in a bamboo tube. Later, from this sacred essence, warrior-gods such as Ayyanar, Ayyappa, and Hanuman were born.

The unfortunate incident involving Indra's deceitful act with Ahalya, the wife of Sage Gautama, is also connected to the birth of Hanuman. According to the narrative, Brahma created a most beautiful woman, Ahalya, who was married to the much older Gautama. They lived in a cottage and eventually became the parents of a daughter named Anjali.

One night, Indra, along with Chandra (the Moon), disguised himself as Gautama, while Chandra took the form of a rooster. At midnight, Chandra crowded loudly, imitating the Brahma-muhurta (the time for early morning rituals), which prompted Gautama to rush to the river for his bath and prayers. Meanwhile, Indra, in the guise of Gautama, entered the cottage and engaged in an illicit act with Ahalya.

The narrative further tells that as Gautama approached the river, the river, disturbed by the untimely bath, questioned why he had come at such an hour and warned him that something was amiss. Suspicious and angry, Gautama rushed back to his cottage, only to find Chandra lingering near the door. In his fury, Gautama threw his animal hide at Chandra, leaving a deep impression, which is believed to be visible on the Moon's surface to this day.

Entering the cottage, Gautama discovered Indra's deceit and cursed him to bear a thousand marks of shame on his body. Although Ahalya was innocent, she was turned to stone for sixty thousand years, destined to be redeemed only by the touch of Lord Rama. Still consumed by anger, Gautama called for his daughter Anjani and demanded to know why she had remained silent during the immoral act. Blinded by rage, Gautama irrationally cursed Anjani to become the unmarried mother of a monkey son, failing to recognize that her silence was out of shyness and respect for her parents' privacy.

Furious at her father's unjust curse, Anjani declared that she would defy it. She then left her home and retreated into the dense forest, determined to remain isolated from any male contact.

Solitary Anjani was praying in a hut in the deep jungle. After some years, Narada, a wandering sage visited there and seeing him, Anjani hid herself in the hut. Narada told her that since he was a celibate sage and wanted to give guru-mantra for successful praying, otherwise her prayers or penance would be futile without a proper guru mantra. Guru-mantra could be given through the bamboo tube by his sitting outside the hut and without physical contact. Anjani received a special blessing from Narada, who imparted a sacred mantra to her. Through this divine act, the essence of Lord Shiva was symbolically conveyed to Anjani, leading to the birth of Lord Hanuman.

Anjani, after receiving the divine blessing, became pregnant and later gave birth to a son, Hanuman. This is why Hanuman is called Rudra-avatar and also Anjani-Putra. However, due to being an unmarried mother, Anjani left her son after instructing him to eat only red fruits that were ripe. This explains why, when the Sun rose in the morning, the young Hanuman jumped and put the red Sun in his mouth, mistaking it for a ripe red fruit.

There is another version of Hanuman's birth. According to Hindu legends, during a meeting organized by Indra in which Rishi Durvasa was participating, all were deeply engrossed in intense discussions. However, Punjikshali, a celestial nymph, was walking around the meeting spot.

Durvasa warned her to stop immediately, but she ignored his warning and continued moving. Angered by her disregard, Durvasa cursed her to be reborn as a monkey.

Devastated, Punjikshali begged Durvasa for forgiveness for her foolish act. Moved by her pleading, Rishi Durvasa modified his curse, saying that in her next birth, she would marry a monkey king and become the mother of a powerful monkey son, who would be an avatar and an ardent devotee of Lord Rama.

Punjikshali was born to the monkey king Viraj and was named Anjali (Anjana). When she reached marriageable age, she was married to monkey king Kesari. They led a happy married life, but after some years, they remained childless. To have a child, Anjali began praying and worshiping Vayu Deva. According to Eknath's Bhavartha Ramayana, while Anjana (Anjali) was worshiping Vayu, King Dasharatha of Ayodhya was performing the Putrakameshti Yagna to have children. As a result, he received some sacred pudding (kheer or payasam) to be shared among his three queens, leading to the birth of Rama, Lakshmana, Bharata, and Shatrughna. It is believed that, by divine decree, a kite snatched a fragment of this pudding and dropped it while flying over the forest where Anjana was engaged in worship. Vayu, the god of wind, delivered the falling pudding to Anjana, who consumed it, resulting in the birth of Hanuman.

According to the Valmiki Ramayana, one morning during his childhood, a hungry Hanuman leaped toward the rising red Sun, thinking it was a ripe fruit, and attempted to take it in his mouth. This caused the entire world to fall into darkness. At the request of the gods, Indra, the king of the deities, intervened and struck Hanuman with his thunderbolt. Hanuman's jaw was broken, and he fell to the ground unconscious. Hence, he was known as Hanumana, meaning "one having a disfigured jaw."

The Ramayana states that Vayu, Hanuman's father (according to one version), was furious upon seeing his injured son with a broken jaw and withdrew all the air on earth. The absence of air created havoc among all living creatures. This suffering prompted Lord Shiva to intervene and revive Hanuman. Subsequently, Vayu restored air to all living beings on earth.

All the gods assembled there. Indra, who had broken Hanuman's jaw, wished that Hanuman's body would be as strong as his Vajra. Similarly, Agni granted Hanuman the boon that no fire would affect him. Vayu wished that Hanuman would be able to fly as fast as the wind. Brahma blessed him with the ability to be unstoppable, and Vishnu granted him immortality and a gada (mace). Thus, Hanuman, the child, possessed many supernatural powers and became "Chiranjivi, " or immortal.

Sometimes, Hanuman used his powers for mischievous activities, playing pranks on innocent passersby and even on meditating sages. One day, he played a prank on a meditating sage who, in anger, cursed Hanuman to forget all his powers until he was reminded of them.

At a young age, Hanuman was a friend and general to the monkey king Sugriva, the younger brother of Bali, who had driven Sugriva out of his kingdom. During his exile, Sugriva lived with Hanuman and his followers in the mountain terrain of Kishkinda. While in exile, Sita was abducted by Ravana, the king of Lanka, and brought to his kingdom. Rama and his brother Lakshmana searched for Sita in the jungle and eventually arrived in Kishkinda. There, they met Sugriva and Hanuman. Sugriva recounted his story of exile and the treacherous act of his brother Vali. It was agreed that Rama would kill the tyrant Bali, and in exchange, Sugriva and his general Hanuman would help Rama in search for Sita.

After Rama killed Bali, Sugriva sent Hanuman along with others, including Jambavan, to search for Sita. Other groups were sent in different directions to continue the search.

This group reached the southernmost end of India, where they found an ocean with the island of Lanka (now Sri Lanka) visible on the horizon. They wanted to explore the island, but none of them could swim across the ocean or leap over it. Only someone with supernatural powers could accomplish this task. Hanuman felt helpless as he and his team could not locate Sita. However, Jambavan knew from previous events that due to the curse, Hanuman had forgotten his supernatural powers. When reminded, he would regain them. Jambavan reminded Hanuman of his powers.

With the curse lifted, Hanuman remembered his immense strength. He immediately transformed into the size of a mountain and flew across the ocean to Lanka. Lanka, the kingdom of Ravana, was populated by demons and was known for its grand palaces made of gold. Hanuman shrank down to the size of a fly and sneaked into the city. After a thorough search, he found Sita in an orchard, sitting under an Ashoka tree, guarded by demon warriors.

Hanuman dropped Rama's ring near Sita from the tree, and she immediately recognized it. Realizing that Rama's messenger was hiding in the tree, she called out. Hanuman jumped down, introduced himself, and explained that he had come to search for her. Sita revealed that Ravana had kidnapped her and was forcing her to marry him soon. Hanuman offered to rescue Sita, but she refused, stating that only her husband, Rama, could free her from Ravana's captivity.

After taking leave from Sita, Hanuman began to wreak havoc, destroying the grove and injuring some of Ravana's demon guards. He was captured and presented before Ravana. When Ravana inquired about his presence, Hanuman boldly declared that Rama was preparing to attack Lanka and reclaim Sita. Ravana ordered his servants to bind Hanuman with oil-soaked clothes and set them on fire. Hanuman's tail was bound with these clothes.

When his tail was ignited, Hanuman extended his tail to escape his bonds and then shrank it back to break free with his superhuman strength. He leaped out of a window and began jumping from roof to roof, causing widespread destruction as his burning tail set the city ablaze.

Hanuman returned to Kishkindha, where Rama awaited news of Sita. Hanuman recounted the events in Lanka, and Rama, with the support of Sugriva's army, marched towards Lanka, leading to the legendary battle. Throughout the battle, Hanuman played a crucial role, acting as a general in the army.

During the battle, Lakshmana was gravely injured, and it was said that he could be saved with the Sanjivani herb found in the Himalayas before sunrise. Hanuman was tasked with retrieving the herb. Instead of searching for the specific herb among many, Hanuman uprooted the entire mountain and flew it back to the battlefield, saving Lakshmana before sunrise.

At the end of the battle, Rama demonstrated his divine power, defeating the mighty Ravana and the demon army. Hanuman, along with Sugriva, Angada, and other monkeys, displayed immense bravery and heroism. Hanuman supported Rama selflessly and wisely.

After Rama's victory and Sita's rescue, Rama returned to Ayodhya and was crowned king. He rewarded everyone who had helped him, giving gifts to all, except Hanuman, who refused them. This act puzzled and angered many court officials and Hanuman's companions. Hanuman explained that rather than accepting gifts as a reminder of Rama, he would always carry Rama in his heart. Despite skepticism, Hanuman proved his devotion by tearing open his chest to reveal an image of Rama and Sita within his heart. This act of devotion is widely documented in mythological literature.

Later, Rama blessed Hanuman with immortality, but Hanuman requested only a place at Rama's feet to worship him. Touched by Hanuman's devotion, Rama granted his request, making Hanuman immortal, or "Chiranjivi." It is believed that wherever Rama's name is uttered, Hanuman is present.

Another story highlights Hanuman's devotion: one day, Hanuman saw Sita applying sindoor (vermilion) to her forehead and asked her why. She explained that sindoor was a sign of a married woman and was believed to ensure her husband's long life. Hanuman, determined to ensure Rama's immortality, smeared his entire body with sindoor and presented himself before Rama. When Rama inquired about his appearance, Hanuman proudly replied, "Lord, if a small amount of sindoor can increase your lifespan, then I apply it all over my body to ensure you live forever."

This story exemplifies the purity and innocence of Hanuman's devotion to Lord Rama. Hanuman, deeply immersed in his devotion, saw Sita applying sindoor to her hair parting and, without caring about the comments and unusual remarks of onlookers, smeared his entire body with sindoor. This act demonstrated his profound and unwavering devotion to Lord Rama. Consequently, Hanuman's idols are painted red with vermillion. It is believed that offering red vermillion mixed with jasmine oil to Hanuman on Tuesdays will help one overcome all problems through his blessings.

As Hanuman is immortal (Chiranjivi), he appeared twice during the Dwapar period (as depicted in the Mahabharata). The first appearance was to meet Bhima and humble his ego, as Bhima considered himself superior due to his immense strength. The second appearance was when Hanuman protected Arjuna's chariot throughout the battle of Kurukshetra by residing on Arjuna's flag.

According to the Mahabharata, while the Pandavas were in exile, Arjuna went to the

Himalayas in search of divine weapons to help him defeat formidable warriors such as Bhishma, Drona, Kripa, Ashwatthama, Karna, and others. During his absence, the remaining four Pandavas and Draupadi moved to a different forest called Narayanasrama and stayed there.

One day, a flower with a captivating fragrance drifted from the northeast direction and fell near Draupadi, enchanting her. Desiring the flower, she asked Bhima to fetch the Saugandhika flower for her. On his way, Bhima encountered a huge, old monkey lying across the path, blocking it. Irritated, Bhima demanded that the monkey move aside and let him pass.

The monkey explained that he was too old and frail to move and requested Bhima to push his tail aside if he wished to pass. Despite Bhima's efforts, he could not budge the tail even an inch, no matter how much strength he applied. Realizing that the old monkey was no ordinary creature, Bhima relented and asked for forgiveness.

The monkey then revealed himself as Hanuman in his true form and blessed Bhima. Hanuman assured Bhima that whenever he roared on the battlefield, Hanuman's voice would join him and strike fear into his enemies. He also warned that ego and arrogance lead to downfall, while modesty and humility bring success, prosperity, and happiness.

According to the Mahabharata, Hanuman met Arjuna in the form of a normal monkey in Rameswaram. During his visit to Rameswaram, Arjuna saw the bridge (Rama Setu) built by Lord Rama to reach Lanka and expressed surprise at why Rama needed the help of monkeys and others to construct the bridge. Being a great archer himself, Arjuna felt he could have built a bridge of arrows without the help of monkeys.

A monkey from a nearby tree then appeared before Arjuna and challenged him to construct a bridge of arrows capable of withstanding the weight of a single monkey, implying himself (Hanuman). Proud of his archery skills, Arjuna confidently agreed to build such a bridge, betting that if it failed to support the monkey's weight, he would immolate himself.

Arjuna, using his inexhaustible supply of arrows, constructed a bridge over the sea and invited the monkey to cross it. As the monkey began to walk on the bridge, it collapsed under his weight. Undeterred, Arjuna built another bridge, but once again, it could not support the monkey and buckled.

Frustrated and ashamed, Arjuna prepared a pyre to end his life when Lord Krishna appeared and instructed him to build another bridge. After the bridge was rebuilt and blessed by Krishna, the monkey (Hanuman in his ordinary form) was invited to step on it. This time, the bridge held firm despite Hanuman's attempts to break it. Overwhelmed with devotion and emotion upon recognizing Rama in Krishna, Hanuman revealed his true form and promised to aid Arjuna in the war.

It is believed that during the Kurukshetra war, Hanuman perched on the flag of Arjuna's chariot and remained there throughout the battle, stabilizing and protecting the chariot. Various accounts offer different reasons for Hanuman's presence on the flag, but his role signifies control over the mind and senses, and his support to the righteous side. Hanuman's presence on the flag symbolizes his backing of the righteous Pandavas against the Kauravas, who had wrongfully exiled the Pandavas and denied them their rightful share of the kingdom.

As an immortal (Chiranjivi), Hanuman is believed to be present wherever Rama's name is mentioned or Rama is worshiped. There is a reference to Tulsidas meeting Hanuman face-to-face. According to Priyadas's version, Tulsidas, who lived in Varanasi, used to visit a jungle outside the city for his morning rituals and would unknowingly offer the remaining water to a particular tree. One day, a ghost (Preta) appeared to Tulsidas and expressed gratitude for quenching his thirst. The ghost offered Tulsidas a boon, and Tulsidas wished to see Rama. Although the ghost could not fulfill this wish, he agreed to guide Tulsidas to meet Hanuman, who could help him glimpse Lord Rama due to his unwavering devotion.

The Preta (ghost) revealed that Hanuman, in disguise as an old leper, used to visit the temple daily to listen to the Ramkatha. Hanuman would arrive before others and leave after the gatherings dispersed. Tulsidas was advised to identify Hanuman and seek his blessing.

Tulsidas went to the temple well before the Ramkatha began and waited for the first arrival. To his surprise, the first visitor was indeed an old leper who sat humbly at the rear end of the gathering. After the Ramkatha ended, Tulsidas quickly followed the leper, who headed towards the forest. Tulsidas approached the leper, fell at his feet, and politely asked who he truly was, urging him not to leave.

The leper claimed to be an ordinary old man suffering from leprosy. Despite this, Tulsidas continued to beg, and ultimately, the leper revealed his true form as Hanuman. The spot where Tulsidas saw Hanuman in his original form is now the Sankat Mochan Temple in Varanasi.

Hanuman blessed Tulsidas and offered him a boon. Tulsidas requested a darshan (glimpse) of Lord Rama. Hanuman informed him that Rama resided in Chitrakuta. Following Hanuman's advice, Tulsidas went to Chitrakuta, where he sat by the path and applied Chandan (sandalwood paste) on the foreheads of visitors.

Two handsome young men came to Tulsidas for a Tilak. Suddenly, Hanuman whispered in Tulsidas' ear the famous couplet:

" Chitrkoot ke ghat pe bhayi santan ki bheer.

Tulsidas chandan ghisein, tilak det Raghuveer, "

Tulsidas had the privilege of meeting Hanuman and, with his help, later meeting Lord Rama. Tulsidas subsequently composed the epic *Ramcharitmanas*, which is a sacred book for Hindus. This episode showcases Hanuman's profound devotion and closeness to Lord Rama.

In both the Valmiki Ramayana and Tulsidas' *Ramcharitmanas*, Hanuman is portrayed as a crucial character—a devoted simian helper and messenger for Rama. He is depicted as an astute devotee with legendary courage, strength, and powers. Hanuman is revered as a divine being (demigod) and an ideal embodiment of Shakti and Bhakti. As an important incarnation of Shiva, he played a pivotal role in both the Ramayana and the Mahabharata.

In Ramayana, Hanuman's role in the battle between Rama and Ravana was huge. He flew across the ocean, located the exact place where Sita was kept captive by Ravana and brought back the information of the whereabouts of Sita. He also set entire palaces on the fire and warned Ravan to return Sita to Rama, unharmed and with pardon in order to avoid the dire consequences. He saved the life of Lakshmana by fetching the Sajivini buti (herb). Hanumana along with a group of monkeys helped Rama build a bridge across the sea and crossed over with the monkey army. He fought bravely and killed many demons and helped Rama kill Ravana and his army and free Sita.

Hanuman is the incarnation of Shiva who helped Rama, an incarnation of Vishnu to defeat the despotic demon king Ravana who was a scholar but adopted the path of adhrama. Shiva always wants to establish the dharma and annihilate the adharma. So, Shiva never tried to save his devotee Ravana even if he gave boons. Shiva doesn't help his devotees if he does adharma activity. Similarly, when Ravana abducted Sita, he was left without the blessing of Shiva. Shiva grants boons to his devotees only as long as they are engaged in righteous activities.

According to the epic Mahabharata, Hanuman's involvement is described as a lesson to Bhima and his perching on Arjuna's flag during the Kurukshetra battle. There are references that Suryadev taught the Vedas and all other scriptures to Hanuman, making him not only a warrior but also a scholar. He is symbolized by strength, devotion, celibacy, and righteousness.

Hanuman is also mentioned in Buddhist literature, where his storyline and character are broadly similar to the Hindu texts. However, in the Tibetan version, Hanuman is portrayed as a carrier of love letters between Rama and Sita, as well as the wedding ring from Rama to Sita. Hanuman is depicted as a monkey messenger and warrior who could read and write. According to the Jataka tales, the Buddha, in one of his earlier births, was described as a monkey king who, despite suffering and abuse, always followed dharma in helping a human in danger.

In Jain literature, Hanuman is depicted not as a divine monkey but as a Vidyadhara (a supernatural being or demigod) who met Rama. Driven by a desire to learn about Sita's abduction by Ravana, Hanuman journeyed to Lanka to persuade Ravana to release her, but his efforts were futile. Nevertheless, he joined Rama in the war against Ravana, exhibiting valor and performing heroic deeds. In Jainism, which upholds non-violence, Rama is revered as Pauma, refraining from harming any living being. In the Jain version of the Ramayana, Ravana meets his end at the hands of Lakshmana. Hanuman ultimately renounced all worldly ties to become a Jain ascetic, symbolizing his complete detachment from social life and devotion to spiritual pursuits.

In Sikhism, the story of Hanuman as Siddha is widely described, with Sikh texts such as *Hanuman Natak* and *Das Gur Katha* portraying his heroic deeds. As a result, Hanuman is a respected figure in Sikhism. Additionally, the character of Hanuman appears in various forms in Southeast Asian texts, alongside the Ramayana. This is due to the influence of Hinduism, which spread to many countries, particularly in Southeast Asia, during ancient times through the rule of Hindu kings and trade. Naturally, with the spread of the Ramayana, the character of Hanuman also became prominent in the literature of these countries.

Generally, Hanuman is worshiped alongside Rama and Sita, but sometimes independently of them. There are numerous Hanuman temples across India and in some neighboring countries. Hanuman's worship is typically performed on Tuesdays and Saturdays, and on these days, the temples are crowded with devotees. There are many famous temples dedicated to Hanuman, both in India and abroad, such as Mahavir Mandir in Patna, Bajrang Bali Hanuman Temple in Hyderabad, Balaji Mandir in Rajasthan, Hanuman Garhi in Ayodhya, and Shri Panchmukhi Hanuman Mandir in Karachi, Pakistan.

Hanuman is very popular among devotees, and it is surprising to find more temples dedicated to Hanuman than to Rama, to whom Hanuman is devoted. This may be because devotees believe that

Hanuman is more easily pleased and is quick to protect and bless them.

Shiva as a tapasvi - Tapa, practiced by all Rishis and sages, cleanses the mind and eliminates all memories and prejudices, leading to the experience of Sat-Chit-Ananda (truth-consciousness-bliss). Tapasya is the process of kindling this inner fire. The Tapasvins are ascetics who metaphorically churn this fire within. Shiva is the greatest Tapasvin, generating immense heat, yet he does not engage with the outward world. All the heat he generates remains contained within his body, naturally causing the world around Shiva to gradually lose its heat and become cold. As a result, water stills and turns to snow, and his mountain becomes the Himalaya, the abode of snow.

As a Tapasvin, Shiva practices celibacy, refuses to engage with women, and refrains from fathering children. He is indifferent to all physical engagements and wanders as a hermit.

But Shakti, or nature, always urges Shiva, who is Purusha, to become a householder for the continuation of humanity. The Goddess, in her various forms, such as the radiant Gauri and fierce Kali, stands in opposition to Shiva for the generation and sustenance of life. While Shiva remains in the north, Shakti emerges from the south as Dakshina Kali, demanding to be seen. Nature cannot be ignored. Though Shiva's eyes are shut, symbolizing his indifference to the outer world, Shakti does not allow him to remain detached. Ultimately, Shiva must generate and sustain life in the world. Thus, he is regarded as "Adideva, " the primordial deity.

Shiva has two forms: the physical and the formless. He is always formless, with neither a beginning nor an end. Physically, he is finite, but in reality, he is infinite, representing the entire universe. His color reflects that of the sky, and the Ganga flows from his matted hair, symbolizing its origin from the Himalayas. The moon, which rises in the sky, is depicted as an ornament of Shiva. The snakes around his neck symbolize creatures that move on the earth. Shiva is limitless and dimensionless, like the universe, as it is impossible to fathom the extent of the cosmos. All galaxies, the sun, planets, stars, Milky Ways, dust clouds, light, and living things are contained within the universe. It is believed that Shiva embodies the entire universe; symbolically, he is depicted with the Ganga River, crescent moon, and snake, indicating that only the universe can contain these elements, not an ordinary deity. Like the universe, Shiva is infinite and beyond the boundaries of time and space. Shiva is regarded as Mahakal, the timeless one, and Jagdish, the lord of the world.

According to Hindu scriptures, Shiva has created the entire universe. He also created the five elements of nature—Earth, Water, Air, Fire, and Sky—and all matter is composed of these basic elements, including the human body. Thus, Shiva is also called "Bhootnath" (Lord of Elements—*Bhoot* meaning element). He created the Sun, the source of energy for the universe, as well as the moon and all species within the cosmos.

Shiva is, in fact, the entire universe and resides in everything, both living and nonliving. Shiva exists within every soul, making him the supreme soul. He imparts the truth about the soul, God, and creation, inspiring humans to purify themselves by connecting their hearts and minds with him. Swami Dayanand Saraswati once said, "Shiva is the one who is bliss and the giver of happiness to all. " The supreme soul, Shiva, brings liberation (*mukti*) and salvation (*jeevan mukti*) to all..

Shiva as Adiguru:-. According to Hindu mythology and scriptures, Shiva is *Adiguru* (the first teacher) who imparted knowledge in various subjects, such as medicine, yoga, science, arts, music, and dance. Initially, he taught 16 types of knowledge related to yoga, lifestyle, and ways of living to each of his seven disciple sages, instructing them to spread this knowledge and tradition to humanity across the world. Through this knowledge, different cultures and civilizations emerged. The tradition of the guru-disciple relationship, which still exists today, was initiated by Shiva. These disciple sages— Brihaspati, Shukra, Agastya, Atri, Bharadvaja, Gautama, and Kashyapa (though there are different versions regarding the names of the seven sages)— are known as the *Saptarishi*. The seven stars surrounding the Pole Star are named the *Saptarishi* stars in their honor.

It is believed that Adiyogi (Lord Shiva) taught 112 branches of the doctrine of yoga, imparting 16 branches to each of his seven disciples, the *Saptarishis*. Additionally, he possessed knowledge of two more branches of yoga, related to experiences beyond the physical body, i. e., in outer space. Yoga, the science of managing the mind, uncrumpling consciousness, and attaining *Sat-Chit-Ananda* (truth-consciousness-bliss), was taught by Shiva to the *Saptarishis* for the betterment of mankind. Today, yoga is highly regarded as a remedy for stress, tension, and physical dysfunctions. Lord Shiva's teachings emphasized the importance of yoga in harmonizing our mental and physical systems. In this context, Maharshi Patanjali is renowned as the author of the *Yoga Sutras*, a classic text on yoga theory and practice. Through this text, yoga has become accessible to the common man. It is believed that Maharshi Patanjali drew inspiration from Shiva's teachings on yoga. It is truly remarkable that Shiva, during the dawn of civilization, taught yoga—knowledge that transcends time. Today, yoga serves as a powerful tool to overcome mental and emotional illnesses, such as anger, lust, greed, and jealousy, and to lead a healthy life.

Shiva as Rudra - Vedic beliefs and practices of the pre-classic era describe three main clans that predominantly existed in the world: the Deities (*Devas, Suras*), the Demons (*Asuras, Danavas*), and the Rudras. There were constant clashes between the Devas and the Demons due to their different cultures, customs, ethics, and approaches to life. The Devas were more civilized and followers of Vedic rituals, whereas the Demons were less educated and did not follow Vedic practices. The Demons were primarily rural-based, living mostly in jungles and scattered across rural areas. The Devas performed Vedic rituals and *yagna*, while the Demons practiced penance (*tapas*). Although there was a clear separation between the two clans, with each having different types of weapons, there were occasional inter-clan marriages. Brihaspati was the guru of the Devas, and Sage Shukra was the guru of the Demons.

In addition to the Devas and Demons, there was also a third clan known as the Rudras. Shiva belongs to the Rudra clan and shares many features with the Vedic god Rudra. According to Hindu scriptures, Shiva and Rudra are often considered the same entity. Shiva, as Rudra—a Rig-Vedic deity with fearsome powers—was the god of the roaring storm, embodying fear and destruction. In Vedic literature, the name Shiva is regarded as an epithet meaning "kind and auspicious. " As Rudra, Shiva is quite distinct from both the Devas and the Demons. His weapon, the trident, is neither a spear nor a sword, and his musical instrument, the *damaru*, is neither a *mridangam* nor a tabla. Instead of adopting the weapons and musical instruments of the Demons, Shiva invented his own, distinct from both.

It is observed that most of the Demons performed penance to Shiva rather than to Vishnu, as Vishnu always favored the Devas and ensured their protection. During the Samudra Manthan (churning of the ocean), after obtaining the nectar, Vishnu took the form of Mohini and deprived the Demons of the nectar. Even Rahu, who was in disguise and managed to taste some of the nectar, was decapitated by Vishnu.

In contrast, Shiva never showed favoritism. As Bholenath, he is easily pleased and grants boons without discrimination. He purely relies on one's devotion, determination, emotion, and meditation. Shiva is a kind and innocent god who does not consider the future consequences of his boons. For example, he granted a boon to Bhasmasura, who undertook penance with nefarious intentions. Consequently, most of the Demons performed severe penance to Shiva and received boons. However, by granting these boons, Shiva, as the god of destruction, accelerates the process of the destruction of evil.

Shiva is also the Adiguru who propagated the doctrine of *Natya Shastra* and made dance a divine expression of happiness and anger. According to Bharata Muni, who composed the famous treatise on *Natyashastra*, this art form emerged with the first performance of dance by Lord Shiva. His dance was dynamic and full of powerful movements, known as *Tandav*. Shiva performs *Tandav* in anger, known as

Rudra Tandav, and in happiness, known as Anand Tandav. Additionally, Goddess Parvati performed the feminine form of dance, characterized by graceful and slow movements, known as *Lasya*.

The sculpture depicts the dance of destruction, with Shiva dancing on the dwarf of ignorance. He holds fire in one hand and a *damaru* (rattle drum) in the other. His front hands are in the mudras (gestures) called *Gajahasta* and *Abhaya Mudra*. It also portrays the moment when Shiva is about to lift his left leg and assume the classic pose of *Nataraj*, an iconic dance posture. Shiva is regarded as the "god of dancers, " and this classic dance posture is not easily replicated.

The sculpture conveys the message of *Nataraj*—the simultaneous processes of creation and destruction. It signifies that coming under Shiva's protection mitigates the fear of both destruction and creation. Change is a fundamental feature of nature, and life is not permanent. The world is full of illusions, and beyond it lies eternity, beauty, and truth. The *Nataraj* symbolizes awareness of the impermanence of worldly life and encourages inner peace and satisfaction.

As First Story Teller

Shiva is considered the first storyteller (Adi Katha Vachaka) in the world, having initiated the art of storytelling. Although Shiva usually prefers silence, he never disappoints Parvati when she requests a story.

One day, Ma Parvati was bored and asked Shiva to entertain her with a story. In response, he recounted the world's first story, which he told in a secret cave somewhere in the Himalayan terrain. Though the first story might have been lost to time, a tiny bird that survived in the cold, isolated site shared the story with a fish, which then passed it on to a Yaksha. Through this chain, the story told by Shiva eventually reached humanity.

The story is rich with numerous episodes, plots, and characters, featuring amazing twists and turns. It is known as the Brihadkatha, or the "vast story." This Brihadkatha later became famous as the Katha-Sarit Sagar, the "ocean of stories." The collection includes stories within stories, exploring the mysteries of life and human relationships. It served as a source of mental satisfaction and provided valuable life lessons. This branch of literature, which includes stories and novels, narrates various aspects of life, emotions, happiness, sorrow, and the complexities of human relationships.

Thus, Shiva is revered as the first storyteller.

According to mythology, Shiva wears a garland of 108 skulls. Once, Parvati asked Shiva when he started wearing this garland. Lord Shiva told Parvati that the skulls in his garland were none other than hers. Before being born as Parvati, she had taken birth as a human 108 times, and each skull represented one of her previous births, woven together in a thread and worn as an ornament. A bewildered Parvati then asked where his skulls were if all the skulls belonged to her. Shiva replied, "You are bound by the cycle of birth and death, but I am free from such a cycle, as I am indestructible.. Parvati then questioned why she is mortal and repeatedly takes birth and dies, while Shiva is immortal. Shiva explained that immortality comes from hearing the

"Amar Katha" (Eternal Story). Parvati desired to hear the Amar Katha to become immortal and live with Shiva eternally, so she persistently requested him to tell the story.

Eventually, Shiva agreed to narrate the story in detail. To ensure that no one could overhear the immortal secret, Shiva sought a solitary place in the Amarnath cave. He left behind the moon, the Ganga, Nandi, his sons, the snakes, and even the Five Elements (earth, water, air, fire, and sky), over which he is the lord. After leaving everything behind, Shiva entered the holy Amarnath cave with Parvati and went into Samadhi. To ensure that no living being could hear the immortal tale, he created Kalagni and instructed him to spread fire to eliminate every living being there.

Despite these precautions, a pair of pigeons overheard the story and became immortal. It is strongly believed that these pigeons can still be seen in the holy shrine today, and remarkably, they manage to survive in the cool, high-altitude area. The cave where Shiva narrated the Amar Katha to

Parvati is known as the Amarnath Shrine and is considered one of the major Hindu pilgrimage sites.

The Amar Katha is a path of knowledge and salvation, and it contains the essence of the immortal story, which holds deep significance for humanity's "code of ethics. " It teaches us to search for the soul rather than being body-conscious. For those who are soul-conscious, realizing that they are souls and not just bodies, they attain awareness of their immortality. To them, there is no need to worry about death, as taking rebirth is akin to changing one's clothes or address. This is the true meaning of immortality, and it is the essence of the Amar Katha.

Through the Amar Katha, Shiva emphasizes the importance of being soul-conscious rather than body-conscious in order to achieve the immortality of the soul. Just as we change our clothes without harming our bodies, souls change physical bodies without being destroyed. Thus, spirituality is more important than materialism in realizing immortality.

Shiva not only narrated the Brihad Katha and the Amar Katha but also recounted the Ramayana to

Parvati. Thus, Lord Shiva is considered the original creator of the great epic Ramayana, long before the birth of Rama. He is also recognized as a great predictor, having foretold the events of the Ramayana era.

Once, Shiva and Parvati were seated on Mount Kailasha. Shiva was in deep meditation, while Parvati, sitting idly, became bored. There was nothing interesting happening on Earth, in Swargaloka, or in Patalloka.

As Shiva emerged from his meditation and opened his eyes, Parvati requested him to tell a story. After some initial hesitation and contemplation of the future, Shiva agreed to tell the story but warned Parvati not to fall asleep until the story was finished. It had happened before that Parvati dozed off before the end of the story, allowing someone else to overhear it. Once Shiva began narrating the story, he became so absorbed in it that he did not notice who was listening. So Shiva began to create and narrate the story of Rama and Sita. The characters and incidents of the Ramayana were born from Shiva's imagination. The story lasted for days, and it was so captivating and vivid that Parvati remained awake, listening attentively. She was so impressed by the story that she insisted on seeing it unfold on Earth.

At Parvati's request, Shiva brought the characters to life on Prithvilok, allowing them to watch the events from Mount Kailasha. Shiva himself became so absorbed in his unique creation that he transferred the story into the mind of Sage Yagnavalkya, who then shared it with others. By the time the story reached Sage Valmiki, he composed the great epic, "Ramayana."

According to the Ram Charit Manas, initially, Shiva narrated the Ramayana, but later, Kak Bhusundi, a crow who spoke with a human voice, took over the narration. Hindu texts describe Kak Bhusundi as a Brahmin who was cursed to become a crow by his guru, Sage Lomas, due to his repeated arguments and ignorance of the sage's teachings.

There is another version which suggests that Kak Bhusundi was born in Ayodhya and showed disrespect for Rama. He was cursed by Shiva for his arrogance and lack of respect towards his guru.

After many lifetimes, he became Kak Bhusundi, renowned for his devotion to Rama. He played a role in helping Garuda overcome his doubts about Rama and narrated the Ramayana.

In Hindu mythology, Kak Bhusundi is said to have been blessed with immortality and continued to live as a crow. He is believed to have witnessed 11 different versions of the Ramayana and 16 different versions of the Mahabharata, each with its own unique ending.

Shiva's Unique Trishul: Lord Shiva is revered as the Destroyer and Transformer among the Tridevas. He belongs to the Rudra clan and is thus also known as Rudra. Traditionally, every clan, tribe, or country has developed its own unique weapons and armor, often varying in design, strength, and method of production. These weapons are crafted based on each group's traditional processes and research. Even today, different countries continue to develop a wide array of weapons and missiles, drawing on their technical and scientific knowledge. These include automatic, biological, and chemical weapons, created for purposes such as self-defense, countering external aggression, and establishing dominance over other nations.

Similarly, in ancient times, the Devas, demons, and humans had different types of weapons. They created some deadly weapons that were indestructible and invincible. Better weapons meant a greater possibility of victory. Some Devas are particularly known for the weapons they wield, such as Vishnu with his Sudarshan Chakra and Indra with his Vajra. Since Shiva is Rudra, he forged his own unique weapons, including the trident, which is neither a spear nor a sword.

Shiva's trident, the most powerful and infallible of weapons, cannot be stopped by anyone except Lord Shiva himself and Goddess Shakti. The three blades of the trident hold deep meanings and significance. According to Hindu mythology, these three blades represent various trinities: creation, maintenance, and destruction; past, present, and future; sattva, rajas, and tamas (the three gunas); and the three worlds created by Brahma and destroyed by Shiva.

Moreover, the three blades of the trident symbolize three stages of the body: 1) the physical body (sthula-sharira), which outlives death; 2) the subtle body (sukshma-sharira), which represents the mind that animates flesh and blood; and 3) the causal body (karana-sharira), which survives death and creates all conditions at the time of rebirth. Thus, the trident carries profound religious and spiritual significance. The trident is exclusively used by Shiva, though sometimes Goddess Durga also wields it, as it is a divine weapon.

As Arms Inventor:- Shiva was an arms researcher and developer who created various weapons with unique features and specifications. Among these, the bow Pinaka, the chakras Sudarshan and Bhavarendu, the Pashupatastra, and the Parashu were all crafted by Shiva.

The Parashu, which was the most lethal close-combat weapon in the epics, was a type of axe with four cutting edges, one on each end of the blade head and the shaft. The Parashu is also one of the weapons used by Goddess Durga, but it is best known for its association with Parashurama, the sixth avatar of Vishnu and a great devotee and disciple of Lord Shiva. Parashurama was renowned for his anger. Pleased with Parashurama's devotion, Shiva bestowed Parashu upon him. Parashurama used the Parashu to annihilate the tyrannical Kshatriya caste twenty-one times across the earth, seeking revenge for the killing of his father by the Kshatriyas. As a result, Parashurama is considered the Adipurush and Adiguru of all Brahmanas, having established the supremacy of the Brahmanas over the Kshatriyas in the world. Moreover, Parashurama's temper has made anger a defining trait of the Brahmanas.

Ravana, the demon king and a clever devotee of Shiva, once performed severe penance to please Shiva. Impressed by Ravana's intense devotion, Shiva granted him a boon. Ravana requested a deadly weapon, and Shiva gave him a divine sword named Chandrahasa, which literally means "the laughter of the moon, " referring to its crescent-moon shape resembling a smile. Ravana later gave the sword to his son Indrajit on various occasions to fight against the deities. The Chandrahasa was invincible and infallible against any weapon, ensuring victory. However, it was given to Ravana with the condition that it must be used righteously, or it would return to Shiva. Consequently, after the abduction of Sita and before the start of the Lanka battle, the Chandrahasa slipped from Ravana's possession and returned to Lord Shiva.

Teen Baan (Three Arrows) was another powerful weapon created by Lord Shiva. A single arrow from the Teen Baan was enough to destroy an entire rival force in battle. Barbarik, the son of Ghatotkacha and grandson of Bhima, was deeply interested in archery from childhood. He performed severe penance to please Shiva, who granted him the divine Teen Baan (arrows) with the assurance that Barbarika could conquer the three worlds using these three arrows. Before the Kurukshetra war, Krishna, aware that Barbarika possessed Shiva's Teen Baan, feared that Barbarika might misuse the powerful weapon.

When Krishna asked Barbarik which side he preferred to fight for—the Pandavas or the Kauravas—Barbarik replied that, as per the promise he made to his mother, he would side with the losing side. In the end, Krishna, disguised as a Brahmana, asked Barbarik for his head. Without any hesitation, Barbarik offered his head to Krishna, thus preventing the use of the Teen Baan by Barbarika, which would have dramatically altered the outcome of the Mahabharata war.

Pinaka was a very powerful bow of Lord Shiva. According to mythology, Shiva, in his avatar as Tripurantaka, destroyed the three cities of Tripura, created by Mayasura, using Pinaka. Shiva is also known as Pinaki because of this divine bow. As per the Valmiki Ramayana, two equally powerful bows were created by Indra and given to Shiva and Vishnu, who were then asked to fight each other to determine who was more powerful. Before the battle could begin, a divine voice (Akashvani) proclaimed that the battle would bring total destruction. Upon hearing this, Shiva threw Pinaka down to Earth. This bow, later known as Shiva Dhanush, was found by King Devaratha, an ancestor of King Janaka.

In the Treta Yuga, King Janaka arranged a swayamvara and announced that whoever wanted to marry Sita must lift and string the divine bow. Ayodhya's prince, Rama, not only lifted the bow but also accidentally broke it while attempting to string it. Thus, he won the swayamvara and became eligible to marry Princess Sita. Upon hearing the sound of the divine bow breaking, Parashurama arrived, enraged, and demanded to know who had broken his guru Shiva's bow. After Rama's polite explanation, Parashurama was satisfied and realized that Rama was an avatar of Vishnu.

Shiva possessed the Pashupatastra, the most powerful, sophisticated, and deadly weapon in Hindu history. It could be operated by the mind, eyes, words, or a bow, making it a truly automatic weapon. In this way, the concept and creation of an automatic weapon can be attributed to Shiva. Indeed, he is the Adi-nirmankarta (first creator) of automatic and sophisticated weapons in the world. This weapon was so powerful and lethal that it was forbidden to be used against less powerful enemies or warriors.

During his exile, Arjuna was advised to obtain divine weapons (divyastras) for the upcoming war.

He decided to pray and perform penance to Lord Shiva to obtain such a weapon. As his penance became more intense, Shiva decided to test Arjuna's capability to handle such a deadly weapon. Disguised as a hunter, Shiva appeared before Arjuna as Kirata while he was performing his penance.

At the same time, a demon named Mukasura, disguised as a wild boar, appeared and attempted to kill Arjuna. Since Arjuna was unarmed while praying, he struggled with the boar. Eventually, he took an arrow and shot the boar, but another arrow struck the boar simultaneously. The boar fell dead, revealing the demon's true form.

The other arrow had been shot by the hunter, Kirata, who claimed to have killed the boar. Arjuna, however, insisted that he had slain the boar. After an argument, Arjuna challenged Kirata to a fight, unaware that Kirata was actually Shiva in disguise. Arjuna used all his weapons but failed to defeat Kirata. Feeling defeated and dejected, Arjuna built a small Shiva Lingam and offered flowers to it. Empowered by his devotion, he challenged Kirata again, only to be surprised to see the flowers he had offered on the lingam adorning the hunter's head. Arjuna then realized that Kirata was actually Shiva. He immediately bowed before Shiva and begged for forgiveness. Pleased with Arjuna, Shiva bestowed upon him the Pashupatastra and taught him its secrets.

However, during the Kurukshetra war, Arjuna never used the Pashupatastra against anyone. He was advised to use it against Jayadratha and Karna, but knowing that the Pashupatastra was an irresistible and destructive weapon associated with Goddess Kali and Lord Shiva, capable of destroying all creation, he refrained from using it. Instead, he used another Brahmastram to defeat them.

Even today, a weapon capable of destroying all creation and annihilating all beings has not been conceived. Not even the most advanced nations, like the USA or Russia, have been able to produce a weapon as powerful and fatal as the Pashupatastra. Indeed, Lord Shiva was the greatest scientist and expert, having created a weapon that could destroy everything in the universe. In terms of weaponry science and technology, the present age lags far behind the achievements of ancient times.

According to Hindu mythology and literature, the Sudarshan Chakra is closely associated with Lord Vishnu and at times, Krishna. Vishnu used the Sudarshan Chakra to defeat demons. There are different versions of how the Sudarshan Chakra was created. According to one version, Vishvakarma, the architect god, made it, and it is described as having 10 million spikes arranged in two rows that move in opposite directions, giving it a saw-like edge.

Another version of the story suggests that the cosmic weapon Sudarshan Chakra was presented to Lord Vishnu by Lord Shiva in recognition of his devotion. The myth states that when the carnage wrought by the demons became unbearable for the deities, they sought help from Vishnu, pleading with him to save them from the demons' tyranny. However, Vishnu lacked an effective and powerful weapon to curb the demons' menace. He decided to seek help from Shiva and went to him. Vishnu found Shiva in deep meditation and did not disturb him, choosing instead to wait and pray. Shiva remained in meditation for many years and did not open his eyes.

Meanwhile, the demons continued their attacks on the deities, and Vishnu was helpless without a powerful weapon. One day, Shiva finally opened his eyes, and Vishnu, overjoyed, began offering him one thousand lotus blossoms. However, Vishnu soon realized that he was one flower short of a thousand. To test Vishnu's devotion, Shiva had hidden one of the flowers. Without hesitation, Vishnu plucked out one of his own eyes and offered it to Shiva. Pleased with Vishnu's absolute devotion, Shiva asked him to request a boon. Vishnu requested a weapon that would allow him to defeat the demons. Shiva then bestowed upon him the most infallible and deadly Sudarshan Chakra, assuring him that it had the power to destroy all enemies.

In the Rigveda, the Chakra is mentioned as Vishnu's weapon, with which he destroys demons. During the Mahabharata period, Krishna, an incarnation of Vishnu, also kept the Sudarshan

Chakra with him. He used it to behead Shishupala. The Sudarshan Chakra was extremely lethal, 100% efficient, and never failed to behead its target. It had an automatic mechanism that allowed it to boomerang back after decapitating its target.

As per the epic Mahabharata, the khaṭvāṅga was a powerful weapon of Lord Shiva. It is described as a long-studded club or staff with a skull on it. The Shaiva tradition and even Vajrayana Buddhists use this weapon as a religious symbol. Besides these weapons, Lord Shiva possesses many other formidable weapons in his armory. The descriptions are as follows:

1. **Ekasha Gada**: The mace of Lord Shiva. One blow from this mace is equivalent to the force of a million elephants.

2. **Jayanta Vel**: A spear imbued with the power of Shiva's third eye. It emits destructive rays that turn any targeted enemy into ashes.

3. **Maheshwara Chakra**: Shiva's chakra, similar to the Sudarshana Chakra.

4. **Shiva Kavach**: The armor of Lord Shiva, which renders its wielder invincible.

5. **Shiva Kaakam**: An unconquerable weapon of Shiva.

6. **Shiva Vajra**: A weapon 100 times mightier than Indra's vajra.

7. **Girish**: A special sword with unique characteristics.

8. **Jaivardhan**: A shield shared by Shiva and Vishnu.

9. **Arrow of Shiva**: A powerful arrow capable of destroying all creation. It contains the destructive power of thousands of hydrogen bombs and automatically returns to the quiver after being used.

10. **Tripurajit Vimana**: A golden chariot used by Shiva to travel anywhere, anytime, and in any manner. It is fully automatic and operates by desire.

11. **Shiva Partham**: A long noose from which even the gods cannot escape.

Shiva possesses an array of highly advanced and sophisticated weapons that are both fatal and destructive. Some of these weapons have power equivalent to thousands of hydrogen bombs, capable of annihilating all beings and destroying the entire creation. Despite the extensive development and research in the field of automatic, highly mechanized arms and missiles in the present day, no weapon—whether biological, atomic, or missile—can match the power of Shiva's arsenal. The ongoing efforts to create weapons equal to those of Shiva have yet to succeed. This highlights the advanced and intricate atomic and technological knowledge that Shiva possessed in creating such unparalleled weapons.

<u>Shiva as first Surgeon</u> -According to Hindu mythology and scriptures, Shiva successfully transplanted Daksha's head with that of a goat and, on another occasion, replaced Vinayaka's head with that of an elephant calf. Daksha, the *manas putra* (mental son) of Brahma, conducted a grand yagna (sacrificial ritual), inviting all the Devas except Shiva to partake in the offerings. When Sati, Shiva's consort, learned that her father Daksha was holding a yagna and that Shiva had not been invited, she was deeply upset. However, Shiva remained indifferent.

Believing that the lack of an invitation was merely an oversight, Sati decided to attend the yagna and insisted on going to her father's house. Despite Shiva's objections, she went, only to be ignored and insulted upon her arrival. Sati demanded to know why Shiva was not invited. Her father, Daksha, scornfully replied that Shiva was not fit to be invited because he did not adhere to the culture and ethics of the Devas. Daksha described Shiva as a wandering hermit who smears his body with ashes, wears animal hides, resides in crematoriums, and takes shelter in caves and mountains. He added that Shiva had no home and was accompanied by dogs, ghosts, goblins, snakes, and *ganas* (followers).

Sati, heartbroken by her father's ignorance of Shiva's true nature, lamented his insult. Overcome with anger and grief, she leaped into the sacrificial fire, immolating herself. When Shiva learned of Sati's death, he was devastated. In his pain and fury, he pulled out a lock of his hair and threw it to the ground. From this hair, Virbhadra, a terrifying warrior, was born. Virbhadra, leading an army of *ganas*, ghosts, goblins, and wild creatures, stormed Daksha's sacrificial hall. They desecrated the holy site, making it unholy with urine, blood, and vomit. Daksha's soldiers and servants were injured or killed, and Daksha himself, terrified by Virbhadra's ferocity and strength, tried to hide but was eventually found and beheaded by Virbhadra.

Shiva, in deep mourning, lifted Sati's lifeless body and wandered through the hills, crying in agony. Consumed by grief, he forgot his *Sanjivini Vidya* (the knowledge of resurrection) and was unable to bring Sati back to life. His intense howling threatened the stability of the universe, terrifying all creatures. Seeing Shiva's state, the Devas and sages became alarmed and rushed to Lord Vishnu, pleading with him to save the earth from Shiva's wrath.

In response to their pleas, Vishnu hurled his Sudarshan Chakra, cutting Sati's body into 51 pieces. Each piece fell to the earth and transformed into a Shakti Pitha, a sacred seat of the Goddess.

After the disposal of Sati's body, Shiva regained his composure. The Devas pleaded with him to forgive Daksha and resurrect him so that the yagna could be completed, as it could not be left unfinished. Shiva, known as Bholenath, pardoned Daksha and replaced his head with that of a male goat. Thus, Daksha, with the head of a goat, was restored to life by Lord Shiva.

After their marriage, Parvati (Shakti) expressed her desire to have a child, but Shiva (Shankara) disagreed. She emphasized the importance of having a child as a powerful metaphor for true involvement with the material world. When she continued to persist, Shankar walked away to meditate in quiet isolation in the dense forest.

Determined, Parvati (Shakti) decided to create a child on her own. She anointed her body with a paste of turmeric and oil, then scraped it off, mixed the rubbings with her sweat, and molded a doll from the mixture. She then breathed life into the doll, creating her son, whom she named Vinayaka (meaning "one born without a man").

Vinayaka was powerful and obedient. After some years, when Shiva returned from meditation, he was blocked by a stranger boy who refused to let him pass. Shiva tried to persuade Vinayaka to move aside, but Vinayaka refused. Enraged by the child's arrogance and disobedience, Shiva raised his trident and severed the boy's head. He then proudly continued on his way, covering his trident with the boy's head.

When Parvati saw this, she was horrified and in anguish. She ran to the headless body of Vinayaka, moaning and beating her chest in distress. She demanded that Shiva resurrect her son, threatening to destroy everything if he did not comply.

Seeing her agony and fury, Shiva realized his mistake and insensitivity. He told Parvati not to be so desperate and decided to resurrect Vinayaka. He ordered his Ganas to fetch the head of the first creature they found in the northern direction. The Ganas found an elephant and brought back its head. Shiva placed the elephant's head on the severed neck of Vinayaka, and he was brought back to life. Shiva then declared Vinayaka to be his son and named him Ganesha, the first among the Ganas and Ganapati, the master of Ganas.

Later, Ganesha became the first god to be worshiped at the commencement of any event, project, or work. Thus, "Shri Ganeshaya Namah" is synonymous with initiation and the starting point of new endeavors.

In both episodes, Shiva successfully transplanted the heads of Daksha and Vinayaka. These episodes may initially appear mythological, hypothetical, and purely unscientific, given that in ancient times, the transplantation of heads—especially between animals and humans—seemed impossible due to the lack of advanced surgical and medical knowledge, specialized tools, and medications. Organ transplantation is a complex medical procedure involving the removal of an organ from one body and its placement into a recipient's body to replace a damaged or missing organ. This intricate procedure includes various tests and surgeries, such as osteopathic techniques.

In contemporary medicine, organ transplants are mostly performed between individuals of the same species, known as "allografts." However, successful heterografts, such as a pig's heart transplanted into a human, have been reported. Shiva's ability to transplant heads demonstrates his role as the first surgeon and medical expert, indicating that he possessed profound knowledge in organ transplantation. Inspired by Shiva, Sage Sushruta, known as the father of surgery and plastic surgery in India, was involved in these practices and authored the famous treatise *Sushruta Samhita*, which is a primary source of ancient surgical knowledge. It is clear that the practice of organ transplantation with animal organs was skillfully known in ancient times, with Shiva being considered the first plastic surgeon and neurologist on Earth.

Different Offerings to Shiva: Lord Shiva is an easily pleased deity who values devotion and sincerity from his worshippers over material offerings. He is not particular about offerings of cooked items, as he lives an ascetic life, wandering the hills and forests, and resides on Mount Kailash, having transcended the need for food. He prefers wild things over cultivated flowers and fruits, which are not typically offered to him. Consequently, plants and ferns liked by Shiva are generally not offered to other deities.

Lord Shiva is worshiped with Bel-patra (leaves of *Aegle marmelos*), Bhang (hemp or Cannabis), Aak (flowers of *Calotropis procera*), Yellow Kaner (Thevetia), Ber (fruit of *Ziziphus mauritiana*), Datura, Rudraksh (*Elaeocarpus ganitrus*), and Sandalwood (*Santalum album*).

Aak, also known as *Calotropis procera*, is revered for its sacred role in offerings to Shiva. It is a wasteland plant with milky latex and purple or white flowers. The plant has antimicrobial, anthelmintic, antioxidant, and analgesic properties. It also improves soil fertility and water retention. Planting an Aak near the main gate of a house is believed to bring prosperity and peace. Shiva's knowledge of the medicinal values of Aak and other wild plants underscores his role as a primal healer.

Bel, also known as Bilva, Sriphal, Bael, Bilpatre, or Stone Apple, is a sacred tree associated with Shiva and has beneficial medicinal properties, particularly as a cooling agent. The Bel tree's three leaves, symbolizing Shiva's three eyes or trident, are placed on his head or on the Shivalingam to cool his temper. Offering Belpatra brings happiness and good health. The spherical fruit has a woody shell and sweet, yellow-orange pulp. The Bel tree is considered auspicious and purifying, with parts of it showing anti-diabetic, antimicrobial, anti-inflammatory, and radio-protectant properties. As medical science advances, further research may reveal additional benefits of these wild fruits and plants offered to Shiva.

Ber (*Ziziphus mauritiana*), known as Badri in Sanskrit and Indian jujube fruit in English, is associated with Shiva, and its worship is considered incomplete without offering Ber, especially during Mahashivaratri. The ripe fruit is sweet, while the unripe fruit is sour and sometimes sweet-sour. Although many believe that Ber exacerbates cough and cold, it has medicinal uses as a hypnotic-sedative, antifungal, antibacterial, and for other healing properties. Once considered an inferior fruit, Ber has been recognized for its multifold medicinal values through research. It is believed that offering Ber (Jujube fruit) to Lord Shiva brings longevity and the fulfillment of desires.

Bhang, commonly known as cannabis, marijuana, or hemp, is a plant with narcotic properties. It grows abundantly in India and is cultivated for both medicinal purposes and recreational use. Bhang is an edible preparation made from the leaves of the cannabis plant. Traditionally, it is consumed in various forms, such as bhang sharbat, lassi, and tanda with milk and dry fruits, as well as bhang sweets and bhang pills during festivals like Maha Shivaratri and Holi. It is believed to treat fever, dysentery, and sunstroke. Additionally, Bhang is used to aid digestion, increase appetite, and address speech imperfections.

Bhang is considered by Hindus as Prasad (offering) to Lord Shiva and is widely consumed as Prasad during Maha Shivaratri. According to Hindu mythology, bhang is linked with Shiva. It is believed that Shiva resides on Mount Kailasha in the cold Himalayas, so bhang helps him stay warm and meditate for long periods. It is also believed that Shiva uses bhang to control his anger and remain detached from his destructive power. Therefore, offering bhang is thought to bring peace, tranquility, and positivity.

Chandan (Sandalwood) paste is smeared on the Shivalingam or applied in three parallel lines after performing a water or milk abhishek. According to mythology, Shiva is often in a highly temperamental state, so water and sandal paste are applied to the Shivling to keep it cool and tranquil. Chandan or sandalwood (*Santalum album*) is a medium-sized evergreen tree known for its fragrant and costly wood, which is used in various products. Sandalwood is considered very sacred and is widely used in religious rituals and social ceremonies. The sandal oil extracted from the wood and its paste have numerous medicinal and religious uses. Sandalwood has antibacterial and anti-inflammatory properties and is used to treat rheumatic pain, joint pain, urinary tract infections, acne, and tuberculosis. Applying chandan paste on the forehead has an immediate cooling effect and can alleviate stress and depression. Sandalwood is also highly valued for art crafting due to its fine-grained properties, earning it the moniker "wooden gold. " In India, cutting sandalwood trees is legally prohibited.

Traditionally, the Shiva Lingam represents the symbol of Shiva as Purusha and Parvati as Prakriti (nature). The vertical part symbolizes Purusha, while the horizontal part represents Prakriti. Together, they embody the life force of the universe and the cosmic balance between Purusha and nature. The lingam is an embodiment of Shiva and a symbol of generative power. Devotees worship the lingam in temples by offering water, milk, or panchamrit to please Lord Shiva. After the jal abhishek, the Shiva Lingam is smeared with chandan paste or marked with three horizontal lines of paste to receive Shiva's blessings.

Dhatura (*Datura stramonium*) is a wild plant that is unsuitable for human or animal consumption. Its leaves are dull green, and its flowers are solitary, erect, and trumpet-shaped. Its fruits are globular shells covered with thorns and are highly toxic. Despite its poisonous nature, Lord Shiva, known for his botanical and Ayurvedic knowledge, understood the medicinal properties of dhatura. Therefore, offering dhatura pleases Shiva. Modern medical science has discovered that despite its toxicity, various parts of dhatura have medicinal properties and are used in Ayurvedic medicine to treat asthma, glaucoma, heart disorders, epilepsy, skin ailments, and urinary problems. It has also been used historically as an anesthetic during surgery and childbirth.

The flowers and fruits of dhatura are considered sanctified for use in the rituals and worship of Shiva. A garland made of dhatura fruits is offered to him for his blessings. According to the Vamana Purana, dhatura is said to have grown from the chest of Shiva. Shiva is also known as Neel-Kantha (Blue Neck) and Vishadhari (Holder of Poison) because, at the request of the Devas, he drank the Halahala (poison) churned from the Samudra-Manthan to benefit the universe. Due to the poison, his neck turned blue. It is believed that offering the poisonous dhatura to Shiva can help remove toxins such as envy, greed, lust for power and money, bad intentions, and dishonesty, thus purifying and cleansing oneself.

Peeli Kaner (yellow oleander, *Thevetia peruviana*), also known as Divyapushpa and Haripriya, is a large evergreen plant. Its funnel-shaped flowers are scented, and all parts of the plant produce a milky liquid that is highly poisonous, including the kernels of the fruit. Despite its toxicity, the seeds and leaves of Peeli Kaner are used in medicine to treat swelling, leprosy, eye diseases, and skin disorders. Its roots are made into a paste and applied to tumors. The fragrance and medicinal properties of its flowers are believed to be favored by Lord Shiva, so devotees offer these flowers to him to seek his blessings and resolve their problems.

Rudraksha is traditionally used as prayer beads in Hinduism, especially in worship of Shiva. According to mythology, when Shiva was grieving over the corpse of Sati, his tears transformed into sacred beads known as Rudraksha (*Rudra + Aksha*), meaning "from the eyes of Rudra (Shiva). " The Rudraksha tree (*Elaeocarpus ganitrus*) is a medium-sized evergreen that grows on the Himalayan slopes of India and Nepal. The fruits are deep bluish-purple, but the Rudraksha stones are typically brown, though white, red, yellow, or black varieties can also be found. The most common Rudraksha seed has five grooves (panch mukhi), while the one with a single groove (eka-mukhi) is rare and believed to be more potent in spiritual power, making it highly valued. Some Rudraksha seeds, called Gauri-Shankar, are naturally conjoined. Different grooved Rudrakshas have unique properties and offer various scientific, medical, and spiritual benefits. Rudraksha is considered a gift from Shiva for the benefit of mankind, and he also adorns himself with Rudraksha garlands. These beads have powerful electromagnetic and inductive properties that are believed to bring auspiciousness and benefit to the wearer. A garland of 108 Rudraksha beads is used by devotees to count the repetitions of divine names during prayers.

Milk is highly valued for its various properties and is considered very pious. Smearing the Shivalingam with milk is a sacred practice. According to the Vishnu Purana, during the churning of the ocean, a pot of poison emerged. The gods and sages requested Shiva to drink it to prevent disaster. Shiva, who was not involved in the churning, drank the poison (Halahala) and stored it in his throat, causing his body to turn blue. To alleviate the effects of the poison, the gods anointed him with milk, which, due to its medicinal and cooling properties, mitigated the poison's impact. Since then, milk has been cherished by Lord Shiva. Offering raw milk to the Shivalingam is considered virtuous and pleases Shiva.

Water, essential for all life, is fundamental to existence. The Dasavatars and Darwin's theory of evolution underscore the importance of water. According to mythology, the gods poured water on Shiva to reduce the effects of the poison he consumed to save creation. Offering water on the Shivalingam while chanting "Om Namah Shivaya" is believed to please Lord Shiva, bringing calm and relaxation to the devotee's mind and fostering a sense of compassion.

Sugar is also offered to the Shivalingam during Mahashivaratri. It is believed that offering sugar to Bholenath on this auspicious occasion brings good luck, fame, and prosperity, and promotes peace and progress in one's household and professional life.

Saffron is used to make a tilak on Shiva and the Shivalingam. It is believed that a saffron tilak brings softness and stability to life and removes all Manglik doshas. Applying saffron tilak to business documents and appliances during Mahashivaratri is thought to remove obstacles in business or profession and ensure its prosperity.

Additionally, offerings of cow ghee, curd, and honey to the Shivalingam are made to please Shiva and seek his blessings for health and success. Pouring water or milk on the Shivalingam is a way to make Shiva happy, as he values the devotion of his worshippers over material offerings. The Panchamrit Abhishek, a ritual involving the offering of a mixture of milk, curd, honey, ghee, and sugar, is believed to help achieve peace, prosperity, and progress.

Third Eye as Fire Missile:- After the self-immolation of Sati and the transplantation of a goat's head onto Daksha's body, Shiva retreated to the snowy mountains beneath the Pole Star. There, he entered into deep and unbroken meditation. Meanwhile, Parvati was born as the daughter of Himavan, the king of the Himalayan region, and she began her devout prayers to win Shiva as her husband. However, Shiva remained in deep meditation with his eyes closed, unmoved by Parvati's continuous prayers.

In the meantime, a demon named Tarakasura had defeated the deities and conquered their kingdoms. He was invincible due to a boon that only a young boy could lead an army to kill him. Such a warrior could only be produced by Shiva (Purusha), but Shiva was deeply absorbed in his meditation. Disturbing Shiva from his meditation was a perilous task, yet the devas were desperate. Ultimately, they approached Kamadeva, the god of desire and love, and requested him to shoot his *kama* arrows (arrows of desire) at Shiva.

Previously, Indra, the king of the gods, would often seek Kamadeva's help to break the penance (tapasya) of ascetics. One arrow from Kamadeva could ignite the desire of any being, making the urge for love and desire overpowering. But Shiva was no ordinary ascetic; he is Pashupatinatha, the lord who controls all animal instincts. When Kamadeva shot his arrows at the meditating Shiva, Shiva remained unmoved. However, he became enraged, realizing that someone had dared to disturb his meditation. Discovering Kamadeva as the culprit, Shiva's fury was unleashed. He opened his third eye, from which a missile of flames emerged, instantly reducing Kamadeva to ashes.

The episode of Kama being reduced to ashes is often regarded as a mythological tale. However, with ongoing research, inventions, and discoveries, the concept of a being turning to ashes through rays has become a reality. For instance, the TV series *Star Trek*, which chronicles the exploits of the crew of the starship USS Enterprise on their mission to explore space, features Captain Kirk, who uses a torch emitting a ray of flames to eliminate attackers.

Today, many types of rays and gasses have been discovered that can cause serious harm or even death to humans, such as gamma rays, excessive X-rays, and alpha and beta particles. Ultraviolet A, B, and C rays, as well as gamma ray guns, have been developed and are capable of killing humans. This leads to the interpretation that Lord Shiva was perhaps a primal scientist who invented a flashlight, torch, or gun emitting highly harmful rays, and that the story of Kamadeva being turned to ashes by Shiva's third eye is symbolic of this.

In Hinduism, mythological stories often have a basis in reality and scientific validity. Ancient times were rich in science and technology, much of which was lost over time. Undoubtedly, the roots of many modern inventions can be traced back to our religious literature and scriptures, especially the mythological stories related to the supreme Lord Shiva. Scientists continue to draw inspiration from Shiva for further inventions and research.

Shiva as Engineer: Bhagiratha was a legendary king of the Ikshvaku dynasty who learned about the tragic death of his forefathers. King Sagara, in his quest to become a Chakravarti (universal monarch), had performed the Ashvamedha Yagna, a ritual in which a sacrificial horse is released, and the land it roams becomes part of the king's domain. However, Indra, the king of the gods, fearing Sagara's growing power, stole the horse and hid it in the ashram of Sage Kapila in the netherworld.

When King Sagara was informed that the horse was missing, he ordered his 60, 000 sons to search for it. They scoured the earth but found nothing. Finally, they discovered the horse's tracks leading to the netherworld. Determined, they dug a vast tunnel and reached Kapila's ashram, where they found the horse. Assuming the sage was the thief, they rushed at him, shouting, "Thief, thief!" Enraged by their accusation, Sage Kapila turned all 60, 000 sons into ashes. Their souls were left to wander, unable to reach heaven because their sins were not absolved.

Determined to bring salvation to his ancestors, Bhagiratha decided to bring the sacred Ganga down to earth to wash away their sins. He began to pray and performed severe penance to Lord Brahma, continuing his devotion for many years.

Brahma agreed to allow Ganga to descend to Earth, but there was a significant problem: the immense force of Ganga's descent would pierce the earth and cause its destruction. Brahma informed Bhagiratha that only Lord Shiva could manage the mighty force of Ganga. Frightened but determined, Bhagiratha prayed to Lord Shiva to break the fall of Ganga. Shiva agreed and positioned himself beneath the descending river.

As Ganga, proud and arrogant, descended, she found herself entangled in Shiva's mighty dreadlocks. The force of her waters was contained within Shiva's hair. Eventually, the mighty river emerged from Shiva's matted locks, flowing gently onto the earth. Bhagiratha then guided the Ganga to flow all the way to Gangasagar (the Bay of Bengal), enabling the souls of his ancestors to attain salvation and either reach heaven or be reborn.

In reality, we see that the Ganga originates from the Gangotri glacier, flowing gradually and growing larger as it traverses distances before finally merging into the Bay of Bengal. The containment of the mighty Ganga by Shiva symbolizes an extraordinary feat of hydraulic and civil engineering. Shiva's matted locks are symbolically represented by the Himalayas, from where the Ganga emanates. When Bhagiratha prayed to Shiva to control Ganga's massive flow, Shiva, as an engineer, invented a flow control device to alter the river's course.

By controlling the immense flow of Ganga, Shiva effectively managed the water resources, allowing the river to flow in a controlled manner that did not harm the ecosystem of the Himalayan terrain or the regions beyond. The episode of Ganga being contained within Shiva's matted hair demonstrates that Shiva is the primeval hydraulic engineer, successfully regulating the flow and conveyance of Ganga. This is a prime example of river management, and modern scientists and civil engineers can draw inspiration from Shiva's method of controlling the Ganga's flow.

As a Householder:- Shiva is known for his untamed passion, which often leads to extreme behavior. At times, he is an ascetic, abstaining from all worldly pleasures and attachments. At other times, he is a devoted householder, deeply attached to his wife and sons. This dual nature is why Shiva is considered the hermit god, yet he is also the only deity often visualized sitting with his family—Parvati, Ganesha, and Kartikeya.

In Hinduism, many gods are depicted with their consorts by their sides—Vishnu with Lakshmi, Ram with Sita, and Krishna with Radha (more than his wives). However, none other than Shiva is visualized or mentioned in any scripture or depicted in any sculpture alongside their children.

Shiva's portrayal with his family exemplifies his role as a careful and ideal householder.

As an Environmentalist:- According to mythology, every god has their own vehicle, often an animal or bird. These vehicles are so closely associated with the gods that they become a way to recognize them: Shiva with his bull, Vishnu with Garuda, and Ganesha with his mouse. Similarly, goddesses have their own vehicles, such as Goddess

Durga with a lion, Lakshmi with an owl, and Saraswati with a swan.

What is particularly striking is that Shiva is often depicted sitting with Parvati, Ganesha, and Kartikeya, despite the fact that the animals and birds associated with each member of Shiva's family are natural enemies. Parvati's lion is a predator and Shiva's bull is its prey; Shiva's snake is a predator and Ganesha's mouse is its prey; Kartikeya's peacock is a predator and Shiva's snake is its prey. Yet, they coexist in harmony, representing an ideal family living within a balanced ecosystem. This coexistence underscores the importance of every creature in maintaining ecological balance. Discrimination between predator and prey is detrimental to the environment, and today's environmental challenges, such as pollution and ecosystem imbalance, are increasingly pressing issues.

Shiva can be seen as the first environmental scientist, as he manages the ecology by balancing species and maintaining their environments. All living creatures in his domain live freely in their natural habitats. Furthermore, Shiva resides atop Mount Kailasha, where no construction or alterations have been made. The Himalayan terrain remains untouched, preserving its natural stability and equilibrium. Shiva's presence there without disturbing the environmental balance highlights his deep understanding of the environment's value on Earth.

It is believed that whenever nature and the ecosystem are encroached upon by heavy construction, habitation, or the mindless exploitation of natural resources, Shiva, as an ecologist, becomes enraged. He then performs the Tandava, a dance that symbolizes the destruction of everything in his path. It is said that the destruction surrounding the Kedarnath temple in Uttarakhand was the result of Shiva's Tandava, triggered by the encroachment on nature. Shiva is seen as the guardian of nature, and any violation of the ecosystem results in punishment, often in the form of natural calamities.

As per Hindu mythology, at the request of Indra, the king of the devas, Vishnu, the supreme god, assembled the deities and demons to churn the ocean for Amrita, the nectar of immortality, and other gems. They used Mount Meru as the rod and Vasuki, the king of snakes, as the rope. Vishnu himself took the form of a tortoise to support the base of the mountain. During this process, the ocean yielded many wonderful gifts, which were shared by the deities, demons, and Vishnu. However, the ocean also produced a deadly poison known as Halahala. This poison was so powerful that it threatened to destroy all creation.

The disposal of the deadly poison was a daunting task, and they turned to Mahayogi Shiva for help. The gods and demons prayed to Shiva and begged him to intervene. As Bholenath, Shiva sees no difference between Amrita and Halahala, and he possessed the power to neutralize the deadly poison. Shiva consumed the poison to protect the three worlds. However, Shakti, disturbed and angry, squeezed Shiva's neck, preventing the poison from passing beyond it. The poison turned Shiva's neck blue, and henceforth he became known as Nilkantha, the blue-throated one.

The mythological story of poison emerging from the ocean of milk during the churning of the ocean, which was then offered to Shiva to drink and dispose of, has a scientific reality when examined closely. According to the legend, a large number of Devas and Demons participated in the churning of the ocean, using Vasuki as a rope to rotate Mount Meru. During this process, Vasuki exhaled vast quantities of poisonous gases, creating harmful pollution that threatened all living beings and vegetation, contaminating the natural environment.

Moreover, the intense churning process to produce various gifts and treasures resulted in significant air, water, and soil pollution. The entire environment became dangerously polluted with Carbon monoxide (CO), Nitrogen oxide (NO_2), Sulfur oxide (SO_2), ground-level Ozone (O_3), and other harmful pollutants. The continuous large-scale churning of the ocean also produced hazardous pollutants, contaminating the ocean water and the surrounding soil.

Mythologically, it is described that gems, gifts, and poison (Halahala) emerged from the Samudra

Manthan, but in reality, this can be interpreted as the accumulation of hazardous pollutants that were difficult to dispose of safely. The magnitude of these pollutants was highly dangerous to all living beings, vegetation, and the earth—similar to the environmental problems we face today.

In the present day, the world is grappling with severe environmental challenges, including global warming, overpopulation, waste disposal, ocean acidification, loss of biodiversity, deforestation, and ozone layer depletion. Humanity is sitting on the brink of destruction due to these environmental problems. The entire world is in search of solutions, and as a response, the United Nations has established the UN Environment Programme (UNEP) to address environmental issues at both global and regional levels.

Upon realizing the adverse effects of the pollution produced during the churning of the ocean and their inability to solve the problem, the Devas sought Lord Shiva's help to mitigate the crisis. They knew that Shiva was an expert environmental scientist and ecologist who could address the issue. Environmental scientists study the effects of human activities on the environment, identify hazards to ecosystems, and determine the causes of pollution. They also help create solutions to protect the environment by eliminating these hazards or at least reducing their harmful effects.

Shiva devised a solution to the pollution and successfully removed the harmful effects of the poisonous pollutants. However, during the process of disposing of the pollution, Shiva inhaled some perilous gasses. He made a conscious effort to prevent these harmful gasses from spreading beyond his neck. Due to the fatal effects of the gasses, his neck turned blue. Despite suffering himself, Shiva saved the creation, along with all living beings and vegetation, from the poison of pollution.

This episode clearly demonstrates that Shiva is the original environmental scientist, who took it upon himself to dispose of the pollution for the welfare of humanity.

Other Episodes:- Brahma creates Shatrupa, a being with countless forms, and desires to control her. According to the Brihadaranyaka Upanishad,

Brahma chases her to exert his dominance, but Shatrupa does not wish to be under his control. As she transforms into various animals to evade him, Brahma follows, taking the corresponding male form—when she becomes a cow, he becomes a bull. This chase continues endlessly, and Brahma, consumed by her beauty and driven by carnal desire, forgets that she is his own creation, akin to his daughter. His mind becomes corrupted, blurring the lines between what is ethically right and wrong.

Shiva, the supreme god of destruction, also destroys ego, ignorance, arrogance, and malignant thinking. As Pashupati, he has mastered the basic animal instincts—sex, greed, ego, violence, and anger. Observing Brahma's mindless pursuit of Shatrupa, Shiva decides to punish him for allowing his mind to become corrupted and deluded.

According to the Linga Purana, Shiva is shocked and horrified when he sees Brahma chasing Shatrupa, lamenting the moral decay that has caused Brahma to forget his ethical responsibilities. Brahma, who initially has four heads facing in different directions to keep Shatrupa in his gaze, sprouts a fifth head on top of the others to look upward. This fifth head symbolizes delusion and ego (aham), reflecting Brahma's self-obsession and his illusion of lordship. Trapped in this imaginary world, Brahma perceives himself as a master or god, lost in his own distorted self-image.

Shiva, also known as Rudra, is the destroyer of ego, arrogance, and illusion. Using his sharp nail, he yanks off Brahma's fifth head, becoming Kapalika, the skull bearer. By doing so, Shiva destroys Brahma's ego and illusion. He then curses Brahma, declaring that he would not be worshiped in the world due to his indulgent act of pursuing his own daughter, an act of incest—a taboo in human society.

In this act, Shiva not only condemns Brahma but also elevates Vishnu as the supreme god, thereby positioning himself as the destroyer of falsehood, ego, illusion, and mental impurity, while upholding truth and purity in conduct. Shiva's judgment is impartial; he rewards honesty and punishes deceit and arrogance.

Shiva, known as Bholenath or Bhole Baba, is regarded as a god of pure heart and innocence. Generally, knowledge and power can distance a person from innocence. A learned and powerful individual may be kind, helpful, and simple, but not necessarily innocent at heart; this is human nature. However, Shiva embodies an ocean of knowledge coupled with innocence. He is easily pleased by anyone who worships him with wholehearted devotion and blesses them in return.

In contrast, Vishnu does not easily respond to a devotee's worship or penance; he differentiates between the good and bad intentions of his followers. Shiva, on the other hand, knows only love and devotion, irrespective of the devotees' intentions.

Shiva's boon to the demon Bhasmasura exemplifies his innocence and purity. Bhasmasura performed severe penance to please Shiva, who, without considering the future consequences, granted him the boon to turn anyone into ashes with a touch of his hand. Shiva, being a pure soul, did not foresee the potential danger. Consequently,

Bhasmasura used this power to chase Shiva, who was ultimately saved by Lord Vishnu.

Once, a tribal youth named Tinnan worshiped a Shiva-lingam in the deep forest. Lacking knowledge of traditions and rituals, he offered the deity whatever he had, including the meat from the day's hunt. To test the sincerity of his devotion, Shiva caused the lingam to sprout a pair of eyes, one of which began to bleed. Despite Tinnan's attempts to stop the bleeding, he was unsuccessful. In desperation, he cut out his own eye and offered it to the lingam. Shiva, moved by Tinnan's genuine emotion and devotion, was pleased and blessed him. Later, Tinnan was brought to Kailasha. Shiva remarked to Parvati, "It is not what I am offered, but the emotion behind the offering that matters to me." Thus, Shiva is drawn not by rituals but by the emotions behind the worship.

Shiva is also known as Ashutosha, meaning he is easily pleased. Demons, who are rivals to the Devas, often worship and perform penance to Shiva for blessings and boons. Shiva does not discriminate between gods and demons, humans and ghosts, or handsome and ugly. All creatures are equal in his eyes, regardless of race, class, or group. Shiva remains impartial and neutral, while Vishnu, a supreme god, actively participates in wars supporting the Devas and defeating the demons. Other gods also side with the Devas against the demons. For the demons, Shiva represents the last resort and refuge. Whenever they seek boons, they turn to Shiva, who values their emotions and devotion above all else, rather than their offerings or affiliations.

Shiva has always supported dharma and destroyed adharma. Ravana, a great devotee of Shiva, received boons from him and became a powerful emperor on earth. When Ravana abducted Sita, the wife of Rama (an avatar of Vishnu), and took her captive in Ashoka Van in Lanka, Rama, along with his younger brother Lakshmana, Sugriva (the monkey king), Hanuman, and others, prepared to attack Lanka to rescue Sita. Before waging war against Ravana, Rama worshiped a Shivling at Rameshwaram to seek Shiva's blessing for victory. Shiva granted Rama's request and blessed him with success against Ravana, who was his devoted follower. Despite Shiva's boon and the powerful weapon, Chandrahasa, Ravana was ultimately defeated and killed, and Sita was freed. This war between Rama and Ravana, or dharma and adharma, saw Shiva supporting Rama and dharma against Ravana and adharma. Shiva always granted boons with the caution that they should be used for righteous purposes; misuse for adharma would render the boon ineffective.

In today's world, there is a strong emphasis on social justice, equality, and fraternity to combat social exploitation, disparity, and inequality. Despite numerous efforts and programs, the gap between the privileged and the underprivileged, as well as between oppressors and the oppressed, continues to widen. This disparity existed in ancient times as well. However, Lord Shiva treated all beings equally, whether deities, demons, humans, ghosts, goblins, yakshas, or outcasts. He never discriminated based on race or class. Shiva, with no permanent home, took refuge in caves and mountains, living among tribes and having ghosts, ganas, goblins, and yakshas as his companions. None felt insulted or neglected in Shiva's presence.

During his marriage to Parvati, Shiva arrived at her house with a retinue of demons, ghosts, goblins, witches, ganas, and yakshas—creatures with claws, fangs, and bloodshot eyes. Despite their appearance, all were free to celebrate in their own ways, and everyone rejoiced at the union. This event marked the first time eternal enemies, demons and devas, danced together in harmony. For Shiva, all living creatures are equal, and he is guided not by appearances but by the emotions accompanying devotion.

Shiva is usually depicted sitting with Parvati and his two sons, Ganesha and Kartikeya. Both sons have distinct dispositions and qualities. Though both are equally powerful, Kartikeya was born from Shiva's energy, while Ganesha was born from Parvati's (Nature's) energy. After receiving the head of an elephant, Ganesha was named Gajapati or Ganesha. He is a composite of both divine and elephant attributes.

According to mythological texts, Ganesha, also known as Ganapati, is an elephant-headed god associated with intelligence, knowledge, memory, and the removal of obstacles. The Ganesha Purana and Ganesha Upanishad describe him as connected to the earth's fertility and arts. He is also depicted as a warrior who vanquishes demons. His corpulent belly symbolizes great affluence and abundance. Ganesha is traditionally worshiped before starting any new enterprise, work, or ritual, representing wisdom and prosperity. He is the patron of intellectuals, bankers, businessmen, and authors. During Deepavali, Ganesha is worshiped alongside Lakshmi, the goddess of wealth and prosperity, as Ganesha, the god of wisdom, guides and controls the prudent use of wealth.

The epic Mahabharata recounts how Sage Vyasa sought Ganesha's assistance to transcribe the epic. Vyasa, having conceived the Mahabharata, prayed to Brahma for help with dictation. Brahma advised Vyasa to seek Ganesha's aid. Ganesha agreed to write down the story without any interruption. This highlights Ganesha's association with intellectual pursuits.

Both Ganesha and Kartikeya are warriors and embodiments of intelligence. Ganesha is especially revered in Maharashtra and North India, while Kartikeya, known as Murugan, is primarily worshiped in Tamil Nadu. It appears that both brothers excel in their respective realms of wisdom and strength.

There are multiple versions of the story about the race around the world. The first version involves the sage Narada, who wanted to determine which of Shiva's sons—Ganesha or Kartikeya—could complete three rounds of the world faster. Although Ganesha was not physically capable of traveling quickly and his vehicle was a mouse, which could not cover long distances, the contest seemed inherently unequal. Kartikeya, on the other hand, was strong and powerful, with a peacock as his vehicle, which could fly long distances.

In the second version, it is believed that the Devas offered a supreme fruit (sometimes referred to as a mango) to Shiva and Parvati. The fruit was said to grant supreme knowledge, and both Ganesha and Kartikeya wanted it. To resolve their dispute, Lord Shiva declared that whoever completed three rounds of the world first would receive the fruit.

The third version describes a Maha Yagna conducted by King Asura Mahabali, who invited all the deities and demons of the world. During the Yagna, a conflict arose over who should be worshipped first. They turned to Lord Shiva for a solution, and he declared that the god who completed three rounds of the world first would be the winner and the first deity to be worshipped. Kartikeya, along with his peacock, Indra with his Airavata, and Vayudeva with his Gazella, started the race.

Ganesha, however, looked at his vehicle—a mouse—which was no match for the speed of the other gods' vehicles. He also realized that he was not physically capable of running or moving fast over long distances. Despite these limitations, he did not feel despondent or irresolute. Instead, he decided to make three rounds around his parents, Shiva (representing the universe and Purusha) and Parvati (representing Shakti and nature). For Ganesha, his parents were his entire world, so completing three rounds around them was a more meaningful accomplishment than traveling the external world.

Ganesha explained, "I circled my emotional world, which is more significant than the external world that Kartikeya traversed." Kartikeya argued that he had completed the three rounds of the world as required. However, Lord Shiva and Parvati were pleased with Ganesha's understanding of the subjective meaning of the task and declared him the winner. Dissatisfied with their decision, Kartikeya felt cheated and left, heading south of the Vindhya mountains.

As a result, Ganesha was declared the god of wisdom, intelligence, and the remover of obstacles, and was honored as "Pratham Pujniya." Since then, every ceremony, worship, and function has begun with prayers to Lord Ganesha. It raises an intriguing question why Shiva organized a race to circle the world three times, fully aware that Ganesha and Kartikeya had vastly different vehicles and physical attributes. Kartikeya, with his peacock, was the god of war, strength, and physical prowess, while Ganesha, with his slow-moving mouse and corpulent body, seemed at a disadvantage. Shiva, however, knew that Ganesha could utilize his limited resources more effectively than Kartikeya could use his abundant ones. Success often depends on the intelligent and optimal use of available resources, rather than the sheer abundance of resources.

This is exemplified by situations where those with fewer resources succeed through clever planning, while those with ample resources may fail due to poor management. Similarly, Ganesha's ability to optimize his limited resources led him to victory in the competition, showcasing that intelligence and resourcefulness can outweigh physical strength.

Moreover, this episode highlights the difference in mindset between Ganesha and Kartikeya. Mindset, or attitude, plays a crucial role in achieving one's goals. Ganesha approached the challenge with a positive attitude and creative thinking, using his insight to devise a plan that involved circling his parents—his true world—three times. Kartikeya, on the other hand, had a fixed mindset, relying on his physical strength and vehicle without considering a strategic approach. This contrast demonstrates that a positive attitude and confidence can be more impactful than physical strength and resources.

Shiva, recognizing Ganesha's creative mindset and optimal use of limited resources, declared him the winner. This decision underscores that a positive attitude and confidence are more important than mere physical strength or resources. Shiva's understanding of human psychology and mindset was evident in his judgment, affirming that the true measure of success lies in the mental and emotional approach rather than just physical attributes.

Jyotirlinga- According to Hindu mythological texts and the Shiva Purana, the Jyotirlinga is a devotional and symbolic representation of Lord Shiva. When Brahma, the god of creation, and Vishnu, the god of preservation, had a dispute over who was supreme, their argument persisted for a long time with neither agreeing to acknowledge the other's supremacy. To settle the debate, a gigantic and infinite pillar appeared between them, stretching up beyond the dome of the sky and down below the foundations of the earth.

As described in the Shiva Purana, Shiva manifested as a massive and infinite pillar of light (Jyotirlinga) and told them to stop fighting and find the ends of its depth and height. Whoever could locate the end of the pillar would be declared the supreme god. Brahma and Vishnu took on the challenge: Brahma transformed into a swan and flew upwards to find the top, while Vishnu transformed into a boar and dug downwards to locate the base. Brahma flew for months and years but could not find the top, and Vishnu dug continuously for the same period without finding the base.

Eventually, both were exhausted and failed to find the ends of the pillar. Brahma, however, deceitfully claimed that he had found the top of the pillar and produced a Ketaki flower and Kamadhenu cow as false witnesses. Vishnu, on the other hand, honestly admitted that he could not find the end of the pillar and acknowledged its infinite nature.

Enraged by Brahma's dishonesty, Shiva cursed him, declaring that he would not be worshipped on earth and that the Ketaki flower would not be used in worship. He also told the cow that her mouth would be deemed unholy for giving false witness, though her dung would remain sacred. Shiva then praised Vishnu, acknowledging his humility and truthfulness. He expressed his appreciation for Vishnu's eagerness to understand the unknown and his acceptance of his limitations, stating that Vishnu was on the path to becoming a god.

Brahma trembled and bowed to Shiva, while Vishnu watched with respect and apprehension. Shiva revealed, "If the formless can be given form, then I am that form. I am Shiva."

Since then, the stone pillar or linga has been worshipped as a reminder of the fiery column of light that appeared between Brahma and Vishnu. To those who view it merely as a stone pillar, it is akin to Brahma's deceitful attitude. Conversely, those who recognize it as a symbolic representation of Shiva, as Vishnu did, understand its true significance. The Jyotirlinga shrine is regarded as the temple where Shiva manifested as a fiery column of light.

According to mythological texts, there were originally 64 Jyotirlingas, of which 12 are considered particularly auspicious and holy. Additionally, there is now one more Jyotirlinga shrine located in Australia. These Jyotirlinga sites, temples, or shrines are named after their respective deities and each is regarded as a different manifestation of Shiva. At all these sites, the primary and important image is the lingam, representing the Adi-Anta (beginningless-endless) pillar symbolizing the infinite nature of Shiva.

According to the Dwadasa Jyotirlinga Stotram, the 12 Jyotirlingas in India and the one in Australia are as follows:

1. **Somnath**, Gir, Gujarat
2. **Mallikarjun**, Srisailam, Andhra Pradesh
3. **Mahakaleshwar**, Ujjain, Madhya Pradesh
4. **Omkareshwar**, Khandwa, Madhya Pradesh
5. **Baidyanath**, Deoghar, Jharkhand

6. **Bhimashankar**, Maharashtra

7. **Ramanathaswamy**, Rameswaram, Tamil Nadu

8. **Nageshwar**, Dwarka, Gujarat

9. **Kashi Vishwanath**, Varanasi, Uttar Pradesh

10. **Trimbakeshwar**, Nashik, Maharashtra

11. **Kedarnath**, Rudraprayag, Uttarakhand

12. **Grishneshwar**, Ellora, Maharashtra

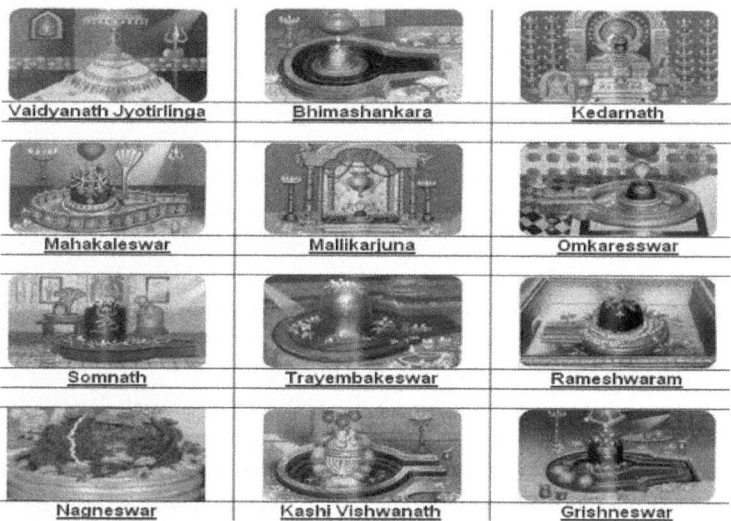

And outside of India:

- **Mukti-Gupteshwar**, Mahadeva, Australia

Jyotirlingas are diverse manifestations of Lord

Shiva, with exactly 12 strategically located across India. Hindu devotees often undertake pilgrimages to visit these Jyotirlingas to seek Shiva's blessings and learn about his many forms and related stories. These sanctums glorify the divine power of Shiva. Scientifically, the locations of the Jyotirlingas are consecrated according to the principles of energizing forms. This science involves using life's energies to enhance existence in a profound way. The arrangement of Jyotirlinga temples forms the shape of a conch shell or follows the Fibonacci pattern—a series found predominantly in nature, such as in sunflowers, pinecones, spider webs, and conch shells. Engineers and architects often use Fibonacci patterns in construction for strength and durability. In financial markets, Fibonacci patterns help traders maximize profits and minimize losses by analyzing trends and price actions.

The importance and significance of each Jyotirlinga differ, and each Jyotirlinga temple has its own story and unique qualities that attract devotees of Shiva to visit, pray, and seek blessings. The descriptions of each Jyotirlinga are as follows:

- **Somnath Jyotirlinga,** situated in Gujarat, is one of the 12 prominent Jyotirlingas of Shiva in India. Revered for its religious importance, the temple has been a pilgrimage site for centuries and is also known for its architectural beauty and grandeur. It stands as a testament to the undying faith and devotion of its devotees, despite being destroyed and looted by invaders and rebuilt multiple times. According to historical records, the temple was repeatedly attacked and plundered by Mahmud Ghazni of Ghaznavid Dynasty, who stole a significant amount of gold, jewelry, and coins. The current Jyotirlinga temple was magnificently rebuilt against the backdrop of the Arabian Sea, and the serene atmosphere of Somnath provides a divine and peaceful experience to pilgrims and tourists.

According to Hindu mythology, the temple was originally constructed by the Moon (Chandra) in pure gold, later rebuilt by Ravana in silver, then by Krishna in sandalwood, and finally by Bhimdeva in stone. The name Somnath means "Master of the Moon" (Som ka Nath). The legend associated with the Somnath Jyotirlinga is as follows: The Moon, who was married to the 27 daughters of King Daksha, Prajapati (a mind-born son of Brahma), loved and favored only one wife, Rohini, neglecting the others. Upset by this, the other wives complained to their father, Daksha, who advised the Moon to treat all his wives equally. The Moon ignored this advice, leading to further complaints from the 26 daughters. Angered by the Moon's behavior, Daksha cursed him with a wasting disease and the loss of his light, causing darkness to spread across the world. In response, the gods gathered and decided that the Moon should pray to Lord Shiva. After long and devoted worship, Shiva, the conqueror of death (Mrityunjaya), appeared and granted the Moon a boon, placing him on his forehead. This allowed the Moon to wax and regain his light. Pleased, the Moon built a golden Somnath Jyotirlinga temple and made offerings of water, milk, ghee, honey, and curd on the top of the Shivalinga. It is widely believed that on moonless nights(amavasya), the Moon dips into the holy water of the shrine to regain his light. Thus, the name 'Somnath' or Jyotirlinga came into existence. Additionally, a holy tank, known as Somkunda or

Papnashak-thirth, was created by the deities at this site.

- **Mallikarjuna Jyotirlinga:** Situated in Srisailam, Andhra Pradesh, the Mallikarjuna Jyotirlinga is also known as the Srisailam Temple and is sometimes referred to as the "Kashi of the South." According to the Shiva Purana, the Mallikarjuna Jyotirlinga represents a unified form of both Shiva and Shakti (Parvati). Here, Mallika refers to Goddess Parvati, while Arjuna signifies Lord Shiva. Located in the Nallamala hill forests along the banks of the Krishna River, the temple is one of the most popular Jyotirlingas among the twelve in India. The temple's beautiful architecture is characterized by intricate carvings, colorful pillars (gopurams), and the Mukh Mandapa hall.

The legend behind the Mallikarjuna Jyotirlinga is as follows: Once, Shiva and Parvati were discussing the marriage of their sons, Ganesh and Kartikeya, and could not decide which son should marry first. They called both sons and asked them who would like to marry first, but neither responded. To resolve the issue, they asked their sons to circumnavigate the world, with the condition that the one who returned first would marry Riddhi and Siddhi, twin sisters. Kartikeya set off to circle the world on his peacock, while Ganesh, considering his physical limitations and his mouse as his vehicle, chose to encircle his parents, as they represented his entire world. This act of devotion and understanding was cherished by Shiva and Parvati, leading them to decide that Ganesh would marry Riddhi and Siddhi first.

Kartikeya was displeased by this decision, as he felt that the outcome should have been based on physical accomplishment rather than emotional connection. He left and went to the mountain named Krauncha to meditate. Shiva and Parvati visited Kartikeya to console him, and the Jyotirlinga is said to have emerged at the spot where they met him.

- **Mahakaleshwar Jyotirlinga:** Located on the banks of the Kshipra River in Ujjain, Madhya Pradesh, the Mahakaleshwar Jyotirlinga is known as the "Destroyer of All Elements" and is considered the most powerful among the twelve Jyotirlingas. It is also one of the seven Mukti-Sthals in India and is unique for being south-facing. According to Hindu mythology, Mahakala is an aspect of Lord Shiva, representing his transcendence beyond time. A prominent feature of the Mahakaleshwar temple is the Bhasma-Aarti, performed early in the morning. During this ritual, the Shivalinga is bathed with ashes from a funeral pyre and then artistically decorated. Thousands of pilgrims visit the temple, especially during the months of Sawan and Nag Panchami. Due to certain tantric practices associated with the temple, the premises are closed to visitors at night.

The Mahakaleshwar Jyotirlinga is believed to be Swayambhu (self-manifested), symbolizing Shiva's eternal nature, which is unaffected by time. According to legend, King Chitrasena of Ujjain, a devoted worshipper of Shiva, faced an invasion by King Ripudamana of a neighboring kingdom, who was assisted by the demon Dushan. As Chitrasena, being weaker, prayed for protection, Shiva, pleased with his devotion, appeared and promised to remain in Ujjain to safeguard the city. Consequently, the

Mahakaleshwar Jyotirlinga temple was established at this location, signifying Shiva's protective presence.

The Mahakaleshwar Jyotirlinga is also regarded as one of the Mukti-Sthals, believed to offer liberation (moksha) and relief from diseases and problems to devotees who worship there.

- **<u>Omkareshwar Jyotirlinga</u>**: This temple is located on an island shaped like the Om symbol, called Shivpuri, on the banks of the Narmada River, in the four-sided hill area of Khanwa, Madhya Pradesh. Omkareshwar Jyotirlinga is a revered Hindu temple and is considered a central site of intense faith and devotion. The temple is a magnificent three-story structure supported by large, intricately carved granite pillars.

Several legends are associated with this sacred site. According to one story from Hindu Puranas, a great war once occurred between the Devas and Danavas. When the Devas were defeated by the Demons, they prayed to Lord Shiva for help. Pleased with their devotion, Shiva manifested as Omkareshwar and defeated the Danavas.

Another legend tells of Vindhya, who controlled the Vindhyachal Mountain range. Vindhya worshipped Shiva by creating a sacred diagram and Lingam of sand and clay. Pleased with his devotion, Shiva appeared in two forms: Omkareshwar and Amareshwar. Amareshwar means "Immortal God" or "God of the Devas," and the temple of Amareshwar is located on the south bank of the Narmada River. Pilgrims often visit both temples, as they are located close to each other and are considered equally divine.

A third legend involves King Mandhata, whose kingdom was attacked by demons. The king, who worshipped Shiva with deep devotion, prayed for protection. Impressed by his sincere faith, Shiva agreed to stay in the region to protect the people, fulfilling the king's request.

- **Vaidyanath Jyotirlinga:** The Vaidyanath Jyotirlinga, also known as Baidyanath or Vaijnath, is a highly revered Jyotirlinga temple situated in Deoghar, Jharkhand. It is one of the twelve Jyotirlingas, considered the most sacred abodes of

Shiva. The temple is also associated with a Shakti Peetha shrine dedicated to Sati.

However, there is some dispute regarding the exact location of the Vaidyanath Jyotirlinga. The claimed locations include:

1. Shri Vaijnath Temple, Parli, Beed, Maharashtra

2. Baidyanath Temple, Deoghar, Jharkhand

3. Baidyanath Temple, Baidyanath, Himachal Pradesh

Currently, the government has not officially confirmed which of these is the actual Baidyanath Jyotirlinga. A significant number of devotees believe that the Shri Baidyanath Temple in Deoghar is the true Jyotirlinga.

Legend: According to legend, Ravana, the king of Lanka, was a great devotee of Shiva. To please Shiva, he performed severe penance and offered his nine heads in sacrifice. As he was about to sacrifice his remaining tenth head, Shiva appeared and, pleased with Ravana's devotion, offered to grant him a boon. Ravana requested permission to take the "Kamna Linga" to Lanka and to bring Shiva from Kailash to Lanka, so that he could worship Shiva and the Lingam there more easily.

Shiva agreed, with the condition that if the Lingam was placed en route, it would become his permanent abode and could never be moved. Concerned about Shiva departing from Mount Kailash and the potential for Ravana to gain powerful boons, the celestial gods sought Vishnu's help to prevent this. Vishnu asked Varuna, the god of water, to enter Ravana's stomach through a ritual called 'Achamana, ' which involves drinking water from the palm of one's hand. As Ravana was traveling with the Lingam. On reaching Deoghar, he felt the need to relieve himself. It is believed that Vishnu took the form of a shepherd named Baiju Gadariya.

He spotted a nearby cowherd and asked him to hold the Shivalinga while he stepped away to relieve himself. The cowherd agreed, and Ravana went on his way.

As the cowherd held the Shivalinga, he noticed it growing heavier with each passing minute. Eventually, it became too heavy for him to hold, so he placed it on the ground and left. When Ravana returned, the cowherd was nowhere in sight. Seeing the Shivalinga on the ground, Ravana attempted to lift it, but no matter how hard he tried, he couldn't move it an inch. In the end, Ravana was forced to admit defeat and left without the Atmalinga, returning to Lanka empty-handed., thus establishing the Baidyanath Jyotirlinga.

A notable feature of the site is the Parvati temple, connected to the main Jyotirlinga temple by a huge red sacred thread, symbolizing the unity of Shiva and Shakti. The Baidyanath temple is renowned for the Shravan Mela and Kanwar Yatra, held during the month of Shravan. Lakhs of pilgrims visit the shrine each year. During the Kanwar Yatra, devotees carry holy water from the Ganga, collected at Ajgaivinath, Sultanganj, and bring it to Baidyanath, walking barefoot and offering it to the Shivalinga.

- **Bhimashankar Jyotirlinga:** According to the Dwadasha Jyotirlinga Stotram, Bhimashankar is the sixth Jyotirlinga among the twelve Jyotirlingas in India. It is located on the banks of the Bhima River near Pune, Maharashtra. The temple, constructed in the Nagara style of Maratha architecture, holds significant religious value among Hindus.

Legend: According to Hindu mythology, Bhima was a cruel demon whose barbarity angered Lord Shiva. Shiva destroyed the demon, turning him to ashes, and decided to reside there in the form of a Jyotirlinga. The Bhimashankar temple is known for its spiritual significance and natural beauty. The surrounding area, designated as a wildlife sanctuary, offers stunning views and tranquility, making it a haven for nature enthusiasts.

Additional Legend: The story also involves Bhima's mother, Karkati, who disclosed to her son that his father, Kumbhakarna, had been killed by Rama. Filled with rage and seeking revenge, Bhima began to worship Brahma to obtain worldly power. Brahma granted him the boon, but Bhima misused his powers to harm others and demanded worship.

He captured Shiva's devotee Kamarupeshwar and forced him to worship him. Angered by this, Shiva appeared and destroyed Bhima, taking away his powers and empowering Kamarupeshwar. The celestial gods then requested Shiva to remain in the region to protect people from demons like Bhima.

Karkati once disclosed to her son, Bhima, that his father, Kumbhakarna (the younger brother of Ravana), had been killed by Rama. Filled with rage and a desire for revenge, Bhima sought to gain worldly power. He worshipped Brahma, who granted him a boon for immense power. However, instead of using this power for the benefit of society, Bhima misused it to harm people and demanded that they worship him.

Bhima captured Shiva's devotee Kamarupeshwar and forced him to worship him. When Kamarupeshwar refused, Bhima became enraged and was about to kill him. At this point, Shiva appeared and defeated Bhima, taking away all his powers and empowering his devotee instead. The celestial gods then requested Shiva to remain in the region to protect people and safeguard them from demons like Bhima.

- **Rameshwaram Jyotirlinga:** This jyotirlinga temple is the seventh in the sequence of the twelve jyotirlingas. It is renowned for its magnificent Dravidian architecture and is located in the small town of Rameswaram on Pamban Island, Tamil Nadu, separated from the mainland. The temple complex is notable for its twenty-two water bodies and features a stunning array of ornate towers and corridors, known as *theerthams*.

The temple has a significant connection to Lord Rama's victory over Ravana. Before Rama set out to Lanka to battle Ravana, he and his army stopped at Rameswaram to drink water. To seek divine blessings for his victory, Rama created a sand linga, which subsequently transformed into a jyotirlinga. It is also believed that Ravana, who was a priest, was invited to perform worship for Shiva on behalf of Rama.

In the temple, there are two Shivlings: one created by Rama and the other brought from the Himalayas by Hanuman. Since Hanuman arrived late with the Shivling he brought, Rama had already created another Shivling. To honor Hanuman's devotion, Rama declared that Hanuman's Shivling would be worshipped first, followed by Rama's Shivling. This tradition of worship continues to this day.

Rameswaram is considered an eternal abode of Lord Shiva, and it is also the place where Lord Rama worshipped Vishnu after defeating Ravana, seeking atonement for the battle.

- **Nageshwar Jyotirlinga:** Nageshwar Jyotirlinga is located on the coast of Saurashtra in Gujarat, between Gomati Dwarka and Bet Dwarka. According to religious texts, Shiva is considered the deity of nagas (poisonous snakes), and Nageshwar means "Ishwar of Nags" (God of Nags). The temple is renowned for its association with protection from venomous creatures. It is constructed with pink stones, and the idol faces south (Dakshinamukhi).

As per the customs of the temple, only Hindus are permitted to enter the sanctum sanctorum to perform Abhishek (ritual bathing) of the idol.

Devotees are also expected to be dressed in customary attire as specified by the priests.

According to the Shiva Purana, Shiva defeated a demon named Daruka and his army to rescue his devotee Supriya, who had been imprisoned. Upon her prayers, Shiva appeared, vanquished Daruka, and liberated her. This event led to the place being known as Nageshwar, as Shiva's body was said to have been covered with snakes at that time. The temple features a large statue of Shiva in a seated posture, which can be seen from a considerable distance.

- **Kashi Vishwanath Jyotirlinga:** Kashi Vishwanath is one of the most important Jyotirlingas in India. Lakhs of devotees visit the temple every year to seek the blessings of Lord Shiva. Historically, this temple has been ransacked several times by Muslim invaders, and a mosque was constructed using materials plundered from the temple, located very close to the original site. Despite these disruptions, the Jyotirlinga temple was later reconstructed.

According to an episode mentioned in the Shiva Purana, Brahma and Vishnu once disputed their supremacy and engaged in a prolonged argument. To test them, Shiva transformed himself into an endless pillar of light and asked them to find its ends. Brahma ascended to find the top end of the pillar, and Vishnu descended to find the bottom end. Both failed in their efforts to locate the end of the pillar. Brahma falsely claimed that he had found the end, while Vishnu admitted his failure to find it. This dishonesty of Brahma angered Lord Shiva, who then cursed Brahma, declaring that he would not be worshipped by Hindus. In contrast, Vishnu was praised for his honesty and was honored with a significant place in Hindu worship.

The place where Shiva's pillar of light is believed to have penetrated the Earth is known as the Jyotirlinga. Kashi (also known as Varanasi) is considered one of the oldest continuously inhabited cities in the world. It is also revered as a place that exists beyond the ordinary realm of Earth. According to Hindu belief, Kashi is the abode of the Trimurti—Brahma, Vishnu, and Shiva (Mahesh).

It is widely believed that a person who is cremated in Kashi is freed from all sins and attains moksha (salvation). The fire used for the cremation is traditionally taken from the Dom Raja, a prominent figure in the city's cremation rituals. Additionally, it is said that Shiva created Kashi on his trident and that the city is imperishable, making it a highly significant and sacred place for devotees and pilgrims.

- **Trimbakeshwar Jyotirlinga-** The Trimbakeshwar Jyotirlinga Temple is situated on the banks of the Godavari River, near Brahmagiri Mountain in Nashik, Maharashtra. The Godavari River originates from this location, giving the temple significant spiritual importance. Trimbak is one of the four locations where the Kumbh Mela is held every 12 years, the others being Haridwar, Prayagraj, and Ujjain.

The temple's architecture is unique and renowned worldwide. Inside the temple, three pillars represent the Trimurti—the three supreme deities of Hinduism: Brahma, Vishnu, and Mahesh (Shiva). According to Hindu mythology, the temple is built on the same site where Lord Rama performed the shraddha ceremony for his forefathers.

As per another legend, Sage Gautama and his wife Ahilya were blessed by Shiva with the boon of never suffering from death. Shiva, pleased with Gautama's devotion, also granted him a pit from which he could produce an abundance of food and grains. This aroused the envy of other sages, who conspired to ruin Gautama's reputation. They sent a cow to his hut, and due to a severe famine, the cow died. The envious sages then falsely accused Gautama of being a cow murderer.

To absolve himself of this false accuracation, Sage Gautama began a penance to Lord Shiva. When Shiva appeared and offered him a boon, Gautama requested that the Ganga River flow through his hut to purify it. Lord Shiva granted this wish, and in addition, Gautama requested Shiva to remain there. Consequently, Shiva manifested in the form of the Trimbakeshwar Jyotirlinga.

- **Kedarnath:-** The Kedarnath Temple is situated in the Garhwal Himalayan range near the Mandakini River in Uttarakhand. It is one of the most important Jyotirlingas and holds a central place in the Char Dham pilgrimage, which also includes Gangotri, Yamunotri, and Badrinath.

The temple's construction is traditionally attributed to the Pandavas, with Adi Shankaracharya credited for its revival. The exact age of the temple is uncertain, but it is believed to be ancient, potentially around 3,000 years old. The Sabha Mandap (assembly hall) of the Kedarnath Temple houses idols of the five Pandavas, along with Kunti, Draupadi, and Shri Krishna. Although the exact date of the temple's construction is not mentioned in ancient literature, it is believed to be around 3,000 years old. Due to its high-altitude location, the temple remains closed for approximately six months each year because of severe and hostile climatic conditions, during which it is covered with snow and experiences extremely cold temperatures.

An episode in the epic *Mahabharata* describes how, after their victory in the Kurukshetra war and the completion of the Ashvamedha Yagna, the five Pandava brothers sought to ascend to heaven physically. Accompanied by Draupadi, they began their journey and worshipped Lord Shiva, who manifested in a vast triangular-shaped Jyotirlinga. The Samadhi (final resting place) of the Hindu sage and religious reformer Adi Shankaracharya is located just behind the Kedarnath Temple.

It is believed that visiting the Kedarnath Temple and bathing there can cleanse one of all sorrow, bad luck, and misfortunes. This Jyotirlinga is mentioned in ancient Hindu scriptures like the *Skanda Purana*. Kedarnath is considered one of the most sacred Jyotirlingas in India and is also one of the four holy sites mentioned in the scriptures as part of the Char Dham Yatra, which every Hindu should undertake at least once in their lifetime to attain Moksha (liberation).

It is worth mentioning that Kedarnath is believed to be ever-vigilant, with Lord Shiva watching over all his devotees. A story often recounted involves a simple villager who was poor but deeply religious. Once, he set out on a pilgrimage to the Kedarnath Temple to see the Shivalinga. After several months, he arrived at

Kedarnath, only to find the temple gates closed for the winter. The priests and others were preparing to leave, as the temple would remain closed for six months. The poor devotee pleaded with the priest to allow him a glimpse of the Kedarnath Shivalinga, but the priest refused and told him to return when the temple reopened in six months. The devotee was forced to stay overnight in the harsh winter conditions, without sufficient clothing or blankets.

At midnight, as he struggled against the freezing cold, a sage appeared and gave him warm blankets, instructing him to sleep comfortably. The next morning, the devotee awoke to find the temple gates open and the priests performing prayers. When the priests saw him, they were surprised and asked if he had returned so quickly. He explained that he had just woken up and had not left. He also mentioned the sage who had given him the blankets. The priests were astonished and realized that Baba Kedarnath (Lord Shiva) had miraculously shortened six months into one night for this poor devotee. They bowed their heads in reverence to the devotee, acknowledging that a pure heart is more important than religious status. This story illustrates how Lord Kedarnath is kind, affectionate, and always attentive to his devotees.

- **Grishneshwar Jyotirlinga:** - Grishneshwar Jyotirlinga is regarded as the Lord of Compassion and is the last among the twelve Jyotirlingas mentioned in the Dwadasha Jyotirlinga Stotram in India. The temple is situated in Aurangabad, Maharashtra, and is splendidly built with red and black stones. The temple has a five-story Shikhara-style construction, which is a mountain-peak style of architecture. Its walls are adorned with beautiful carvings depicting the Dashavatara of Vishnu. In the main court hall of the temple, there is a giant Nandi Bull, symbolizing purity and justice. The temple is located near the Ellora Caves, a UNESCO World Heritage Site, and is also known as the Dhushmeshwar Temple.

The legend behind the Grishneshwar Jyotirlinga, as described in Hindu mythology, involves a woman named Kusuma, who worshipped Lord Shiva by immersing his idol in a water pool. Her husband and the villagers did not understand her unique method of worship and objected to it. In a fit of anger, her husband killed their son, but despite this tragedy, Kusuma continued her worship. One day, Lord Shiva appeared before her, and miraculously, her son emerged alive from the water pool. Moved by her devotion, Lord Shiva manifested as the Jyotirlinga at that spot. The temple is said to have been constructed by Kusuma. The serene ambiance and spiritual aura of Grishneshwar attract both devotees and tourists alike.

- **Mukti Gupteshwar jyotirlinga: -** In addition, there is a belief in the existence of a 13th Jyotirlinga at the Mukti Gupteshwar Temple in Minto, Australia. This temple, located in a serene environment surrounded by mountains, is believed to house Gupteshwar, an incarnation of Lord Shiva, in a man-made cave temple. Notably, it is considered the world's first and only man-made cave temple, attracting a large number of pilgrims and visitors. The main deity of the temple is the 13th Jyotirlinga, and replicas of the 12 other Jyotirlingas are also installed within the temple. This temple was gifted to the Australian people in 1999 by King Birendra Bir Bikram Shah Dev of Nepal.

The story of the formation of the 13th Jyotirlinga, Mukti-Gupteshwar Mahadev, is mentioned in the *Mahabharata*. After losing in the game of dice, the Pandavas were exiled to the forest for twelve years, followed by one year of living in disguise. During their exile, they arrived at an ashram in Nepal, where they stayed and meditated.

According to the legend, during this time, the 13th Jyotirlinga lay hidden since the Mahabharata age. While living in the ashram, Arjuna, one of the Pandava warriors, went hunting and encountered a wild boar. As he prepared to shoot the boar, another hunter appeared and claimed it as his own. Both hunters shot their arrows at the same time, killing the boar. They argued over who had killed the boar and fought each other for 21 days. As Arjuna began to weaken, he quickly fashioned a Linga from mud, prayed, and offered flowers on it. To his astonishment, the flowers he offered appeared on the head of the hunter, revealing that the hunter was actually Lord Shiva in disguise. Realizing this,

Arjuna immediately bowed before Shiva. Pleased with Arjuna's valor and devotion, Shiva promised to be with him and with anyone who worships the Linga.

According to Hindu scriptures, Australia is considered to be at the "mouth of the snake, " a symbol of protection and an ornament of Lord Shiva. This belief is reinforced by the fact that an arrow from the Somnath Temple points directly along an unobstructed path of light towards the South Pole, leading to the view that the 13th Jyotirlinga should be sanctified in Australia. As a result, the Linga that Arjuna made has been housed in the sanctified prayer room within the man-made cave temple in Minto, Sydney.

Besides these 13 Jyotirlinga temples, there are many other significant temples dedicated to Lord Shiva and numerous places associated with him. Shiva's temples are not only located in India but also in other parts of the world. According to Hinduism, there are 33 *koti* gods, though the interpretation of the word *koti* varies. Some interpret *koti* as meaning 'type' or 'kind, ' suggesting that there are 33 types of gods, while others interpret it as 'crore,' leading to the belief that there are 33 crore gods. The religious plurality inherent in Hinduism allows for a multiplicity of beliefs, faiths, and views.

In contrast, other religions such as Islam and Christianity are more monotheistic, adhering to the worship of one God and generally not permitting their followers to believe in another deity. This religious plurality is a hallmark of Hinduism, which is inclusive and non-exclusive in its approach to divinity.

Among all gods, Lord Shiva is especially revered, and according to various surveys, the number of Shiva temples is the highest in India, followed by temples dedicated to Hanuman. Shiva is considered the de facto god of the Earth, and most of his divine activities are believed to have occurred on Earth. Unlike other deities whose abodes are often imagined in the sky or other celestial realms, Shiva's abode is traditionally considered to be Mount Kailash.

Lord Shiva is worshipped in many forms and at numerous places, and he is revered by the majority of Hindus as *Bholenath*—a deity who is easily pleased and non-discriminatory. A simple offering of water on a Shivalinga is believed to be sufficient to please him. Shiva is worshipped as a primary deity in both India and Nepal, and he is also considered a crucial aspect of Hinduism, often regarded as the supreme lord.

In addition to the Jyotirlingas, there are many other significant Shiva temples in India, including:

- Brihadeeswarar Temple, Thanjavur, Tamil Nadu
- Vadakkunnathan Temple, Thrissur, Kerala
- Lingaraja Temple, Bhubaneswar, Odisha
- Mangueshi Temple, Goa
- Neelkanth Mahadev Temple, Rishikesh, Uttarakhand
- Amarnath Cave Temple, Anantnag, Jammu & Kashmir
- Nellaiappar Temple, Tirunelveli, Tamil Nadu
- Chenkal Maheswaram Sri Sivaparvathi Temple in Thiruvananthapuram, Kerala

- Tarakeshwar Temple, West Bengal
- Chidambaram Nataraja Temple, Tamil Nadu
- Koteshwar Mahadev Temple, Rudraprayag, Uttarakhand
- Shore Temple, Mahabalipuram, Tamil Nadu

These temples, along with many others across India, are central to the worship of Lord Shiva.

One of the most important places associated with Lord Shiva is Mount Kailash, which Hindus believe to be his divine abode. Mount Kailash is often referred to as the center of the universe. Many Hindus and Buddhists alike consider it a place of immense spiritual power. According to Hindu belief, Mount Kailash lies directly beneath the Pole Star, which is unique among celestial bodies as it remains relatively immovable, while other stars and planets move across the sky.

Mount Kailash is located in Tibet and stands at an elevation of 22, 028 feet (6, 714 meters) above sea level. The area surrounding the mountain is extremely rugged and remote, making it very difficult to access. Despite numerous attempts, no human has ever successfully reached its peak, even though Mount Everest has been conquered many times. Mountaineers who have tried to scale Mount Kailash have reported being forced to turn back by strong winds, falling ice, or other insurmountable obstacles. This has led to the belief that the mountain is simply unconquerable, adding to its mystical and supernatural aura as the home of Lord Shiva.

In Tibetan Buddhism, Mount Kailash is considered the abode of the Buddha Demchok, who represents supreme bliss. Legend has it that Milarepa, one of Tibet's most revered saints, meditated on the mountain for three years, three months, three days, and three hours.

Every year, thousands of pilgrims from around the world undertake the arduous journey to Mount Kailash, often also visiting the nearby Lake Manasarovar. The 52-kilometer circumambulation (kora) of the mountain is believed to cleanse a person of all their sins, making it a once-in-a-lifetime pilgrimage for many. A remarkable and mysterious feature of Mount Kailash is the appearance of the "Om" symbol on its surface. While some believe that the symbol was created by ancient Indian sages, the exact origin of the Om symbol remains unknown. Nevertheless, its presence is seen as a glorification of Lord Shiva's abode.

There are several other mysteries surrounding Mount Kailash, including the peculiar similarity between the two nearby lakes, which are associated with the sun and the moon. Lake Manasarovar, representing the sun, is said to be the birthplace of Lord Brahma, while Rakshas Tal Lake, associated with the moon, is believed to be the residence of Lord Shiva. Devotees of Shiva traditionally take a holy dip in Lake Manasarovar but avoid bathing in Rakshas Tal.

The mysteries of Mount Kailash have long fascinated explorers, scientists, and others. Despite centuries of speculation, one fact remains clear: the mountain is sacred and revered as the abode of Lord Shiva. NASA has noted unusual features on Mount Kailash, including what some interpret as the face of Lord Shiva. However, NASA scientists have attributed these phenomena to magnetic forces in the area.

Another significant Hindu shrine is the Amarnath Temple, located in a cave at Anantnag in Jammu and Kashmir, at an altitude of 3,888 meters above sea level. One of India's most important Shiva temples, the Amarnath Cave is also known as the abode of Mahamaya Shakti Pitha. The Shiva-Lingam at this shrine is a natural stalagmite formation inside a 40-meter-tall cave on the Anantnag mountain, which rises to a height of 5,186 meters. This stalagmite, formed by the freezing of water droplets falling from the cave's roof, represents Lord Shiva and is a physical and religious manifestation of him. Two additional ice stalagmites are believed to symbolize Ganesh and Parvati.

According to the Mahabharata and various Puranas, the lingam symbolizes Shiva. The ice lingam typically forms and grows during the month of Shravan (July-August) and starts melting about a month later, reaching its full height during the summer festival. It is believed that this is the place where Shiva revealed the secrets of life and eternity to Parvati. During this time, a pair of pigeons, which were mating in the cave, overheard the divine discourse and became immortal. They are still said to be seen during the pilgrimage.

The phenomenon of the self-forming ice pillar or ice lingam, and its subsequent melting, has been occurring since ancient times. The earliest reference to this is found in Kalhan's historical text *Rajatarangini*, where it is mentioned as Krishnanath or Amarnath.

Legend has it that Sage Bhrigu was the first to discover this holy site. At that time, the entire Kashmir Valley was submerged under water, and it was Sage Kashyap who drained the waters with his divine powers. As the waters receded, Bhrigu was the first to reach the site of the Shiva Lingam.

The formation of the ice pillar or Shivalinga is a natural and unique wonder. While there are many caves in the Shivalik and Himalayan terrains, Amarnath Cave is unique in its natural formation of stalagmites. This makes the site particularly holy for Shiva's devotees and pilgrims. During the Shravan

Mela festival, pilgrims visit the site to witness the ice Shivalinga.

Shiva Temples Outside India: As Lord Shiva is an ancient and supreme deity, his worship extends beyond India. Shiva's devotees, believers, and followers can be found worldwide. Consequently, there are numerous temples dedicated to Shiva not only in India but also internationally. Notable Shiva temples outside India include:

1. Prambanan Temple, Java, Indonesia
2. Pashupatinath Temple, Nepal
3. Sagar Shiv Temple, Mauritius
4. Katas Raj Temple, Pakistan
5. Munneswaram Temple, Sri Lanka
6. Arulmigu Sri Raja Kaliamman Temple, Malaysia
7. Mukti Gupteshwar Temple, Minto, Australia
8. Tirta Empul Temple, Bali, Indonesia
9. Madhya Kailash Temple, Midrand, South Africa
10. Shiva Temple, Auckland, New Zealand

11. Sivan Kovil Temple, Lewisham, London, United Kingdom
12. Shiva Temple, Zurich, Switzerland
13. Shiva Hindu Temple, Zuidoost, Netherlands
14. Shiva Temple, Oman
15. Shiva Vishnu Temple, Melbourne, Australia

Shiva's Simplicity:- Lord Shiva is known as Bholenath (innocent and simple), yet he is also Mahadev, the God of gods, and is associated with the creation, preservation, and destruction of the universe. Despite his divine status, he is characterized by his gullible nature and lack of discrimination among any creature, whether deva, demon, or man. He leads a very simple life, wearing no clothing except animal hide, and lacks the jewelry that adorns other gods. He has no permanent home and resides under the open sky on the snowy Mount Kailash. His body is smeared with ashes, his hair is matted, and he lives like a hermit, wandering the stony hills of the mountain with bare feet. He has no attachment to physical comforts or amenities like other gods.

His nature is very innocent and he is easily pleased by anyone who approaches him, often bestowing blessings even for accidental offerings. An episode illustrating Shiva's simplicity and positive nature is as follows:

Once, a thief was fleeing from soldiers who were chasing him. To escape, he climbed a bilva tree and spent the entire night hiding there to avoid detection. Beneath the tree was a Shiva-linga. The thief, terrified and pale with fear, inadvertently dropped a few bilva leaves onto the Shiva-linga. Despite his situation, Shiva was pleased with this accidental offering and forgave the thief, appreciating that the leaves were offered at a time when most people were asleep.

There was a thief who used to steal in a town where there was a Shivalaya (temple of Shiva). The people of that location worshiped Lord Shiva and offered milk and water on the Shivlinga. Inside the temple, there were two bells: a small bell near the gate and a larger bell hanging above the Shivlinga.

One day, the thief entered the temple secretly to steal and took money from the donation box and around the Shivlinga. He also attempted to steal the bells, but the larger bell was too high for him to reach. Greedy and unable to leave it behind, he tried hard but was unsuccessful. Ultimately, he climbed onto the Shivlinga to attempt to reach the bell. Riding on the Shivlinga is considered a grave offense, but Shiva, in his innocence and simplicity, thought that the thief must be very devoted to him. Instead of offering fruits and flowers, the thief had offered himself and placed himself on the Shivlinga. Shiva, being the god of simplicity and positivity, appeared and blessed the thief, pleased by his accidental offering.

In the Mahabharata, Draupadi asked Lord Krishna why she had five husbands when it was customary in that era to have only one husband, and polyandry was taboo. Krishna replied that in her previous birth, she had been a princess who performed intense penance for Shiva. Impressed by her devotion, Shiva asked her to choose a boon. Draupadi requested a husband who was honest, strong, skilled, handsome, and intelligent. Instead of giving her one husband with all these qualities, Shiva granted her five husbands, each embodying one quality. This decision disregarded the social customs of that time, which considered polyandry unacceptable. Shiva's action was not a challenge to the social system but a reflection of his innocence and ignorance of societal norms. He acted according to Draupadi's request, demonstrating his nature as Bholenath, a simple and innocent sage.

After their marriage, Shiva and Parvati reached Mount Kailash. Parvati expressed her desire for a house to protect her from the heat of summer, the cold of winter, the rains, and the night. However, Shiva, who was accustomed to living as a hermit without material possessions, did not see the need for a house. Nevertheless, Parvati persisted, so Shiva called upon Ravana to build a house for her. Ravana used his knowledge of Vastu Shastra to construct a magnificent palace. Once the palace was built, Ravana became attached to it and requested it as his reward. Innocent Shiva agreed, and the Ganas informed Parvati of the situation. Parvati was initially upset but came to understand that Shiva, in his innocent nature, was not aware of the significance of property and was simply following his nature.

Ravana, knowing Shiva's innocent and gullible nature, once requested Shiva to give him Parvati as his wife. Shiva, unfazed, replied that if Parvati wished to go with him, she was free to do so. Even though such a request would have angered most people, Shiva, being Bholenath, did not understand the concepts of marital loyalty or property. To teach Ravana a lesson, Parvati transformed a frog named Mandoka into a beautiful maiden named Mandodari and placed her on Mount Kailash. When Ravana saw Mandodari, he mistakenly believed she was Parvati and took her to Lanka as his queen. Shiva and Parvati watched with amusement as Ravana, the demon king, made love to the frog disguised as a woman, believing he had won Parvati.

According to the Tamil Pariyar Puranam, Tinnan was a young hunter and a devoted follower of Shiva, although he did not know the proper way to worship. Every evening, after his hunt, he offered forest flowers to a Shiva-linga and poured water from his mouth on it, along with any animals he had hunted. Despite the unconventional offerings, Shiva accepted Tinnan's devotion because it was sincere and pure. Once, Shiva tested Tinnan's devotion by creating a quiver that caused the temple roof to collapse. All the priests fled, except Tinnan, who protected the linga with his body. Impressed by Tinnan's dedication, Shiva appeared before him, stopped him from plucking his eyes to fix the linga, restored his sight, and made him the tenth of the 63 Nayanars, known as Kannappar. Shiva values the genuine emotions and devotion behind the offerings rather than the rituals themselves.

A famous folktale describes that, unlike other gods who have mounts, Shiva moves on foot. Parvati, seeing Shiva's bare feet suffering on the stony paths of the Himalayas, requested him to have a mount. Shiva agreed and called all the deities and animals to choose one to be his mount. When no deities volunteered, Shiva invited the animals. Nandi, the bull, stealthily overheard Shiva's conversation and prepared by collecting dry wood and keeping it covered during the rainy season. When Shiva asked for dry wood, Nandi was the only one able to provide it. Pleased with Nandi's resourcefulness, Shiva accepted him as his mount. This story reflects Shiva's simplicity and his preference for living as a hermit, without comparing himself to other deities.

Lord Shiva's nature is so vast and beyond complete description. As Adi Shankaracharya expressed it:

"Forgive me, Oh Shiva! My three great sins! I came on a pilgrimage to Kashi Forgetting that you are omnipresent. In thinking about you, I forgot that You are beyond thought. In praying to you, I forgot that You are beyond words."

(Note: The respectful address for deities such as Saraswati, Lakshmi, and Parvati may include "Maa" for reverence.)

The married life of the Trinity :- As per Hindu mythology, the universe and its affairs are managed and operated by the Trinity i. e. **Brahma, Vishnu and Shiva.** The universe and the earth, along with humans and other creatures undergo the repeated cycles of creation and destruction. The universe contains living and nonliving creatures, stars, planets, galaxies, the milky ways and meteoroids. The universe is very vast and may be infinite and the Earth is a tiny part of the universe. As per Hindu belief, Brahma, the first God of the Trinity (Trimurti) has created the universe. Vishnu is one of the most important gods of the holy trinity and he is the preserver and guardian of the human and other creatures. He is also a protector of the order of things (dharma). Shiva, the third God in the Hindu triumvirate, is a god who destroys the universe to recreate it. So, the destruction is actually deconstruction and the destruction is not arbitrary, but constructive. The cycle of creation, preservation and destruction is continuous and everlasting.

Brahma, Vishnu and Shiva are married Gods. Goddess Saraswati, who is the wife of Brahma, is the goddess of knowledge and learning. She embodies intelligence, education, music and arts. Goddess Laxmi who is the goddess of wealth, fortune and prosperity, is the wife of Vishnu. Parvati is Shiva's wife and she is the goddess of strength, power, fertility and devotion and known by different names like Durga, Kali, Shakti and Parashakti. The married life of these three gods Brahma, Vishnu and Shiva is evaluated with a sense of reverence and respect.

The married life of Brahma:- Brahma is the creator of the Universe and god of wisdom whereas his wife Saraswati is the goddess of knowledge, arts, music and literature. Brahma is depicted as an elderly god with a beard, adorned in white robes and riding on a goose or a swan. He has four heads and four arms in which he carries the Vedas. It is Hindu belief that four Vedas have been composed by him and simultaneously he reads all Vedas with his four heads. He is very scholarly and learned and is always involved in creation and study. He has grown too old and looks like a Rishi (sage) and hence is regarded as 'Father of all'. His consort is Saraswati, goddess of knowledge, music and poetry. Clad in white attire, she is often holding or playing a musical instrument i. e Veena, so she is also called Veena Pani. She is gracious and a scholarly goddess dressed in pure white, often seated on a white lotus which symbolizes light, knowledge and truth. Her mount is white swan which is the embodiment of knowledge. She is known by many names in ancient Hindu literature as Brahmi, Vani, Viyadatri, Vagdevi, Varneshvari etc. The Rigveda, the first Veda describes her as the best of mothers, of rivers and of goddesses. Her white clad, white lotus and white swan, all white color symbolizes purity and true knowledge, insight and wisdom. If Brahma is the creator of one and all then Saraswati is goddess of knowledge which makes living creatures to live, adopt and preserve wisely.

Saraswati is generally shown to have four hands but there are some instances where there are sometimes just two hands. It is believed that when she is shown with four hands, those hands symbolically mirror her husband Brahma's four heads, representing manas, buddhi, chitta and ahamkara (mind, intellect, imagination and ego). A hansa or swan is often shown near her feet and the swan is said to drink a mixture of water and milk, symbolizing its ability to discriminate between good and evil. She is wife of the first God and the relation between wife and husband is considered solid and concrete which could not be crushed in the time of difficulty and dispute. As per the Hindu belief and culture, the nuptial life is a constant relationship which continues for at least seven births, otherwise eternal. There is no room for divorce as there is no conception or tradition for divorce in the Hindu marriage. It is usually found and described in ancient Hindu literature, scriptures and mural paintings or archaeological sculptures that Brahma and Saraswati are never seen together and never sitting or standing together. For a successful marital life, togetherness is very essential. It gives bonding strength to the couple and aloneness can make married life awful and also causes the gap between the spouses. It is depicted that Brahma is an aged god, with white beard, involved in the marathon and strenuous job of creation and creation within the time. Brahma studies the four Vedas with help of his four heads. Continuous studies and the exhausting job of creation has made him old and his youthfulness has faded. The physical strength and glow have diminished. The physical weakness makes married life less romantic and decreases corporal closeness.. On the other hand, spirituality might have increased. The feeling of apathy and lack of concern is on the way to grow.

Saraswati, goddess of wisdom, knowledge, arts and literature wears a very simple and white attire and minimal jewelry and she is involved in playing the veena (musical instrument). She is very gracious and abstemious. The white dress worn by her marks her indifferent to the physical charm as well as material attachments. There is a lack of any carnal inclination due to rare meeting with her husband, Brahma seems to have lost his interest in the physical pleasure due to being old and continuous work pursuits. So, goddess Saraswati is also called 'Brahmancharni' and old age affects sensual strength adversely. It is natural that increasing age and mental involvement reduces the strength of a man for producing the next generation. The physical weakness and losing muscle power results in fading carnal desire. Consequently the couple may be issueless and the child plays a vital role of more closeness and biding of the couples. On the contrary, the couples without children might feel a lack of feeling of togetherness and nearness. Childlessness is one of the main reasons for an unsuccessful marital life, because a successful and happy marriage requires bonding over their own child / children. The natural purpose of marital life is to reproduce and preserve the next generation for the continual cycle of death & birth and birth & death. The phenomenon of the married life of Brahma and Saraswati is true in the present time as these days the marriage is usually solemnized at the later age of couples due to various factors.

In today's society, it has become increasingly important for both men and women to establish themselves financially and socially before entering into marriage. To achieve financial independence, individuals often prioritize their education, striving to attain higher degrees that can lead to well-paying jobs with attractive benefits. However, this pursuit of professional success requires a significant investment of time and energy.

As men focus on their education and career advancement, it is often observed that they may begin to lose some of their physical vitality during these crucial years. This can coincide with what would otherwise be the peak of their physical strength and optimal time for reproduction. On the other hand, women today are equally capable and encouraged to pursue higher education and professional goals, matching the achievements of their male counterparts. As a result, the age at which individuals typically marry has increased.

Both men and women now dedicate themselves to their professional goals, often postponing marriage and parenthood until later in life. By the time they feel ready to settle down, they may find that their physical capabilities for conception have diminished. This can lead to fewer children or, in some cases, challenges in conceiving altogether. Additionally, the demands of professional life can leave couples with less time and energy for one another, impacting their romantic and physical intimacy.

Moreover, the stress and fatigue that accompany demanding careers can further diminish a couple's desire for physical closeness. When couples are posted or work in different locations, it can lead to extended periods of separation, reducing the time they spend together and weakening the emotional and physical bonds that are vital to a healthy marriage. The pressures of work and distance may also reduce the couple's focus on shared activities, mutual celebrations, and even the care of their children.

For many professionals, such as college teachers, officers, and businesspeople, the combination of increased age, job-related stress, and time constraints can result in a less fulfilling romantic life. The responsibilities and demands of their careers may lead them to postpone having children, sometimes indefinitely, which can ultimately result in missed opportunities for parenthood. This, in turn, may lead to feelings of detachment or indifference within the marriage.

In today's fast-paced world, many educated and working couples face these challenges in their married life. This can result in reduced physical intimacy, diminished emotional warmth, and a decreased sense of dependence on one another. In some cases, couples may choose to live more independently, with each partner pursuing their own interests and desires without much interference from the other. Over time, marriage may become more of a formality than a deeply fulfilling partnership.

As per Hindu mythology, Brahma and Saraswati have no son or daughter, Brahma has 16 manasaputras (mental sons) and 1 manas putri (mental daughter). As per Bhagavata Purana, these are Brahma's manas putras Angiras, Attri, Pulastya, Marichi, Pulaha, Kratu, Bhrigu, Vashistha, Daksha, Narada, Chitragupta and Kardama Muni and 1 manas putri Shatarupa. These manasputras are famous Rishis (sagas) or kings. With due reverence and regard to the married life of Brahma, it is said that decline in physical power for reproduction due to growing age, indifference between spouses and incessant involvement in the duty and study increases the mental activity in place of physical activity. The aged people are more active mentally rather than physically. The mental engagement is consequent of manas putra or putri. It is psychotically correct that when physical activity is at ebb, then the mental activity is at rise like a tide. The late marriage enables the couple to achieve the target and to accomplish themselves for acquiring the better position in the society and the establishment and to be independent financially, but on the other side, the late marriage discomforts in the field of sensual activities, mutual physical engagements, romance and reproduction. In a late marriage, less conjugated life and fewer children/ issueless compensates for the financial advantage, social credibility, luxurious life and well status. In light of these considerations, young people today must carefully evaluate the potential outcomes and decide whether to pursue marriage earlier or later in life.

The married life of Vishnu:- Vishnu is the supreme God and one of the three important gods in

Hinduism. As per Hindu belief that he is a member of the holy Trinity (Trimurti). Vishnu is the preserver and protector who protects the universe from being destroyed and keeps it continuing. As mythological text says that Vishnu is the Preserver and guardian of men (Narayana) and protects the order of things (Dharma). Whenever, there is danger on the Dharma, he appears on the earth as various incarnations or Avatars in the any form to destroy the demons, who torture, kill and involve in heinous activities against the mankind and Dharma. By annihilating the wicked demons /persons, he maintains a cosmic harmony. As per Hindu literature and Puranas, Vishnu's ten avatars or worldly incarnations in the form of man or animal or mixed, like Ram, Krishna, Buddha etc. are human-beings, Matsya (fish), Kurma (tortoise) are animals and Nar-Simha (mix of man and lion). It is also predicted that his last incarnation would be Kalki who will take birth when the crimes, corruptions, moral decay, bloody fighting and jealousy are at their peak and humanity is in danger. Kalki will come riding on the white horse and the world will end and a new world will start. The Bhagavata

Purana contains a collection of stories relating to his incarnations and his magnificent works which have greatly affected mankind, inspiring all to live ethically and morally.

The importance of God Vishnu is manifold in the Hindu religious books. He is said to manifest a portion of himself anytime he is needed to fight evil and to protect dharma (moral and religious laws). His supremacy lies in the protection from evil and for this purpose to take Avatars whenever the moral and religious laws are in acute danger due to the prominence and threats of evil, chaos and destructive forces in the world. He is worshiped by a hundred names. In the trinity, he occupies an important position. In Hinduism, a separate sect was formed as Vaishnavism where Vishnu is revered as supreme God and it is believed that the followers of vaishnavism (vaishnavs) would be taken by Vishnu to Baikund Dham where Vishnu lives.

In Hindu art and literature, Vishnu is differently depicted depending on the specific cultures like Indian, Cambodian or Javanese, but he is most often portrayed with blue skin, four hands holding Sudarshan Chakra, conch shell, lotus and Gada or sword. His mount is Guruda who is half man and half bird (eagle). It is found that Vishnu is depicted as standing or reclining on the coils of the serpent Sheshnag in the sea. Sometimes Vishnu is lying down on the coils of the serpent and Laxmi, goddess of wealth and his wife is pressing his legs, and some deities are standing there in reverence. As per Hindu mythology, during the rainy season Vishnu sleeps for four months in the Kshir Sagar and during this period, the annual pralaya (holocaust) takes place and the world gets a new life. He sleeps as he is tired of his nonstop work and needs a break. It is believed that he wakes during the Deepavali when goddess Laxmi is worshiped and he marries Laxmi, ending his siesta and the marriage season starts in the Hindu calendar.

Goddess Lakshmi, wife of Vishnu is the goddess of wealth, prosperity, fortune, love, beauty and joy. She emerged from the churning of the ocean (Samudra manthan) by the gods and demons and chose Vishnu as her consort. As per the Vishnu Purana, whenever Vishnu takes avatar on the earth as Ram and Krishna, Laxmi also descends as Sita, Rukmani and Radha. She is also honored as Shri and represents the material world of the earthly dominion as the mother goddess and Bhumi.

Lakshmi is often depicted in the Hindu art and scripture as gracefully dressed, prosperity-showering golden coloured lady with owl as her vehicle. She normally stands or sits on the lotus podium, while holding a lotus in her hand, symbolizing fortune, wealth and growth. She has four hands which represent four aspects of life i. e dharma, karma, artha and moksha (religious laws, action, finance and salvation). These are very important elements or purposes of human life as per the Hindu philosophy.

Lakshmi is a member of the Tridevi along with goddesses Saraswati and Durga. She represents the Rajas guna and iccha-shakti (will- power). She is often portrayed with two elephants which symbolize work, activity and strength with rain, water, fertility and abundant prosperity. She holds a kalasha (pot) full of gold coins, representing the material and spiritual wealth which are very essential for a prosperous and peaceful life.

Wealth is a very important element for the prosperity, development and progress of man, society and country. This affluence solely depends on wealth. In the absence of wealth, either man or society or country cannot stand, develop, make progress and get respect. Life is miserable without wealth. So, Laxmi is widely worshiped and Lakshmi –puja (deepavali) is celebrated with pomp and show, and the people spend handsomely for the pleasure and blessings of Goddess Lakshmi. She is the most respected and essential goddess of all time and every age. Goddess Lakshmi has an important place not only in Hinduism but also in the other religions too, may be in any other form. There is a strong and firm belief that without blessings and pleasure of Lakshmi, improvement, blissful life, success, development, progress and prosperity is not possible. Her kindness and blessings are a must for a flourishing life, society and country. Money makes credibility, capability and acceptability.

If Vishnu is the preserver and guardian of the world, Lakshmi is goddess of wealth and prosperity. Living on the earth and enjoying a wealthy life without any scarcity is both significant. So, Vishnu and Lakshmi are at par in their fields. Both are supreme for human beings, society and country. It is found that Vishnu and Lakshmi are rarely seen sitting together like Shiva & Parvati. Usually, Laxmi is seen sitting next to Vishnu's feet and Vishnu is lying on the coils of a serpent. Such posture distinctly displays that there is no equality between them and the relationship between this couple may lack parity.

Many stories are narrated to explain why Lakshmi, the goddess of wealth, is depicted sitting at the feet of Vishnu, who is lying down. These stories suggest that wealth can bring ego into any soul, while Vishnu, as the Supreme God, symbolizes the humility that keeps ego in check. As per Hinduism, God and soul represent master and servant, so servants should serve God. But in reality, it is considered that men generally have more ego

In the context of a marital relationship, it is observed that if the spouse is educated, holding a good position and financially independent, then the husband usually exerts effort to dominate his wife in private or in public. Since the wife is not financially dependent on her husband and also holds a good post, she does not easily submit. Consequently, disputes arise causing lack of mutual understanding and sometimes mental as well as physical harassment. If such conflicts persist, divorce/separation is inevitable. These days cases of divorce and harassment are reported significantly in affluent, educated and well -earning families, because of husband's desire for domination and super ordination. Moreover, due to the male ego, the husband never wants to be subordinated and feels inferior to his wife. A successful and long marital life depends on equal and mutual understanding, at par behavior, mutual respect, free conversation, sharing of feelings and most importantly nonexistence of ego. Here Vishnu is the preserver and supreme god of preservation, nourishment and protection, whereas Lakshmi is supreme goddess of wealth and prosperity. It may be said that both are CEOs of their own faculties and naturally both are at equal footing and independent. Both Vishnu and Lakshmi have great responsibility and have to do their duties. God Vishnu is continuously involved in protecting, maintaining and preserving, whereas Goddess Lakshmi is also engaged in bringing prosperity to the nation, society and men. Both bear great responsibilities to mankind and the world. The protection of life with prosperity is the main accomplishment. So, people worship and respect both Vishnu and Lakshmi for protection and prosperity. Since both are independently engaged in the separate field of responsibility. It is observed if spouses are working independently, consequently they become independent of each other. The feeling of subordination diminishes, leading to a decrease in the husband's dominance over his wife. As a result, the husband's ego may clash with the wife's growing sense of independence, causing tension in the relationship. This can naturally lead to a decline in closeness, frequency of communication, physical intimacy, and mutual understanding, widening the gap between the spouses.

In some cases, the husband may try to assert his dominance by demanding tasks from his wife that reinforce his sense of superiority. This behavior may satisfy the husband's ego but can strain the relationship.

According to Hindu mythology and scriptures, Goddess Lakshmi is often depicted sitting at the feet of Lord Vishnu, pressing his legs while he reclines on the coils of a serpent in the presence of other deities. This imagery has been interpreted as reflecting a traditional view of marital roles, where the wife is seen as serving her husband. However, it is important to recognize that in modern relationships, both spouses are equal and should share equal status and authority.

Disrespectful behavior from the husband can lead to indifference, a lack of mutual interest, and emotional distance, making married life unpleasant and challenging. Consequently, physical intimacy may decrease, which could affect the couple's ability to have children, potentially resulting in fewer or no children. The feeling of subordination diminishes, leading to a decrease in the husband's dominance over his wife. As a result, the husband's ego may clash with the wife's growing sense of independence, causing tension in the relationship. This can naturally lead to a decline in closeness, frequency of communication, physical intimacy, and mutual understanding, widening the gap between the spouses.

In some cases, the husband may try to assert his dominance by demanding tasks from his wife that reinforce his sense of superiority. This behavior may satisfy the husband's ego but can strain the relationship.

According to Hindu mythology and scriptures, Goddess Lakshmi is often depicted sitting at the feet of Lord Vishnu, pressing his legs while he reclines on the coils of a serpent in the presence of other deities. This imagery has been interpreted as reflecting a traditional view of marital roles, where the wife is seen as serving her husband. However, it is important to recognize that in modern relationships, both spouses are equal and should share equal status and authority.

Disrespectful behavior from the husband can lead to indifference, a lack of mutual interest, and emotional distance, making married life unpleasant and challenging. Consequently, physical intimacy may decrease, which could affect the couple's ability to have children, potentially resulting in fewer or no children.

And it is pertinent to mention that Vishnu and Lakshmi have no son or daughter.

It is believed that Lakshmi requests Goddess Parvati to give Ganesha to her, because she is in need of a progeny. Parvati gives her son Ganesha to Lakshmi with some conditions. This is why on the occasion of Deepawali, goddess Lakshmi is worshiped with God Ganesha. It is said that the followers who are known as Vaishanav would never be prosperous and be poor and deprived from physical attachment and enjoyment. And similarly, Lakshmi bhakts (devotees) would be far from Vishnu's blessing. Consequently, they will not be able to go to Vaikunth Dham where the Vishnu Bhakts can visit easily. This is the outcome of the sullenness of Vishnu and Lakshmi to each other's devotees due to mutual bitterness and aloofness between the divine couples.

In the present age, the dynamics of Vishnu and Lakshmi's marital life can be seen in many modern couples, especially where both spouses are highly educated and hold demanding professional positions. Both partners are often duty-bound, work-focused, and so busy with their hectic schedules that they struggle to find time for frequent romantic interactions and the enjoyment of togetherness.

Moreover, there may be a possibility that the wife's financial independence hurts the ego and feeling of supremacy of the husband and due to constraints of profession / office work the wife may not follow the whims and fancies of the husband. The ego and clash of personality widens the gap between the spouses. This gap between the spouses makes the marriage life dull, bitter and the lack of interest causes indifference among each other. In such a situation, both spouses understandably agree to live independently at their willingness and no interference is required from either side as both are bound to live as their requirements, otherwise mutual disputes, stoppage of exchange of views, discontinuation of conversations and bodily relations will broaden. The distance and indifference adversely affects the health of the marital life and sometimes they drift so apart and aloof from each other that it becomes the reason for separation or divorce or living separately. And in such conditions, married life turns to a tragic end.

If both spouses are career-oriented and decide to postpone having a child due to their professional commitments, they may find it challenging to devote the necessary time and attention to raising a child. This postponement can sometimes lead to a situation where the couple remains childless. However, it is often believed that having children is an essential part of a fulfilling and successful marital life. Without children, some may feel that their marriage is incomplete or lacking in vitality.

In Hindu tradition, having a son is particularly significant, as he is traditionally responsible for performing the cremation rites for his parents, which is believed to help their souls attain salvation

(Moksha). Additionally, a son or daughter continues the family lineage and heritage, taking on family responsibilities after the parents' passing.

Even in today's world, the dynamics seen in the marital life of Vishnu and Lakshmi still resonate with many educated and working couples. Factors such as ego, a sense of superiority, lack of interest, demanding careers, diminished physical intimacy, and an unplanned approach to family planning can all negatively impact a marriage. These days, there is an increasing prevalence of divorces, separations, and couples having fewer or no children.

To sustain a happy and successful marriage, it is important for both partners to set aside ego and recognize the value of their spouse. Mutual understanding, honesty, and cooperation are crucial for a strong marital bond. Couples must carefully consider whether their careers or professions are more important than the happiness of their family and the possibility of having children. If both are important, they must strive to maintain a healthy balance; otherwise, the marriage may suffer.

Married life of Shiva:- Shiva is a principal God in the family of Trimurti and he is known as the destroyer who destroys the universe in order to recreate a new universe. He also destroys evil, misconception and darkness. He is considered to be the most divine among all Hindu gods and is also regarded as "Mahadev" which means supreme god or deity of all deities. It is believed that Shiva is the father of the whole universe. His destruction represents reconstruction, development and regeneration of thing/ new world. Unlike other gods, he leads a very ascetic life on Mount Kailash as an omniscient Yogi. He lives under the open sky and has no home to live in. He wears the skin of animals, garland of serpents around his neck, crescent moon on his forehead, holy Ganga flowing from his matted hair, smeared with ash and the third eye on his forehead. He keeps the Trishul or trident as a weapon and at same time the Damroo or rattle drum in his hand. He very often is seen to sit alone in meditation, but sometimes he is with his wife, goddess Parvati and sons Ganesh and Kartikey. Nandi, his mount, is also present.

Shiva means auspicious, gracious, kind, benevolent, friendly and welfare. Also in the Rig-Veda, Shiva is mentioned and addressed as Rudra. He is praised as" the mightiest of the mighty. " He is worshiped widely in nearly the whole world and Shiva-Lingams are represented as Shiva as Purush and Shakti as Prakriti (nature). The sculptures of Shiva have been found in many countries. He is known by many names such as Viswanatha, Shankara. Shambhu, Bholenath, Rudra, Nilkantha and so on. As per Hindu mythology, Shiva is not limited to three things i. e. name, time and form, He is timeless, formless and nameless, He represents the body with life and motion. He is omnipresent, omniscient and omnipotent.

God Shiva has contradictory nature and behavior. On one hand he is Bholenath (king of innocents), having no sense of malice, ego, power and prejudice. He is easily pleased and showers his blessings on his devotees without distinguishing the status and position of the devotees. He does not see the rituals but the feelings and faith of the devotees. All deities, ghosts, goblins, ganas, gandharvas etc find shelter equally with Shiva without any discrimination unlike other deities who prefer only deities. On the other hand, Shiva is also called Rudra (fearsome) who does Tandav after losing his temper and destroys the things around him. The sooner he is pleased, the sooner he gets angered depending on the activities of men/demons.

It is believed that Shiva is absolute and nothingness as everything begins with Shiva and ends with him. He is like a cipher which is infinite having no start point and no end point. Shiva is the universe which contains numerous stars, planets, galaxies, constellations of celestial bodies and meteoroids, appears infinite or zero, but seems real. So, Shiva is everything and tangible, but infinite and zero. Shiva is a husband, a father and a house holder, but he is also a hermit, apathetic to the earthly world and involved in meditation. He is a householder but a mendicant and yogi too. He is a father and sitting with family, but no physical attachments and easement. He is the start point (aadi) and the end point (anta).

Shiva has married twice, at first he got married with Sati, daughter of king Daksha, who is manasputra of god Brahma. Daksha was Prajapati and master of the people. His youngest daughter Sati sees Shiva wandering in the mountains as a mendicant and falls in love with him. She expresses her desire to be his wife without knowing his willingness and desire. Being fearless, she approaches her father Daksha for permission, he reluctantly refuses to grant permission as Daksha has some reservations against Shiva as Shiva does not follow the culture and ethics of the deity and he lives like a hermit. But Sati is adamant and firm on marrying Shiva. It goes without saying that Sati is the first daughter who revolts against her father Daksha and her wedding with Shiva is the first love marriage on the earth. After her fathers' refusal, she leaves her father's house to become Shiva's wife.

Sati follows Shiva as a devoted wife and expects nothing from him, because she does it out of unconditional love. On the other hand, Shiva does not want to be a house holder and remains to be a hermit. Sati does not try to convince Shiva to be householder and only serves him without expecting anything from him. Shiva remains the wandering mendicant. Sati accepts him as he is, and this is why Sati means a devoted wife who sacrifices her life for her husband. Once upon a time, Daksha conducted a Yagna and all deities were invited, except Shiva, because Daksha was angry with Shiva for his daughter's revolt. He did not consider Shiva as God, as Shiva belongs to the Rudra family. Shiva does not follow the culture, moral principles and rituals of the deities. Despite the no-invitation from her father, Sati goes to her father's house to participate in Yagna. But she is not treated well and humiliated by her father there.

She demanded why Shiva or Mahadeva was not invited. Her father Daksa told her that Shiva does not follow culture and customs of the deities, wanders as hermit, smears his body with ash, lives in caves and has dogs, ghosts and snakes as his companions and he is not welcomed here. She wonders that her father does not know the reality of Shiva, that is why he has such a disgusting opinion against Shiva. Sati out of anger leaps into the sacrificial fire and sets herself in flames. She died there leaving all as mere spectators, and none of them came forward to save her.

When Shiva gets the news of the sudden demise of Sati, he becomes restless, weeps in agony and howls in pain. He felt a sudden vacuum due to the absence of Sati in his life. It is the very first and unique instance of a husband or lover in the world who took his wife's body on his shoulder and wandered in the hills, crying in pain forgetting everything that he is one who has restored Chandra and can resurrect anyone by Sanjivini Vidya. His howling and anguish is so intense that the universe is unable to bear its burden. So the deities requested Vishnu to save the universe from the anger and pain of Shiva. Sati's body was cut into 51 pieces by Vishnu with help of his Sudarshan Chakra. Each piece falls on the earth and is transformed into Shaktipeetha, seat of the Goddess. After Sati's body parts fell, Shiva retreated to the mountains for a long and deep meditation.

On the other side, Shiva takes the form of Virabhadra, a fearsome warrior who leads an army of ghosts, goblins. and other wild creatures into Daksha's Yagna hall and destroys the precinct and makes everything dirty. Virabhadra catches Daksha and chops his head. It is believed that yagna is not left unfinished, so the deities beg Shiva to forgive Daksha and resurrect him to complete the Yagna. Shiva replaced Daksha's head with that of a male goat which is supposed to be a sacrificial offering, showing that Daksha is prevented from having a dominating feeling as Prajapati, but to realize he has to be as humble as a goat. Beheading of Daksha who insults his married daughter, Shiva's crying in agony for Sati, wandering with the body of sati for her resurrection and withdrawing himself to mountains displays the highest form of love, affection and faithfulness of Shiva as a husband towards his wife. These elements are very essential for a good marital life. After a long period of time, Parvati, daughter of Himavan, king of mountains, gets married to Shiva after her long and severe tapasya and praying. Shiva always behaved with great respect towards Parvati, treating her as an equal. He had a deep understanding with his consort. Once Shiva and goddess Parvati were sitting together and Bhringi, a devotee of Shiva wanted to go around him, Shiva told him that he had to go around Parvati also as she is an inseparable part of him. He as Purush is incomplete without Parvati as Shakti or Prakriti (nature). But Bhringi refused and tried to slip between him and her. Shiva took the goddess on his thigh,. Bhringi then took the form of a bee to fly through the gap between their necks. Finding this, Shiva merged his body with Shakti. Thus, Shiva became Ardhanarishwara, half male and half female, therefore Bhringi failed to go around Shiva, excluding Shakti. This episode shows that spouses are inseparable parts of each other, not separate, not unequal and not inferior. So, in Shiva temples, Shiva cannot be worshiped without goddess Parvati as Shiv- Linga is embodiment of Linga and Yoni, merger of Purusha (Shiva) with Shakti (nature, Parvati) which is essential for generation, preservation and development of nature. Shiva is a caring husband who practices equality and respects his wife. This is why, on any occasion and especially on Shivaratri, damsels are generally advised to offer water and Bilva patra (leaves of Indian Bael [*Aegle marmelos]* to Shivalinga to get a good husband like Shiva.

After marriage and coming to Mount Kailash, Parvati sets up her kitchen in Mount Kailash. She collects vegetables, grains and spices in the baskets and makes a wood stove. She collected water in pots and was busy preparing food. But Shiva wondered about watching her do these things, because he had transcended the need for food and water and did not require cooked food.. Goddess Parvati in spite of his disapproval, cooks tasty and delicious foods and distributes it to all ganas, ghosts, goblins and other creatures. They enjoyed food for the first time in their lives. Many flavors and textures excited their senses, and they experienced the diversity of nature. All ganas and others used to wait for the cooked foods and naturally they are growing closer to Parvati and away from Shiva. There was one time when Shiva told Parvati angrily that there is no need for cooking, no one requires food as everyone will die eventually. On hearing this, goddess Parvati became angry. The annoyed goddess instantly disappears from her kitchen. In absence of the food,

Shiva's ganas weep and the food tasted by them provides satisfaction and allows their minds to keep away from fear. Now they don't desire to eat the raw substances as they used to eat earlier. Seeing them hungry and dying of starvation, Shiva feels their pain and tells them that he is going to search for Parvati and bring her back. He moves as a hermit, wandering here and there in search of her and comes to know in the city of Kashi that one lady is providing food to all who come to her. She is respected as goddess Annapurna. Shiva goes there and extends his begging bowl before her. The goddess fills it with hot and delicious food.

Shiva does not hesitate to bow before his wife for the sake of his Ganas and realizes that food is very essential for the activities of life. Food plays a key role in the human journey from Prakriti to Purusha (from nature to soul). Moreover, it is believed that Shiva as Purusha or soul acknowledges the importance of food in sustaining flesh and Shakti as nature or provider of food is sustainer of the flesh. Hence Shiva and Shakti are inseparable from each other.

As per mythology and literature, there are some different versions of how goddess Kali comes into existence. Main version is that there is a demon named Raktabija by name who got a boon that every drop of his blood will spawn a new Raktabija. He has created havoc on the earth and defeated almost all deities in the battle and seized most of the kingdoms. He becomes invincible due to producing innumerous Raktabija owing to dropping the blood of his wounds fallen on the earth. No deity was capable of defeating and killing Rakatbija. They decided to combine their divine powers and bestow the same and weapons to Goddess Durga. They requested her to destroy Raktabija. Durga converts into fierce and fearsome Kali gradually. Goddess Kali has four hands carrying Khadga (crescent shaped sword), a trident, a chopped head and a bowl collecting the blood of the severed head. She has a garland of chopped heads around her neck and wears a skirt of ripped out arms. Kali kills innumerable clones of Raktabija and drinks the blood out of chopped heads, so that no drop of blood would fall on the earth to produce another Raktabija. The wild creatures like jackals, vampires etc are following Kali to eat the killed demons. After continuous killing of demons and drinking the blood, she became more powerful, fierce and brutal. It is psychologically true that brutality and power deprive rationality, justification, morality and consciousness. It means that the dark side of man comes out in light, so fair Durga becomes dark Kali. Since Kali loses consciousness and mental rationality, she uses it to kill all demons or deities who come in her way. No deities have the power to stop Kali and the wild creatures. They come to Shiva and request him to stop Kali for the unmindful killings of the deities and pacify her as Raktabija has already been destroyed.

Shiva agrees to pacify the terrifying Kali. On a no moon night, he asks the ganas to inform the whereabouts of Kali and after getting informed, Shiva alone goes to the path where Kali is about to arrive. He lays down on the path and puts the trident in the ground near his head. On the night of the new moon, the dense darkness makes everything invisible. After a few moments, the sounds of wild and cannibalistic creatures, cries of the wounded, the screams of the dying, and the smell of blood and flesh fill the air. Footsteps draw closer as Kali reaches the place where Shiva is lying. She places one foot on Shiva's chest, and immediately realizes that she has stepped on a body that is deeply revered and dear to her, one she should never tread uponKali sees that Shiva is under her foot and immediately realizes her mistake. Out of embarrassment and shame, her tongue instinctively sticks out. She then calms down and returns to her original form, Durga or Gauri. This episode illustrates that Shiva is a considerate husband who knows how to calm a fierce and formidable wife. Arguing with your wife at such a moment can be dangerous, as it may escalate the situation and make things worse.

Shiva knew how to implement the psychological remedy to bring back the soft and fair Durga from the fearsome and blood-thirsty Kali. By awakening her gentle feelings and emotions, he lay down beneath Kali's foot.

Shiva does not hesitate to let ferocious Kali step on his chest to calm her rage. For an ideal married life, mutual understanding, passion, forgiveness, integrity, communication, and equality are essential ingredients. Shiva easily understands the ferocity of goddess Kali and intends to bring her back to her original state. He did not show his male ego or supremacy. A spouse should share and understand the mental and physical problem of the other and make an effort for its remedy.

Even in the present context, women's empowerment is looked down upon. Shiva always practices the empowerment of his wife. When the terror and attacks of demon Mahishasura was at peak and no deity was capable to stop or fight with or defeat Mahishasura. Shiva and other gods convert Parvati into Durga by crafting parts of her form by different gods and her face is created by Shiva. She has become the supreme power created with a combination of the powers of all other gods. Thus, Parvati becomes very powerful and kills the demon Mahishasura who can change his form into demon, animal etc. When he is in the form of buffalo, Goddess Durga kills him after a long and terrible combat. Shiva in all situations stood firmly with Durga.

Shiva is regarded as Mahayogi (Great Yogi) and Param Sadhu (Great Sage) who has no desire for worldly attachment and enjoyment, but at same time he is a very amicable householder (Shankara). Hermit and householder are apart from each other, but Shiva skillfully plays both roles. There is a concrete love and relationship between him and goddess Parvati, they sit together in a cave or on Mount Kailash. Whenever Parvati asks about Sri Ram and secrets of immorality, Shiva first describes the story of Ram and then Ram Katha is retold. He tells her the world's first story containing hundreds of stories with myriad plots and characters with amazing twists and turns. It is called the Brihatkatha or the Katha-Sarit Sagar, the ocean of stories. While narrating the story, Parvati falls asleep. whereas Shiva is completely absorbed in telling the stories and keeps on telling. Meanwhile, some birds which are residing in the cave listen to the same stories and Ram-Katha or Katha Sarit Sagar have reached to humanity through the birds and others. A conversation between spouses is a perfect step for cordial relations in marital life.

Shiva is also known as Natraj (Master of Dancers). Shiva shares his wife 's hobbies and sometimes he competes with Parvati (Shakti) for enjoyment. Once he was dancing with Shakti, the dancing became more and more competitive and intensive. Shiva felt that Shakti may win in the bout. Shakti was dancing perfectly and swiftly. In the midst of being defeated, Shiva suddenly changes his dancing posture, and he moves his left foot upward in such a manner that no one can do it. The raising of the left foot leaves the body imbalanced, but Shiva remains balanced, calm and composed. Seeing some of his secret parts uncovered, Shakti feels bashful and withdraws herself from dancing. This incident shows that during tough competition or under the impulse of losing the contest, such an act is natural to take place, and this was no ulterior motive. Shiva performs a difficult form of dance, and his pose of dance is the rarest. He never hesitates to share with his consort, either in dance or game. Caring and cooperation are very essential ingredients of a happy nuptial life.

It is very interesting that Shiva, the hermit-god of Hinduism, is the only Hindu god to be envisaged and believed as a householder with a wife and children (i. e Parvati and Ganesha & Kartikey). All gods have their consorts by their side –Vishnu with Lakshmi, Ram with Sita and Krishna with Radha, but on one is visualized with their children apart from Shiva. Shiva knows how to balance his life as a hermit and a householder and he maintains a close relationship with his wife and sons. The different and contrasting qualities in Shiva makes him very unique and a multiple faceted God. Shiva knows how to calm the fearsome Kali, to behave with the warrior Durga and how to treat demurred Gauri. He has the capacity to cope with different forms of Parvati.

In the modern age, a successful married life can be achieved by following the suit of Shiva. The ego, lack of mutual understanding, unfaithfulness, rude behaviors and less conversation are main hurdles to a good marital life and the spouses are required to break these hurdles. Mutual understanding, cooperation and sincerity are a few requirements for successful married life. The married life of Shiva and Parvati is both successful and revered. This is why spinsters are encouraged to worship and offer prayers to the Shivalinga, hoping for a good and discerning husband.

About Book

In Hinduism, the gods Brahma, Vishnu, and Shiva form the holy Trinity. Together, they create, maintain, and destroy the universe. Among them, Shiva stands out with his unique and mysterious nature. He is the "God of Gods, " yet lives like an ascetic hermit, without a permanent home. His body is smeared with ashes, he wears animal hides, and he is known to dance in crematoriums. Despite his austere appearance, Shiva is a highly auspicious and easily pleased deity.

The text describes his multifaceted personality, activities, and charisma, which demonstrate that Lord Shiva is, in many ways, a universe unto himself—absolute and infinite. It covers stories of his marriage, his granting of boons, his defeats of demons, his incarnations, the Jyotirlingas, and other fascinating aspects of Shiva. This book serves as a mini-encyclopedia of Shiva and is a must-read to add meaning and relevance to your life.

About Author

Mr. P. C. Sharma, a graduate in Science and Law, retired as an Income Tax Officer after more than 36 years of dedicated service in the Income Tax Department. With a wealth of experience and expertise in taxation, he is also a well-read individual with a deep understanding of diverse ideologies, viewpoints, and circumstances. His broad intellectual curiosity has led him to develop an independent way of thinking, always seeking the deeper truths of life.

Through this journey of exploration, he realized a profound connection between Lord Shiva and the concept of truth. During his career, Mr. Sharma actively participated in literary competitions, earning numerous awards and accolades. His poems and stories have been regularly featured in newspapers and magazines. Now, he has authored a book on Lord Shiva, a god he believes embodies the universe itself.

www.ingramcontent.com/pod-product-compliance
Lightning Source LLC
LaVergne TN
LVHW061538070526
838199LV00077B/6825